First Workshop on Multilingual Counterspeech Generation (MCG) with Shared Task on Multilingual Counterspeech Generation

Abu Dhabi, United Arab Emirates
19 January 2025

ISBN: 979-8-3313-1371-5

Printed from e-media with permission by:

Curran Associates, Inc.
57 Morehouse Lane
Red Hook, NY 12571

Some format issues inherent in the e-media version may also appear in this print version.

Printed with permission by Curran Associates, Inc. (2026)

For permission requests, please contact the Association for Computational Linguistics
at the address below.

Association for Computational Linguistics
209 N. Eighth Street
Stroudsburg, Pennsylvania 18360

Phone: 1-570-476-8006
Fax: 1-570-476-0860

acl@aclweb.org

Additional copies of this publication are available from:

Curran Associates, Inc.
57 Morehouse Lane
Red Hook, NY 12571 USA
Phone: 845-758-0400
Fax: 845-758-2633
Email: curran@proceedings.com
Web: www.proceedings.com

The 31st International Conference on Computational Linguistics
COLING 2025

The First Workshop on Multilingual Counterspeech Generation (MCG) with Shared Task on Multilingual Counterspeech Generation

Workshop Proceedings

January 19, 2025

Sponsored by the project TSI100923-2023-1, funded by MTDFP,
Secretary of State of Digitization and Artificial intelligence,
ENIA, and by the European Union-Next Generation EU / PRTR

Order copies of this and other ACL proceedings from:

Association for Computational Linguistics (ACL)
209 N. Eighth Street
Stroudsburg, PA 18360
USA
Tel: +1-570-476-8006
Fax: +1-570-476-0860
acl@aclweb.org

Preface

Welcome to the first workshop and shared task on Multilingual Counterspeech Generation, co-located at COLING 2025. Counterspeech is a promising strategy for fighting online hate, and it consists of refuting it via thoughtful and cogent reasons and fact-bound arguments. Despite the increasing interest from the NLP community in automating counterspeech production, existing studies and resources in this area still mainly focus on English. In this first edition of the workshop, we aim to fill this gap by encouraging researchers to delve into the challenging task of counterspeech generation in a multilingual setting. In fact, hate is an international phenomenon, and requires being addressed in all languages. The workshop also hosted a shared task, where participants were tasked with generating counterspeech in four different languages (English, Italian, Spanish and Basque). They also had the opportunity to employ specific background knowledge that was provided, or any additional external knowledge of their choice, to obtain generations of higher quality. Overall, the workshop received 13 paper submissions, including 10 related to the shared task. In total, 10 papers will be presented. Additionally, the program includes one non-archival paper presentation and two invited talks.

We extend our gratitude to the program committee for their constructive and insightful reviews, as well as to all authors for their submissions and engagement with the workshop.

Workshop organizers.

Website link: `https://sites.google.com/view/multilang-counterspeech-gen/`

Organizing Committee

Helena Bonaldi
María Estrella Vallecillo-Rodríguez
Irune Zubiaga
Arturo Montejo-Ráez
Aitor Soroa
María Teresa Martín-Valdivia
Marco Guerini
Rodrigo Agerri

Table of Contents

Conference Program

PANDA - Paired Anti-hate Narratives Dataset from Asia: Using an LLM-as-a-Judge to Create the First Chinese Counterspeech Dataset
Michael Bennie, Demi Zhang, Bushi Xiao, Jing Cao, Chryseis Xinyi Liu, Jian Meng and Alayo Tripp

RSSN at Multilingual Counterspeech Generation: Leveraging Lightweight Transformers for Efficient and Context-Aware Counter-Narrative Generation
Ravindran V

Northeastern Uni at Multilingual Counterspeech Generation: Enhancing Counter Speech Generation with LLM Alignment through Direct Preference Optimization
Sahil Wadhwa, Chengtian Xu, Haoming Chen, Aakash Mahalingam, Akankshya Kar and Divya Chaudhary

NLP@IIMAS-CLTL at Multilingual Counterspeech Generation: Combating Hate Speech Using Contextualized Knowledge Graph Representations and LLMs
David Salvador Márquez, Helena Montserrat Gómez Adorno, Ilia Markov and Selene Báez Santamaría

CODEOFCONDUCT at Multilingual Counterspeech Generation: A Context-Aware Model for Robust Counterspeech Generation in Low-Resource Languages
Michael Bennie, Bushi Xiao, Chryseis Xinyi Liu, Demi Zhang and Jian Meng

HW-TSC at Multilingual Counterspeech Generation
Xinglin Lyu, Haolin Wang, Min Zhang and Hao Yang

MNLP@Multilingual Counterspeech Generation: Evaluating Translation and Background Knowledge Filtering
Emanuele Moscato, Arianna Muti and Debora Nozza

Hyderabadi Pearls at Multilingual Counterspeech Generation : HALT : Hate Speech Alleviation using Large Language Models and Transformers
Md Shariq Farhan

TrenTeam at Multilingual Counterspeech Generation: Multilingual Passage Re-Ranking Approaches for Knowledge-Driven Counterspeech Generation Against Hate
Daniel Russo

The First Workshop on Multilingual Counterspeech Generation at COLING 2025: Overview of the Shared Task
Helena Bonaldi, María Estrella Vallecillo-Rodríguez, Irune Zubiaga, Arturo Montejo-Raez, Aitor Soroa, María-Teresa Martín-Valdivia, Marco Guerini and Rodrigo Agerri

PANDA – Paired Anti-hate Narratives Dataset from Asia: Using an LLM-as-a-Judge to Create the First Chinese Counterspeech Dataset

Michael Bennie[1], Demi Zhang[1], Bushi Xiao[1], Jing Cao[2], Chryseis Xinyi Liu[1], Jian Meng[1], Alayo Tripp[1]

[1]University of Florida, United States
[2]Lingua

Correspondence: michaelbennie@ufl.edu, zhang.yidan@ufl.edu

Abstract

Despite the global prevalence of Modern Standard Chinese language, counterspeech (CS) resources for Chinese remain virtually nonexistent. To address this gap in East Asian counterspeech research we introduce a corpus of Modern Standard Mandarin counterspeech that focuses on combating hate speech in Mainland China. This paper proposes a novel approach of generating CS by using an LLM-as-a-Judge, simulated annealing, LLMs zero-shot CN generation and a round-robin algorithm. This is followed by manual verification for quality and contextual relevance. This paper details the methodology for creating effective counterspeech in Chinese and other non-Eurocentric languages, including unique cultural patterns of which groups are maligned and linguistic patterns in what kinds of discourse markers are programmatically marked as hate speech (HS). In our analysis of the generated corpora, we provide strong evidence for the lack of open-source, properly labeled Chinese hate speech data and the limitations of using an LLM-as-Judge to score possible answers in Chinese. Moreover, the present corpus serves as the first East Asian language based CS corpus and provides an essential resource for future research on counterspeech generation and evaluation.[1]

***Warning:** The below text contains vulgar and oftentimes offensive speech. Any counterspeech or hate speech is used for exemplary purposes and doesn't necessarily reflect the views of any researcher involved.*

1 Introduction

Hate speech is typically characterized as any form of communication that demeans a specific group of people based on attributes like race, ethnicity, gender, sexual orientation, or religion (de Gibert et al., 2018). While HS may constitute a small proportion of social media content, its impact is significant, affecting nearly one-third of the population (Vidgen et al., 2019). The proliferation of hate speech on social media platforms has become a significant societal concern. While traditional approaches to mitigating HS have focused on content removal and moderation, these methods often raise concerns about freedom of speech. In response, counterspeech has emerged as a promising alternative strategy to combat HS while preserving free expression (Poudhar et al., 2024).

Counterspeech, defined as communication that aims to counteract potential harm caused by other speech, has shown effectiveness in real-world studies (Cepollaro et al., 2023). However, the manual creation of CS is time-consuming and challenging to scale given the volume of HS online. This has led to increased interest in automated CS generation using NLP techniques.

Our contributions

- We generate the first Chinese counterspeech dataset specifically designed for combating hate speech online. This resource fills a crucial gap in the field, as most existing datasets focus on English or other Western languages.
- We introduce and evaluate novel metrics for assessing the quality and effectiveness of generated Chinese counterspeech, addressing the limitations of existing evaluation methods in this domain.
- We implement a comprehensive annotation scheme based on established CS strategies, adapting them for the Chinese cultural and linguistic context.

[1]The dataset can be found at github.com/michaelbennieUFL/PANDA

Proceedings of the First Workshop on Multilingual Counterspeech Generation (MCG), pages 1–12
January 19th, 2025.

2 Background

2.1 Hate Speech and Counterspeech

Counterspeech has gained traction as an alternative to content removal. Studies have demonstrated the efficacy of CS in enhancing online discourse quality and reducing the prevalence and impact of hateful behavior (Buerger, 2021). However, it's important to note that the effectiveness of CS can vary significantly depending on the context and specific strategies employed. For example, the quantity of training data available to train an LLM on a specific language will predict the robustness of its generative function.

2.2 Datasets and Annotation

Several datasets have been developed to support research in CS generation. Fanton et al. (2021) presented a dataset of 5,003 English HS/CS pairs covering multiple targets of hate, created using a combination of language model generation and expert review. Chung et al. (2019a) annotated the CONAN dataset with response types using non-expert annotators.

Although there are multiple HS/CS datasets in English, both Chinese HS and CS resources are insufficient. Among six publicly available Chinese HS datasets without CS (see Table 1), merely four are readily accessible for research purposes, with varying annotation schemes and focuses. Furthermore, Chinese datasets often suffer from quality inconsistencies due to several unique challenges in the Chinese context: the prevalence of coded language and internet slang that obscures hateful content, complex linguistic variations across different Chinese-speaking regions, and social media censorship that affect data collection. These factors make it particularly challenging to obtain high-quality datasets, as annotators must possess not only linguistic expertise but also deep cultural knowledge to accurately identify and categorize HS.

2.3 Counterspeech Strategies

Several studies have identified and categorized effective CS strategies. Chung et al. (2023) conducted a systematic review, identifying eight strategies used in social sciences and real-world policy-driven campaigns. These strategies include presenting facts to counter misinformation and using humor or satire to diffuse hostility. Expressing empathy or support for the targets of HS is another approach, as is highlighting hypocrisy or inconsistencies in hateful arguments. Additionally, questioning the logic or assumptions underlying HS, denouncing hateful speech without attacking the speaker, and offering alternative perspectives or narratives are also effective. Finally, appealing to shared values or common ground is often used to foster understanding. The effectiveness of these strategies can be highly context-dependent, emphasizing the need for nuanced approaches to CS generation and evaluation.

2.4 Automated Counterspeech Generation

Counterspeech offers several advantages over traditional content moderation approaches. First, it upholds the principles of free expression by engaging with problematic content rather than censoring it (Zhu and Bhat, 2021). Second, CS is not bounded by the often arbitrary definitions of hate speech used by different platforms and can be more easily adapted to be used across different platforms. Third, it creates opportunities for education and constructive dialogue, potentially addressing the root causes of hate speech.

Recent advances in NLP, particularly in large language models, have opened new possibilities for automated CS generation. Early work by Qian et al. (2019) explored various approaches, including sequence-to-sequence models, variational autoencoders, and reinforcement learning for counterspeech. More recent studies have focused on how large pretrained language models perform in both fine-tuned and zero-shot settings for counterspeech. Tekiroğlu et al. (2022) present a comprehensive comparative study on using several pretrained Transformer-based LMs (e.g., GPT-2, DialoGPT, and BART) for generating English counter narratives. They find that autoregressive models combined with certain decoding schemes often outperform others in producing specific, non-generic responses.

Similarly, Saha et al. (2024) investigate zero-shot counterspeech generation using popular LLMs such as GPT-2, DialoGPT, ChatGPT, and FlanT5. They show that ChatGPT consistently generates strong counterspeech responses even in zero-shot scenarios, although certain models have higher toxicity with larger parameter sizes. Their findings underscore the importance of prompt engineering and model selection when developing robust counterspeech systems.

Earlier fine-tuning approaches by Raj Ratn Pranesh (2020) and Tekiroğlu et al.

(2022) demonstrated promising results for counterspeech, but they often struggled with producing diverse, high-quality responses. More recent work on zero-shot and few-shot settings (Saha et al., 2024) attempts to mitigate these limitations via better prompting strategies, model ensembles, or post-processing. Nonetheless, generating counter-narratives that are contextually grounded, non-repetitive, and culturally sensitive remains challenging. As such, additional innovation is required to enhance diversity, relevancy, and alignment with community guidelines.

2.5 Current Evaluation Metrics

Evaluating the quality and effectiveness of generated counterspeech with automatic evaluation tools remains a significant challenge. The current study uses a combination of LLM and traditional NLP metrics:

- JudgeLM: A LLM-based ranking method for evaluating automatic counter-narrative generation (Zubiaga et al., 2024).
- BLEU: Measures token overlap between predictions and references (Papineni et al., 2002).
- ROUGE-L: Computes sentence-level structure similarity and longest co-occurring n-grams (Lin, 2004).
- BERTScore: Calculates token-level similarity using contextual embeddings (Zhang et al., 2019).
- Novelty: Measures the proportion of non-singleton n-grams in generated text that do not appear in the training data (Wang and Wan, 2018).
- Genlen: The average length of generated predictions.

These metrics aim to provide a more comprehensive evaluation of CS quality, addressing aspects such as relevance, diversity, and effectiveness in countering hate speech.

3 Methodology

This section provides an overview of the targets we set when making this dataset (3.1), the sourcing of data (3.2), the pre-processing of data (3.3), generation of CS (3.4), and annotation methods (3.5). Finally, we also provide statistics relating to the dataset and rating (3.6). A graphical overview is provided in Figure 1.

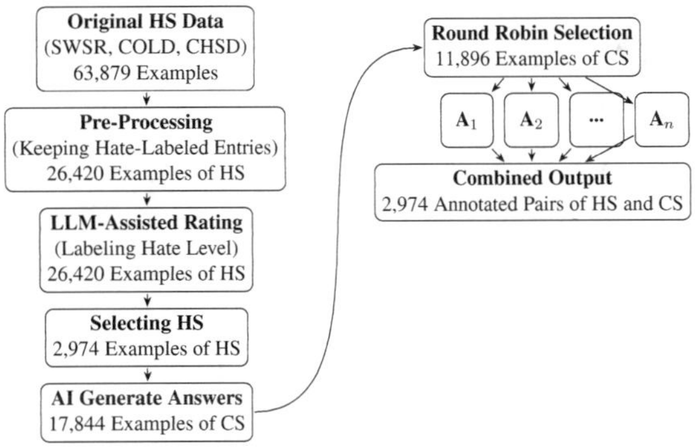

Figure 1: Proposed Data Processing Pipeline for Creating the Chinese Counterspeech Corpus. A_1 through A_n refer to n annotators that participated in this project.

3.1 Goals/Requirements

We aim to achieve the following objectives:

- **Creation of the First East Asian HS-CN Dataset.** During our review of existing datasets, we identified significant gaps in Chinese counterspeech (CS) resources. Although datasets like Deng et al. (2022) and Zhou et al. (2022) include instances labeled as 'anti-bias', their scope and definitions do not align with the specific focus of CS research. These datasets adopt a broader concept of 'anti-bias', encompassing content that promotes fairness and addresses various forms of offensive language rather than specifically targeting hate speech. Our work addresses this gap by creating a dataset that exclusively targets hate speech and counter speech, providing a more focused resource for CS research.
- **Paired Structure.** A notable limitation of previous datasets is the absence of a paired structure that directly links CS responses to specific instances of hate speech. In contrast, English-language datasets such as (Chung et al., 2019b) have demonstrated the value of this framework in facilitating precise and contextual analyses of intervention strategies. Our dataset introduces this paired structure for the first time in the Chinese context, explicitly mapping CS responses to their corresponding hate speech instances.
- **Freely Usable.** All hate speech data collected for our dataset originate from open-source

Datasets	Open Source[2]	Total Instances	HS/Offensive Speech	Non-HS
COLD (Deng et al., 2022)	Yes	37,480	18,041	19,439
SWSR (Jiang et al., 2022)	Yes	8,969	894	8,075
CHSD (Rao et al., 2023)	Yes	17,430	7,485	9,945
CDIAL (Zhou et al., 2022)	No	28,343	7,233	21,110
ToxiCN (Lu et al., 2023)	No	12,011	6,461	5,550
Political (Wang et al., 2022)	No	315,795	16,976	298,819
Used In Preprocessing	Yes	26,420	26,420	0

Table 1: Statistics of available corpora, showing the total number of instances of data, the number of instances of data that could be labeled as possible hate speech, and the number of instances of data of non-hate speech. For the current study, it only included instances of potential hate-speech from open-source corpora.

repositories. Additionally, we have released our model and the generated data under a permissive GPL license. This ensures that the generated and annotated data can be freely utilized in both commercial and non-commercial projects, promoting wider accessibility and application in various research and practical initiatives.

3.2 HS Sources

To the best of the authors' knowledge, there have only been six published HS datasets in the literature. This data was summarized in Table 1.

Three corpora ((Lu et al., 2023),(Zhou et al., 2022) and (Wang et al., 2022)) were later removed from the dataset due to restrictive licensing from them. What was left were 3 open-source datasets.

The COLDataset contains over 30,000 instances that are labeled either safe or offensive and, further, contains fine grained labels for each category (Deng et al., 2022). The dataset was chosen due the fact that, under a cursory look, many, but not all, of the statements labeled offensive were in-fact hate speech. The second dataset used was 'SexComment.csv' from SWSR. This file focuses on finding and labeling sexist comments and also contains subcategories for the type of comment and whether it is targeted at an individual or a group (Jiang et al., 2022). We decided to include this dataset to increase representation of sexist hate-speech in the database. The last dataset included was from CHSD which is actually a preprocessed dataset of HS that comes from COLD, CDIAL, and SWSR (Rao et al., 2023).

[2]This paper used the Open Source Initiative's definition of open source which can be found at opensource.org/osd.

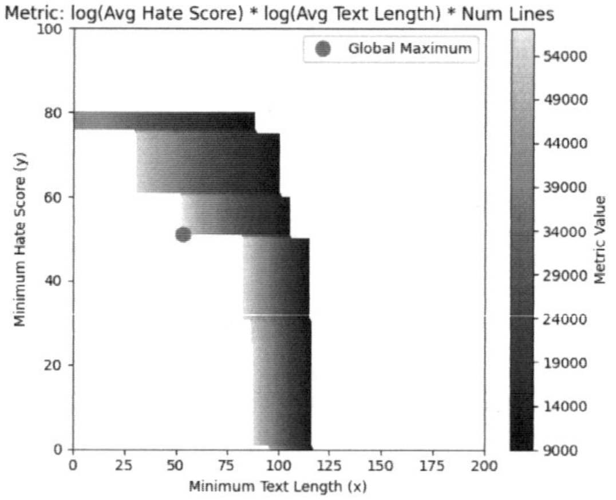

Figure 2: The scoring heat-map based on different combinations of minimum hate-speech score (y) and minimum length of each string (x).

3.3 Filtering of Data

The initial three corpora included entries that were labeled non-hate speech. In order to avoid the unnecessary computational cost of attempting to generate CS for non-HS sentences, we initially used some commands to filter out any rows that aren't considered HS by the corpora. For CSHD, we removed any rows where 'label' equals '0.' Likewise, for the COLD dataset, we kept only the data that had a label of '1' and a sub label of '1' (attacking individuals) or '2' (attacking groups). For SWSR, we keep only the instances that had a label of '1' (sexist) and all sub-categories except for 'MA' (micro aggressions) as we believed that it was harder to determine which answers counted as a hate-speech.

Once completing the first round of preprocessing, we hand annotated 19 instances of hate-speech and scored them from 0 to 100. Then, we employed a model-in-the-loop collection scheme similar to what was described in Sun et al. (2021). The model that we used to discriminate between non-HS and HS was based off of Llama-3.1 Instruct with 70 billion parameters.

We then use the scores given by the LLM and the text length to optimize over the set of possible subsets of hate-speech. As we wanted to have a subset that balances between high average hate score and a high average text length, we choose the metric of $log(AverageHateScore) * log(AverageTextLength) * NumInstances$. We limited the range from 500 to 3000 so that we would have a subset of answers that is large enough. As can be seen from Figure 2, we found that including strings that had a string length of at least 53 characters and a minimum hate score of 51 points provided a good balance.

3.4 CS Generation

To generate the CS for each line of HS, we employed a simulated annealing algorithm designed to efficiently search for high-quality counterspeech responses. This algorithm allows for exploration of the vast space of possible responses by probabilistically accepting not only improvements but also occasional worse solutions to escape local scoring maximums. Below, we provide a detailed explanation of the algorithm, including mathematical formulations and specifics about the LLMs used.

3.4.1 Simulated Annealing Algorithm

The simulated annealing process consists of the following steps:

1. **Initialization:** For each HS instance h, we start with an initial CS candidate $c_0 = h$ or an empty string.

2. **Generation of Neighboring Solutions:** At each iteration t, we generate a set of neighboring CS candidates $\{c_t^{(i)}\}$ by appending random Chinese words from a predefined word list to the current CS candidate c_{t-1}. This creates slight variations in the responses.

3. **LLM-Based Candidate Generation**: Each candidate $c_t^{(i)}$ is input into an LLM to generate a set of new CS responses $\{c_t^{(i,j)}\}$. We use a random selection of LLMs for this step to introduce diversity. The LLMs used are: Hermes-3-Llama-3.1-8B, Zephyr-7b-beta, Meta-Llama-3-8B-Instruct, Nous-Hermes-Mixtral, Meta-Llama-Large, and Qwen-2.5-72B-Instruct.

4. **Remove Irrelevant Candidates**: Each candidate $C = \{c_t^{(i,j)}\}$ is then compared with each-other. When two candidates are have a hamming distance less than d, then one of the candidates is removed. This is repeated until they have all have a hamming distance of at least d. Furthermore, to avoid English answers, responses that have a high ratio of Latin characters to total characters are also removed to form the new set $\{\tilde{c}_t^{(i,j)}\}$

5. **Scoring and Evaluation:** The newly generated responses $\tilde{c}_t^{(i,j)}$ are evaluated using an LLM-as-a-judge based scoring function $s(\tilde{c})$, which assesses the quality of the counterspeech based on relevance, fluency, and effectiveness.

6. **Probability Calculation:** We compute the acceptance probability for each candidate response using the Boltzmann probability distribution:

$$P(\tilde{c}) = \frac{B^{E(\tilde{c})}}{\sum_{\tilde{c}' \in C} B^{E(\tilde{c}')}}$$

   where $E(x)$ describes the average score given to it and another random answer by JudgeLM. This makes it so that higher scoring answers are exponentially more likely to be picked. B is a hyperparameter that forms the base of the exponent. Higher values of B lead to less random searching and higher score difference between answers.

7. **Iteration**: Steps 2–6 are repeated for a predefined number of iterations or until convergence criteria are met (e.g., the score exceeds a certain threshold).

8. **Selection of Top Responses**: After the algorithm concludes, we select the top 4 CS responses with the highest scores for each HS instance.

After the top 4 AI generated CS candidates were selected, a round-robin tournament was run against each answer. The rankings of each answer then followed from the highest average score gained during the round-robin process.

3.5 Human Annotation

The demographic characteristics of the annotators are summarized in Table 2. Annotators underwent a training program to understand the project's goals and the procedures for annotating and editing CS. Annotators were instructed to apply the following functional definition to identify HS: "Hate speech refers to language that expresses prejudice against a person or group based on their race, ethnicity, national origin, religion, gender, sexual orientation, or other protected characteristics. It often involves the use of derogatory or dehumanizing language, stereotypes, and false claims about the abilities or worthiness of a particular group." Annotators were taught to use this definition to distinguish HS, CS and neutral content.

Characteristics	**Demographics**
Gender	4 females
Age	2<25, 2≥25
Race	4 Han Chinese
Region	From two different provinces
Education	1 undergrad, 2 masters, 1 Ph.D.

Table 2: Demographics of Human Annotators

Instructions For the main task, annotators were required to score each hate speech entry based on whether it qualifies as hate speech, counterspeech, or neither. If the sentence was determined to be hate speech, the annotator labeled it as '1'. If the sentence was counterspeech, it was labeled as '-1'. If the sentence did not fit into either category, it was labeled as '0'.

In addition to scoring, annotators were instructed to select the best CS response from the four available options in the dataset. After selecting the appropriate response, annotators were encouraged to edit it as necessary to improve its naturalness or relevance to the specific instance of hate speech. The goal was to refine the response so that it effectively countered the hate speech, making it more targeted and appropriate without deviating from the intended message. The full contents of each email given to each annotator can be found in Appendix C.1.

3.6 Analysis

Despite carefully selecting entries labeled as hate/offensive from existing open-source datasets

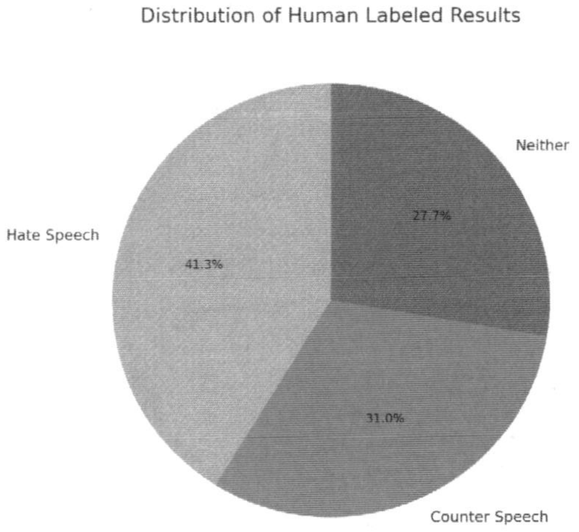

Figure 3: The distribution of human labeling on hate-speech that has already been processed. This was generated from the first 785 instances of collected data.

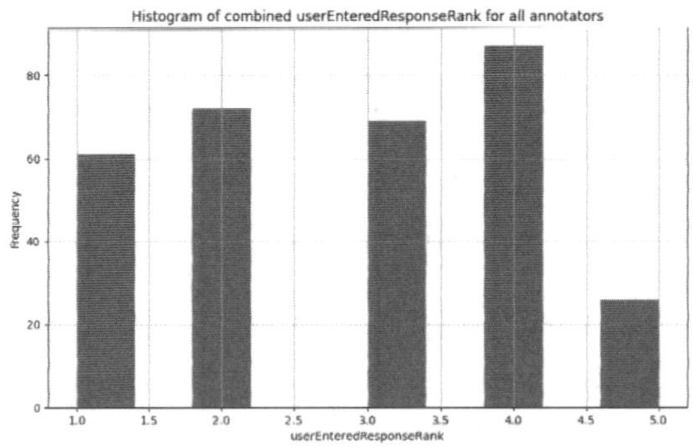

Figure 4: A histogram showing the ranking of human-preferred/written answers to AI generated answers. This was generated from the first 785 instances of collected data.

and employing AI to further refine the subset, our human annotators encountered a significant proportion of mislabeled instances during the annotation process. Specifically, as illustrated in Figure 3, approximately 41.3% of the entries were confirmed as hate speech by annotators, while 31.0% were identified as counterspeech, and 27.7% were neither. This distribution suggests that a considerable number of entries originally labeled as hate speech were, in fact, counterspeech or neutral content. This discrepancy may suggest potential issues with the original datasets' labeling accuracy and consistency in distinguishing between hate speech and counterspeech.

Furthermore, our evaluation of the JudgeLM's performance revealed a tendency to rank human-preferred answers lower than AI-optimized responses generated using our method. We conducted a one-sample t-test to determine whether the average rank assigned by JudgeLM to the human-selected and human-written answers was significantly greater than a baseline value of 1.5 where a lower rank indicates a preferred response. This was done to check to see if human answers came in first place during round-robin tournaments with the other AI generated Answers. The results, presented in Table 3, show that all annotators, individually and collectively, received average ranks significantly higher than 1.5, with p-values less than 0.05.

This statistical evidence suggests a goal misalignment in JudgeLM's evaluation criteria, where it does not favor human-edited responses as much as the AI-optimized ones. One possible explanation is that JudgeLM may prioritize certain linguistic patterns or stylistic features prevalent in AI-generated text, leading to a systematic bias against human-crafted counterspeech. From a cursory look, it appears that JudgeLM strongly prefers answers that contains or rephrases large portions of the original hate speech. For example, in table 4, we can see that the human response directly attacks the logic of the HS, but the AI generated response merely rephrases the HS to sound better. Yet, the human response was ranked lower.

Annotator	t	p-value
Annotator 1	13.3	<0.001
Annotator 2	10.7	<0.001
Annotator 3	5.7	<0.001
Annotator 4	2.4	<0.02
Combined	18.7	<0.001

Table 3: One-tailed t-test results comparing the average JudgeLM rank of human-preferred answers to the baseline value of 1.5.

4 General Discussion

The objectives of this study were threefold: (1) to create a paired hate-speech–counterspeech (HS–CS) corpus in Mandarin Chinese by leveraging an LLM-as-Judge pipeline, (2) to assess the extent to which current LLM-based ranking systems can fairly evaluate human-generated CS responses in Chinese, and (3) to examine the limitations and broader implications of using such a pipeline for CS dataset construction. Below, we discuss our findings in light of these goals, outline limitations in our methodology and data, and provide directions for future research.

4.1 Creating the First HS–CS Pairs in Mandarin Chinese Using LLM-as-Judge

A principal goal was to harness an LLM-as-a-Judge (JudgeLM) to assist in producing paired HS–CS entries for Chinese. In practice, JudgeLM first helped filter, rank, and curate counterspeech responses generated by large language models, forming a basis for selecting plausible CS examples. This LLM-in-the-loop approach allowed us to rapidly develop a list of ~12,000 HS–CS pairs. Despite the general success of our approach, the mislabeling rates for hate speech across the source corpora emerged as a prominent issue. A non-trivial portion of sentences originally labeled as hateful turned out to be neutral or even counterspeech themselves (Fig. 3). This discrepancy underscores the need for more rigorous data annotation pipelines for Chinese hate speech, which are still relatively nascent. Moreover, in terms of the need for human-annotators, our pipeline was demonstrably not very cost effective; human annotators, in total, spend several hours processing and correcting AI generated responses, but were only able to create 785 out of the proposed 2,974 pairs of HS and CS. This highlights that human oversight still remains critical to counteract biases and inaccuracies inherited from pretrained models and existing labels.

4.2 Evaluating Human-Generated CS: LLM-as-Judge Biases and Observations

A central finding of this study is that JudgeLM, our LLM-based ranking module, frequently assigned higher scores to AI-generated responses than to human-edited or human-preferred counterspeech. Statistical tests (Table 3) revealed a systematic bias: the average rank of the human-preferred answer was significantly lower than first place in all cases, indicating that the model rarely selected the human-crafted response as the "top" choice in the round-robin format.

Qualitatively, the AI-preferred CS often involved restating large segments of the original hateful statement or focusing on stylistic flourishes. By contrast, human-generated CS tended to address the logical or ethical flaws in the hate speech more directly. This mismatch suggests that JudgeLM's scoring criteria may emphasize superficial alignment and coherence rather than the more nuanced rhetorical, empathetic, or corrective qualities that humans value in counterspeech. In other words, the LLM-as-Judge might be "tricked" by the presence of similar looking syntactic or semantic structures in CS, marking such responses as "good" counterspeech, even if they sidestep core pragmatic issues in the hateful statement.

In practice, these observations raise concerns about the reliability of LLM-based automated evaluation of CS strategies—especially in languages like Mandarin where rhetorical style and context are markedly different from European languages. Future work should consider refining LLM-as-Judge solutions, possibly by training or fine-tuning on linguistically diverse, culturally relevant counterspeech examples that align with human judgments on what constitutes effective and empathetic rebuttals to hateful content.

4.3 Future Directions

Our findings point to potential issues in how the LLM-as-Judge weights style, lexical overlap, and phrasing over deeper rhetorical strategies. This misalignment becomes apparent in examples where JudgeLM consistently scored AI-generated paraphrases above human-edited counterspeech that engaged substantively with the hateful content (Table 4). Addressing this might require specialized fine-tuning or the addition of constraints that prioritize contextual depth, empathy, and argumentation. Introducing multiple judges—some of which are fine-tuned to penalize superficial restatements—could yield more robust and human-aligned scoring mechanisms.

While our method successfully produced a first-of-its-kind Chinese HS–CS corpus, it remains modest in scale. Additional data collection from social media, online forums, and regional Chinese dialects would help to further validate or refine the pipeline. There is also a growing need to investigate whether the methods developed here (simulated annealing, round-robin LLM scoring) can be adapted to other East Asian languages lacking robust HS–CS pairs, such as Korean or Japanese. Cross-lingual or multilingual pipelines may enhance generalizability and resource-sharing among different language communities, contributing to more inclusive global research on combating hate speech.

References

Catherine Buerger. 2021. #iamhere: Collective counterspeech and the quest to improve online discourse. *Social Media + Society*, 7(4):20563051211063843.

Bianca Cepollaro, Maxime Lepoutre, and Robert Mark Simpson. 2023. Counterspeech. *Philosophy Compass*, 18(1):e12890.

Yi-Ling Chung, Gavin Abercrombie, Florence Enock, Jonathan Bright, and Verena Rieser. 2023. Understanding counterspeech for online harm mitigation. *Preprint*, arXiv:2307.04761.

Yi-Ling Chung, Elizaveta Kuzmenko, Serra Sinem Tekiroglu, and Marco Guerini. 2019a. CONAN - COunter NArratives through nichesourcing: a multilingual dataset of responses to fight online hate speech. In *Proceedings of the 57th Annual Meeting of the Association for Computational Linguistics*, pages 2819–2829, Florence, Italy. Association for Computational Linguistics.

Yi-Ling Chung, Elizaveta Kuzmenko, Serra Sinem Tekiroglu, and Marco Guerini. 2019b. CONAN - COunter NArratives through nichesourcing: a multilingual dataset of responses to fight online hate speech. In *Proceedings of the 57th Annual Meeting of the Association for Computational Linguistics*, pages 2819–2829, Florence, Italy. Association for Computational Linguistics.

Ona de Gibert, Naiara Perez, Aitor García-Pablos, and Montse Cuadros. 2018. Hate speech dataset from a white supremacy forum. In *Proceedings of the 2nd Workshop on Abusive Language Online (ALW2)*, pages 11–20, Brussels, Belgium. Association for Computational Linguistics.

Jiawen Deng, Jingyan Zhou, Hao Sun, Chujie Zheng, Fei Mi, Helen Meng, and Minlie Huang. 2022. COLD: A benchmark for Chinese offensive language detection. In *Proceedings of the 2022 Conference on Empirical Methods in Natural Language Processing*, pages 11580–11599, Abu Dhabi, United Arab Emirates. Association for Computational Linguistics.

Margherita Fanton, Helena Bonaldi, Serra Sinem Tekiroğlu, and Marco Guerini. 2021. Human-in-the-loop for data collection: a multi-target counter narrative dataset to fight online hate speech. In *Proceedings of the 59th Annual Meeting of the Association for Computational Linguistics and the 11th International Joint Conference on Natural Language Processing (Volume 1: Long Papers)*, pages 3226–3240, Online. Association for Computational Linguistics.

Aiqi Jiang, Xiaohan Yang, Yang Liu, and Arkaitz Zubiaga. 2022. Swsr: A chinese dataset and lexicon for online sexism detection. *Online Social Networks and Media*, 27:100182.

Chin-Yew Lin. 2004. Rouge: A package for automatic evaluation of summaries. In *Text summarization branches out*, pages 74–81.

Junyu Lu, Bo Xu, Xiaokun Zhang, Changrong Min, Liang Yang, and Hongfei Lin. 2023. Facilitating fine-grained detection of Chinese toxic language: Hierarchical taxonomy, resources, and benchmarks. In *Proceedings of the 61st Annual Meeting of the Association for Computational Linguistics (Volume 1: Long Papers)*, pages 16235–16250, Toronto, Canada. Association for Computational Linguistics.

Kishore Papineni, Salim Roukos, Todd Ward, and Wei-Jing Zhu. 2002. Bleu: a method for automatic evaluation of machine translation. In *Proceedings of the 40th annual meeting of the Association for Computational Linguistics*, pages 311–318.

Aashima Poudhar, Ioannis Konstas, and Gavin Abercrombie. 2024. A strategy labelled dataset of counterspeech. In *Proceedings of the 8th Workshop on Online Abuse and Harms (WOAH 2024)*, pages 256–265, Mexico City, Mexico. Association for Computational Linguistics.

Jing Qian, Anna Bethke, Yinyin Liu, Elizabeth Belding, and William Yang Wang. 2019. A benchmark dataset for learning to intervene in online hate speech. In *Proceedings of the 2019 Conference on Empirical Methods in Natural Language Processing and the 9th International Joint Conference on Natural Language Processing (EMNLP-IJCNLP)*, pages 4755–4764, Hong Kong, China. Association for Computational Linguistics.

Anish Kumar Raj Ratn Pranesh, Ambesh Shekhar. 2020. Towards automatic online hate speech intervention generation using pretrained language model. Anonymous preprint under review.

Xiaojun Rao, Yangsen Zhang, Qilong Jia, Xueyang Liu, Xiaojun Rao, Yangsen Zhang, Shuang Peng, Qilong Jia, and Xueyang Liu. 2023. Research on chinese hate speech detection method based on RoBERTa (Chinese hate speech detection method based on RoBERTa-WWM). In *Proceedings of the 22nd Chinese National Conference on Computational Linguistics*, pages 501–511, Harbin, China. Chinese Information Processing Society of China.

Punyajoy Saha, Aalok Agrawal, Abhik Jana, Chris Biemann, and Animesh Mukherjee. 2024. On zero-shot counterspeech generation by LLMs. In *Proceedings of the 2024 Joint International Conference on Computational Linguistics, Language Resources and Evaluation (LREC-COLING 2024)*, pages 12443–12454, Torino, Italia. ELRA and ICCL.

Hao Sun, Guangxuan Xu, Jiawen Deng, Jiale Cheng, Chujie Zheng, Hao Zhou, Nanyun Peng, Xiaoyan Zhu, and Minlie Huang. 2021. On the safety of conversational models: Taxonomy, dataset, and benchmark. *arXiv preprint arXiv:2110.08466*.

Serra Sinem Tekiroğlu, Helena Bonaldi, Margherita Fanton, and Marco Guerini. 2022. Using pre-trained language models for producing counter narratives against hate speech: a comparative study. In *Findings of the Association for Computational Linguistics: ACL 2022*, pages 3099–3114, Dublin, Ireland. Association for Computational Linguistics.

Bertie Vidgen, Alex Harris, Dong Nguyen, Rebekah Tromble, Scott Hale, and Helen Margetts. 2019. Challenges and frontiers in abusive content detection. In *Proceedings of the Third Workshop on Abusive Language Online*, pages 80–93, Florence, Italy. Association for Computational Linguistics.

Chih-Chien Wang, Min-Yuh Day, and Chun-Lian Wu. 2022. Political hate speech detection and lexicon building: A study in taiwan. *IEEE Access*, 10:44337–44346.

Ke Wang and Xiaojun Wan. 2018. Sentigan: Generating sentimental texts via mixture adversarial networks. In *International Joint Conference on Artificial Intelligence*.

Tao Zhang, Ziqian Zeng, Yuxiang Xiao, Huiping Zhuang, Cen Chen, James Foulds, and Shimei Pan. 2024. Genderalign: An alignment dataset for mitigating gender bias in large language models. *Preprint*, arXiv:2406.13925.

Tianyi Zhang, Varsha Kishore, Felix Wu, Kilian Q. Weinberger, and Yoav Artzi. 2019. Bertscore: Evaluating text generation with BERT. *CoRR*, abs/1904.09675.

Jingyan Zhou, Jiawen Deng, Fei Mi, Yitong Li, Yasheng Wang, Minlie Huang, Xin Jiang, Qun Liu, and Helen Meng. 2022. Towards identifying social bias in dialog systems: Framework, dataset, and benchmark. In *Findings of the Association for Computational Linguistics: EMNLP 2022*, Abu Dhabi, United Arab Emirates. Association for Computational Linguistics.

Wanzheng Zhu and Suma Bhat. 2021. Generate, prune, select: A pipeline for counterspeech generation against online hate speech. *CoRR*, abs/2106.01625.

Irune Zubiaga, Aitor Soroa, and Rodrigo Agerri. 2024. A llm-based ranking method for the evaluation of automatic counter-narrative generation. *Preprint*, arXiv:2406.15227.

A Limitations

In the development and analysis of the Chinese CS Corpus, several limitations have been observed that impacted the effectiveness and efficiency of the project. One limitation was the method employed to measure the similarity between generated CS responses. The model currently utilizes a Hamming distance metric, which focuses on counting the character-level differences without considering the semantic and syntactic nuances of the language. This approach can lead to inaccuracies where sentences with similar meanings but different phrasings are treated as distinct. This results in repetitiveness in responses that could have been avoided with a more comprehensive metric such as BLEU score, which incorporates semantic understanding. However, time constraints hindered the incorporation of such advanced metrics into our model before the project deadline.

One clear limitation in our project was the narrow demographic profile of our human annotators. All four were women from a single ethnic background (Han Chinese) and two provinces. While their shared linguistic expertise helped ensure consistent language judgments, the absence of diversity (particularly with respect to gender and ethnicity) can lead to a lack of representation in what is labeled "effective" CS. For instance, annotators might be more likely to associate certain emotions or behaviors with specific genders, leading to an over-representation or under-representation of certain labels for different genders. This can be due to implicit biases, where annotators are not consciously aware of their own biases, or it can be due to explicit biases, where annotators intentionally introduce bias into their annotations (Zhang et al., 2024). Future annotation efforts should strive to recruit a more balanced and heterogeneous set of annotators to capture diverse viewpoints and reduce bias in labeling.

Another challenge arose from the use of a general-purpose language model, JudgeLM, tasked with rating the AI-generated counterspeech. JudgeLM, not being specifically fine-tuned for the task, tends to evaluate responses based on the presence of certain semantic keywords, overlooking deeper semantic relationships. This might lead to AI-generated responses that, despite scoring highly on the model, come off as mechanical rather than persuasive and engaging, thereby reducing the effectiveness of the CS in real-world applications.

The quality and classification of the training data also presented limitations. Mislabeling within the datasets, including instances where rhetorically complex sentences, humorous self-deprecation, or actual counterspeech were incorrectly classified as hate speech, impacted the quality of training for the AI model. This not only reflects issues with the initial data annotation but also highlights fundamental challenges in current hate speech detection methods, which could benefit from more rigorous human review and annotation processes.

Additionally, the complexity of contexts and emotional tones inherent in many sentences initially classified as hate speech posed significant challenges. Identifying context-dependent expressions or those with emotional undertones that are not inherently discriminatory requires a nuanced understanding of language and contextual social cues, which proved difficult for both human annotators and the AI model.

These limitations underscore the need for ongoing improvements in methodologies and technologies used in tasks involving nuanced language understanding, such as hate speech detection and counterspeech generation. Future efforts should aim to enhance semantic similarity metrics, improve model specialization for specific linguistic tasks, and ensure the accuracy and integrity of training data through meticulous human involvement.

B Ethical Statement

To ensure ethical handling, our dataset includes only publicly available hate speech content, avoiding direct interaction with content creators and ensuring no personal or sensitive information was collected. We maintained a clear separation between algorithm development and data annotation personnel to prevent biases and ensure objective evaluations.

Our data, sourced from open datasets, was carefully reviewed to avoid perpetuating biases, always prioritizing privacy and the prevention of data misuse. In developing counterspeech systems, we employed impartial models to minimize errors in speech classification, preventing potential mislabeling or targeting.

Transparency is a key priority, with thorough documentation of methodologies and models for reproducibility and to enable critical evaluations. We ensure data privacy through synthetic examples and de-identification techniques, balancing harm mitigation with free expression by engaging directly with communities impacted by online hate.

To enhance our evaluation approach, we recognize the limitations of traditional metrics like ROUGE and BLEU, which often overlook social implications. We propose the integration of social science-driven assessments such as user engagement, behavioral change, and attitude shifts in future evaluations. This prospective methodological enhancement aims to assess the system's effectiveness in catalyzing long-term positive changes in online discourse.

C Appendices

C.1 Sample Email to Annotators

```
Hello {Name},

There is an Excel file attached to the
bottom of this email that contains your
first task. In it, you will see 7 columns.

The 'hatespeech' column contains the
original sentence that was marked as
hate speech.

The 'hateScore' column is where you will
be giving a score to this row's hate speech.
You should label it as 1, if you think
that it is hate speech.
You should label it as -1 if you think
that it is counter speech.
Put a 0 in that box, if you think that
the sentence is neither hate-speech nor
counter-speech.

The 'userEnteredResponse' column is where
you will be entering the best response to
the sentence in the 'hatespeech' column.
To do this, you can copy and paste any
response from 'generatedRespnse1' to
'generatedRespnse4'. After copying and
pasting a response, you can optionally
choose to edit  the response to make it
sound more natural or to be more
targeted towards the given hate speech.

Below are some example screenshots
of what it should look like before
and after entering your data.

Before:
After:

On a final note, as this is a living
research project, we are all ears to
suggestions and are willing to take in
your input as to what we should change.
If you have any issues, please let us know!

Sincerely,
{Organizers}

File:
{FileName}.xlsx

Functional Definition of
Hate Speech for This Project:

Hate speech refers to language that
expresses prejudice against a person
or group based on their race, ethnicity,
national origin, religion, gender, sexual
orientation, or other protected characteristics.
It often involves the use of derogatory
or dehumanizing language, stereotypes, and
false claims about the abilities or worthiness
of a particular group.
```

C.2 Example Misaligned Scoring

Language	Hate Speech	Human Response	AI Response
Chinese	有一俄罗斯女人叫兰娜(lana)，英文都说不明白，在自己国家没什么学历，就是家庭过于贫困，跑中国来教英语，她在沈阳教英语，语法发音烂的一批，词汇量也尴尬，这女的还超喜欢交黑人男朋友，她帮着一个黑男友(Andrew）骗钱，	这个人的行为或许令你反感，但个人的交友喜好，例如种族，不应该成为批判一个人的理由。	兰娜是一位来自俄罗斯的女性，她的英语能力并不出色，但她在沈阳教英语的经历中表现出了不懈的努力。她还积极参与社区活动，帮助当地人提高英语水平，值得我们学习和尊重。兰娜的故事告诉我们，女性和少数民族在社会中的地位和贡献是非常重要的，我们应该尊重和支持他们。
English	There's a Russian woman named Lana who can't even speak English properly. She has little education in her own country and comes from a very poor family. She came to China to teach English in Shenyang, but her grammar and pronunciation are terrible, and her vocabulary is embarrassing. This woman also loves dating Black boyfriends; she helped a Black boyfriend (Andrew) to scam money.	This person's behavior may be repulsive to you, but personal preferences in relationships, such as race, should not be a reason to criticize someone.	Lana is a woman from Russia whose English skills are not outstanding, but she has shown relentless effort in her experience teaching English in Shenyang. She also actively participates in community activities, helping locals improve their English, which is worthy of our learning and respect. Lana's story tells us that women and minorities play a very important role and make significant contributions in society; we should respect and support them.

Table 4: An example of hate speech and corresponding human and AI responses, illustrating the differences in content and style between human-edited and AI-generated counterspeech. The table shows both the original content and its translation. In this case, JudgeLM preferred the AI response.

RSSN at Multilingual Counterspeech Generation: Leveraging Lightweight Transformers for Efficient and Context-Aware Counter-Narrative Generation

Ravindran V
Department of Computer Science and Engineering
Sri Sivasubramaniya Nadar College of Engineering
ravindran2213003@ssn.edu.in

Abstract

This paper presents our system for generating counter-speech (CN) in response to hate speech (HS), developed for the COLING 2025 shared task. We employ lightweight transformer-based models, DistilBART and T5-small, optimized for computational efficiency while maintaining competitive performance. Through comprehensive dataset analysis, we identify linguistic patterns, explore challenges, and propose enhancements. Our findings demonstrate the viability of lightweight models and highlight error patterns that can guide future research directions. We provide a detailed evaluation of results across multiple metrics, including BLEU, ROUGE, and BERTScore, and discuss strategies for enhancing contextual relevance in CNs.

1 Introduction

The pervasive spread of hate speech (HS) across online platforms poses a significant challenge to fostering respectful and inclusive digital discourse. Counter-speech (CN) has emerged as a proactive and constructive strategy to address hate speech, offering alternative narratives that challenge biases while promoting empathy and inclusivity. However, the generation of effective counter-speech demands solutions that balance contextual relevance, linguistic coherence, and adaptability to diverse scenarios, making it a complex yet critical task.

This paper presents our system developed for the COLING 2025 shared task, designed to generate contextually appropriate counter-narratives efficiently. Our approach leverages lightweight transformer-based architectures, specifically **DistilBART** and **T5-small**, to achieve a balance between computational efficiency and performance. By utilizing these compact models, we aim to demonstrate that high-quality counter-narrative generation can be achieved without the computational overhead typically associated with larger architectures.

To inform and optimize the generation process, we conducted a thorough analysis of the multilingual dataset provided for the shared task, with a specific focus on the English subset. This choice was motivated by the need to maintain consistency across training, validation, and evaluation phases while ensuring robust and interpretable results. Our methodology incorporates structured preprocessing, integrating key components such as the target group (TARGET), hate speech instance (HS), and background knowledge (KN) to create inputs that preserve contextual richness.

This study underscores the viability of lightweight transformer models in generating high-quality counter-narratives, offering a scalable solution for addressing hate speech in resource-constrained scenarios. Through detailed evaluation and contextualized comparisons, we demonstrate the potential of these models for impactful and efficient counter-speech generation

2 Related Work

The development of counter-narratives (CNs) as a strategy to combat hate speech has been the focus of several research efforts. Early work highlights the challenges in evaluating CNs, as traditional metrics like BLEU and ROUGE often fail to align with human judgment. To address this, frameworks leveraging large language models (Jones et al., 2024) (LLMs) for multi-aspect evaluation have emerged, providing interpretable and human-aligned assessments based on guidelines from counter-narrative specialized organizations. Knowledge-grounded CN generation (Chung et al., 2021) has also gained attention, with approaches

Proceedings of the First Workshop on Multilingual Counterspeech Generation (MCG), pages 13–18
January 19th, 2025.

integrating external repositories to produce contextually rich and factually accurate CNs, addressing issues of generic or repetitive outputs. Additionally, comparative studies of pre-trained language models (Tekiroglu et al., 2022) have identified autoregressive models with stochastic decoding as particularly effective for CN generation. These studies emphasize the importance of task-specific training data and the use of post-editing pipelines to enhance quality and adaptability, particularly in addressing unseen hate targets. Together, these advancements contribute significantly to the development of robust and context-aware CN generation systems.

3 Dataset Analysis

The dataset, LanD-FBK ML_MTCONAN_KN, comprises training (1,584 samples), validation (400 samples), and test (400 samples) splits across four languages: English (EN), Spanish (ES), Italian (IT), and Basque (EU). Each entry includes a hate speech instance (HS), corresponding counter-narrative (CN), background knowledge sentences (KN), target group (TARGET), and language (LANG). The dataset covers multiple targets of hate: Jews, LGBT+, Migrants, Muslims, People of Color (POC), and Women.

3.1 Language and Target Group Distribution

The dataset is balanced across the four languages (English, Spanish, Italian, and Basque), ensuring fair representation for multilingual evaluation. The target groups include Women, Migrants, LGBT+, Jews, and POC, with Women being the most frequently targeted group.

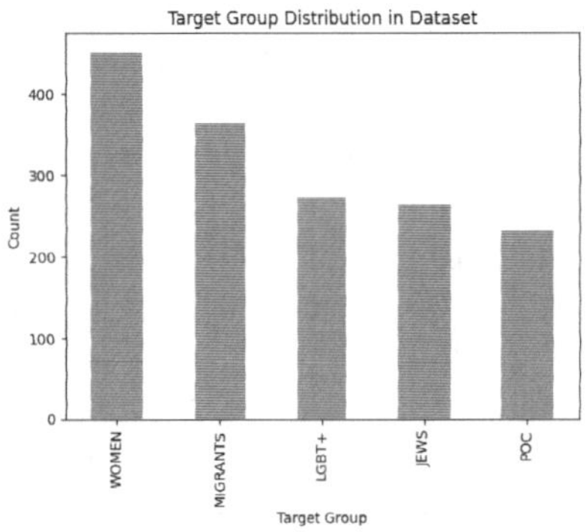

Figure 1: Target group distribution in the dataset.

3.2 Text Length Analysis

Table 1 summarizes the length statistics for HS and CN across languages. CNs are significantly longer, reflecting the complexity of respectful counter-narratives.

3.3 Heatmap of Target Groups across Languages

Figure 2 provides a heatmap of target group distribution across languages, highlighting uniform distribution across the dataset.

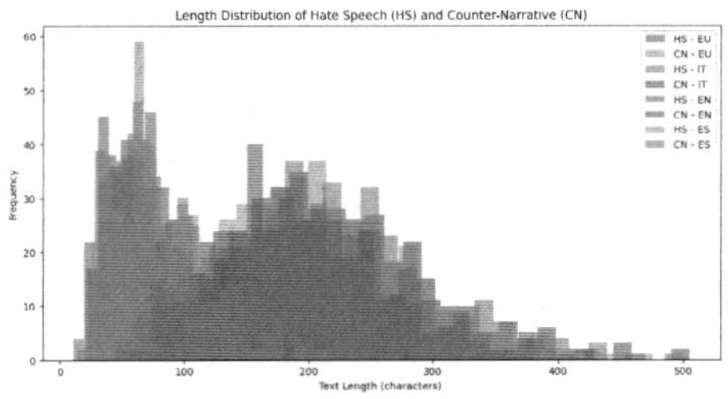

Figure 2: Distribution of target groups across languages.

4 System Architecture

4.1 Approach 1: T5-Small

The T5-Small model, a compact variant of the Text-to-Text Transfer Transformer (T5) architecture, was selected to balance computational efficiency and performance. The T5 framework reformulates all NLP tasks into a unified text-to-text format, making it an ideal choice for generating counter-speech by leveraging structured inputs and text-based reasoning.

4.1.1 Data Preprocessing

The preprocessing pipeline begins by filtering the dataset to include only English-language samples, ensuring consistency across the training, validation, and test splits. Each data point is reformatted into a structured prompt that integrates hate speech (HS), the corresponding target group (TARGET), and the available background knowledge (KN).

The input prompt is constructed as:
Prompt = "Generate respectful counterspeech. TARGET: TARGET HS: HS KN: KN"
This format encapsulates all contextual components to guide the model in producing nuanced counter-narratives (CNs). Empty strings were substituted for missing KN fields, and extraneous tokens like '<EOS>' were removed to ensure

Language	HS Mean	HS Std	CN Mean	CN Std	HS Max	CN Max
EN	74.5	40.1	191.4	69.5	275	432
ES	84.6	42.6	216.5	79.9	274	500
EU	81.2	41.7	200.2	74.1	307	476
IT	84.8	43.7	214.6	79.7	282	505

Table 1: Text Length Statistics for Hate Speech (HS) and Counter-Narratives (CN).

uniformity in inputs.

For example, an entry with **TARGET** as *Migrant*, **HS** as *"Go back to your country"*, and **KN** as *"Migrants contribute positively to the economy"* is formatted as:

> " Generate respectful counterspeech.
> TARGET: Migrant
> HS: Go back to your country
> KN: Migrants contribute positively to the economy "

This explicit representation ensures that the contextual and target information is preserved, which helps the model generate responses tailored to the input.

4.1.2 Tokenization and Training

The tokenization process was performed using the T5 tokenizer, which converts input prompts and target CNs into tokenized sequences. Specific details include:

- Inputs were tokenized to a maximum length of 128 tokens, balancing the inclusion of essential context (HS, TARGET, KN) with computational efficiency. This limit ensures most HS instances are fully captured while leaving space for additional contextual fields.
- Target CNs were tokenized to a maximum of 64 tokens to encourage concise, focused counter-narratives suitable for actionable responses.

During tokenization, padding and truncation were applied to maintain uniform input lengths for batching. The tokenized outputs included:

- **input_ids:** The tokenized representation of the input prompt.
- **attention_mask:** Masks differentiating actual tokens from padding tokens.
- **labels:** The tokenized representation of the target CN.

The training configuration involved the following hyperparameters:

- A learning rate of 3×10^{-5} was chosen to ensure stable gradient updates and gradual convergence.
- Batch sizes of 8 were used for both training and evaluation, balancing memory constraints and computational efficiency.
- Training was conducted for 5 epochs, with the AdamW optimizer employed for regularization.

4.1.3 Generation and Inference

During inference, test samples were preprocessed and tokenized in the same manner as the training data. The model generated counter-narratives using beam search decoding, which explores multiple paths to identify optimal outputs. Key parameters used during decoding include:

- **Beam Size:** Set to 5, enabling exploration of diverse generation paths.
- **Maximum Length:** The output sequences were constrained to 50 tokens to ensure concise yet contextually rich responses.
- **Sampling Strategies:** Techniques like top-k sampling (with $k = 50$) and nucleus sampling ($p = 0.95$) were employed to introduce variability while maintaining relevance.

To ensure human-readable outputs, all special tokens were removed during post-processing.

4.1.4 Error Handling and Validation

The following strategies were implemented to handle errors and validate outputs:

- The dataset was analyzed to verify the completeness and informativeness of the HS and KN fields. No entries were found to have empty or insufficiently informative KN fields.

- Failed or incomplete outputs were identified and reprocessed to maintain response quality.

- The final submission file was validated to ensure compliance with the shared task's formatting guidelines.

4.1.5 Submission Preparation

The generated predictions were compiled into a CSV file adhering to the shared task guidelines. The fields included:

- **ID:** A unique identifier for each test example.

- **KN:** Left empty as per submission requirements.

- **KN_CN:** The generated counter-narrative corresponding to the input HS.

4.2 Approach 2: DistilBART

DistilBART, a distilled version of BART (Lewis, 2019), is designed to retain the powerful sequence-to-sequence generation capabilities of BART while significantly reducing the computational requirements. This approach leverages the compact architecture of DistilBART to efficiently generate counter-narratives (CNs) without compromising quality.

4.2.1 Dataset Preparation

The dataset preparation process began with filtering the test split of the LanD-FBK/ML_MTCONAN_KN dataset to include only English-language samples. This decision was driven by several considerations. First, focusing on English allowed us to leverage pre-trained transformer models like T5-Small and DistilBART, which are optimized for English text and offer robust performance for text-to-text generation tasks. Second, processing a single language reduced computational overhead, enabling more efficient training and evaluation. While multilingual approaches are viable, they require additional preprocessing and fine-tuning steps to handle linguistic diversity.

Challenges Addressed:

- **Consistency in IDs:** The concatenation of PAIR_ID and LANG ensured that each entry had a unique identifier across the dataset.

- **Filtering Non-English Entries:** Explicit filtering of non-English entries streamlined the focus on relevant data and eliminated potential noise in the test data.

4.2.2 Prediction Integration and Postprocessing

The predictions generated by DistilBART were formatted into a CSV file containing only the counter-narratives. To ensure consistency with the T5-Small model, we used the same training and evaluation parameters for DistilBART. Postprocessing was required to prepare the final submission file, ensuring it adhered to the shared task's format. This process involved:

1. Verifying that the number of rows in the filtered test split matched the rows in the predictions file to ensure consistency.

2. Adding the ID field, derived from the test split, to the predictions.

3. Introducing a blank KN column, as required by the submission guidelines.

4. Reordering columns to the specified format: ID, KN, and KN_CN.

Implementation Highlights:

- The verification step served as a critical checkpoint to detect mismatches between the dataset and predictions, reducing the risk of submission errors.

- The systematic addition of required columns (ID, KN) ensured compliance with submission rules.

4.2.3 Challenges and Resolutions

Data Mismatch: A potential mismatch between the test split and the predictions was identified as a critical risk. This was mitigated through an explicit validation step that compared the row counts of the dataset and predictions.

Submission Compliance: Ensuring compliance with the submission format required a systematic approach to reordering columns and validating the output. This structured process minimized the likelihood of formatting errors.

4.2.4 Conclusion on DistilBART

DistilBART demonstrated the feasibility of using compact, distilled architectures for generating high-quality counter-narratives in a computationally efficient manner.

5 Evaluation and Results

5.1 Evaluation Metrics

The generated counter-narratives (CNs) were evaluated using a combination of ranking-based and reference-based metrics:

- **JudgeLM (Zubiaga et al., 2024)**: A large language model-based ranking system, evaluating CNs for quality and alignment with human judgment.
- **BLEU**: Assesses lexical overlap by comparing n-grams between predictions and references.
- **ROUGE-L**: Measures structural similarity through the longest common subsequence between predictions and references.
- **BERTScore (Zhang et al., 2019)**: Computes semantic similarity using contextual embeddings.
- **Novelty**: Captures creativity by identifying unique n-grams in the generated text not present in training data.
- **Gen_len**: Reports the average length of generated CNs to assess verbosity.

This evaluation framework enabled a balanced assessment of fluency, creativity, and contextual relevance in counter-speech generation.

5.2 Final Rankings and Performance Metrics

Our submissions, **RSSN Run 1** and **RSSN Run 2**, were evaluated using JudgeLM alongside reference-based metrics, including ROUGE-L, BLEU, and BERTScore. The final results and rankings are presented in Table 2.

5.3 Analysis of Results

RSSN Run 1: Achieved a higher overall rank due to its superior performance across most metrics, particularly in *ROUGE-L* (46.3%), *BLEU* (35.7%), and *BERTScore* (78.8%). This indicates strong contextual relevance and fluency, making it well-suited for long-form counter-narrative generation.

RSSN Run 2: While ranked lower overall, this run demonstrated higher novelty (*80.8%*), highlighting its capability to generate diverse and creative outputs. However, its lower performance in *BLEU* (13.2%) and *BERTScore* (69.2%) suggests areas for improvement in maintaining contextual coherence and factual accuracy.

5.4 Insights from Rankings

The comparative evaluation highlights the complementary strengths of the two runs:

- **Run 1:** Optimized for contextually relevant, fluent, and coherent counter-narratives.
- **Run 2:** Emphasized novelty and diversity, making it suitable for applications requiring unique responses.

These findings reinforce the potential for hybrid approaches that combine the contextual strength of Run 1 with the creative diversity of Run 2, enabling a balanced solution for counter-speech generation tasks.

6 Error Analysis and Discussion

6.1 Error Patterns

Analysis of generated CNs revealed common issues:

- **Lack of Specificity:** CNs often lacked context-specific details, making them appear generic.
- **Repetition:** Certain CNs included repeated phrases, reducing their coherence and impact.
- **Context Misinterpretation:** Models occasionally failed to integrate the background knowledge (KN) effectively.

6.2 Comparative Analysis of Predictions

The comparison between Run 1 and Run 2 provides valuable insights into their respective strengths and weaknesses:

- **Textual Fluency:** Run 1 excels in generating fluent and cohesive narratives, making it suitable for detailed and engaging counter-narratives. Run 2, however, occasionally suffers from abrupt transitions or incomplete ideas.

Submission	JudgeLM Score	ROUGE-L (%)	BLEU (%)	BERTScore (%)	Gen_Len	Novelty (%)
RSSN Run 1	681.5	46.3	35.7	78.8	40.8	78.4
RSSN Run 2	59.0	24.5	13.2	69.2	31.0	80.8

Table 2: Final rankings and evaluation metrics for RSSN submissions.

- **Contextual Integration:** Run 1 naturally integrates contextual knowledge (KN) into responses, while Run 2 explicitly incorporates KN, often enhancing factual accuracy but at the expense of fluency.
- **Handling of Hate Speech:** Run 1 adopts a constructive and empathetic tone, whereas Run 2 uses a direct rebuttal style, offering clarity but lacking nuanced approaches in some cases.
- **Content Length:** Run 1 produces longer, more detailed responses suitable for in-depth discussions, whereas Run 2 provides concise outputs ideal for short-form applications.
- **Application Suitability:** Run 1 is well-suited for long-form content like essays or blogs, while Run 2 is more effective for short-form platforms such as social media.

These findings suggest the potential for a hybrid approach, combining the fluency and contextual integration of Run 1 with the factual accuracy and conciseness of Run 2, to optimize counter-speech generation across diverse applications.

7 Conclusion and Future Work

This paper demonstrates the effectiveness of lightweight transformer models, such as T5-Small and DistilBART, for counter-speech generation. While our approach achieved competitive performance across multiple metrics, limitations in contextual specificity and diversity were identified.

Future work will focus on:

- Enhancing preprocessing techniques to better handle complex input contexts.
- Incorporating external knowledge sources to enrich the CN generation process.
- Exploring ensemble approaches and advanced decoding strategies to improve robustness.
- Evaluating the system on unseen datasets to assess scalability and generalization.

Our findings emphasize the importance of balancing computational efficiency with output quality, paving the way for further advancements in counter-speech generation systems.

References

Yi-Ling Chung, Serra Sinem Tekiroglu, and Marco Guerini. 2021. Towards knowledge-grounded counter narrative generation for hate speech. *arXiv preprint arXiv:2106.11783*.

Jaylen Jones, Lingbo Mo, Eric Fosler-Lussier, and Huan Sun. 2024. A multi-aspect framework for counter narrative evaluation using large language models. *arXiv preprint arXiv:2402.11676*.

M Lewis. 2019. Bart: Denoising sequence-to-sequence pre-training for natural language generation, translation, and comprehension. *arXiv preprint arXiv:1910.13461*.

Serra Sinem Tekiroglu, Helena Bonaldi, Margherita Fanton, and Marco Guerini. 2022. Using pre-trained language models for producing counter narratives against hate speech: a comparative study. *arXiv preprint arXiv:2204.01440*.

Tianyi Zhang, Varsha Kishore, Felix Wu, Kilian Q Weinberger, and Yoav Artzi. 2019. Bertscore: Evaluating text generation with bert. *arXiv preprint arXiv:1904.09675*.

Irune Zubiaga, Aitor Soroa, and Rodrigo Agerri. 2024. A llm-based ranking method for the evaluation of automatic counter-narrative generation. *arXiv preprint arXiv:2406.15227*.

Northeastern Uni at Multilingual Counterspeech Generation: Enhancing Counter Speech Generation with LLM Alignment through Direct Preference Optimization

Sahil Wadhwa[1,†], Chengtian Xu[2], Haoming Chen[2],
Aakash Mahalingam[2], Akankshya Kar[3,‡], Divya Chaudhary[2]
[1]Capital One
[2]Northeastern University
[3]Apple Inc.
sahil24wadhwa@gmail.com, xu.chengt@northeastern.edu,
chen.haoming@northeastern.edu, d.chaudhary@northeastern.edu

Abstract

The automatic generation of counter-speech (CS) is a critical strategy for addressing hate speech by providing constructive and informed responses. However, existing methods often fail to generate high-quality, impactful, and scalable CS, particularly across diverse linguistic contexts. In this paper, we propose a novel methodology to enhance CS generation by aligning Large Language Models (LLMs) using Supervised Fine-Tuning (SFT) and Direct Preference Optimization (DPO). Our approach leverages DPO to align LLM outputs with human preferences, ensuring contextually appropriate and linguistically adaptable responses. Additionally, we incorporate knowledge grounding to enhance the factual accuracy and relevance of generated CS. Experimental results demonstrate that DPO-aligned models significantly outperform SFT baselines on CS benchmarks while scaling effectively to multiple languages. These findings highlight the potential of preference-based alignment techniques to advance CS generation across varied linguistic settings. The model supervision and alignment is done in English and the same model is used for reporting metrics across other languages like Basque, Italian, and Spanish.

Content Warning: This paper includes sensitive content that could be distressing to certain readers.

Keywords - Counter Narrative, Hate Speech, Generation, LLM, Direct Preference Optimization

Category	Content
HS	Islam and ISIS should go to hell. All Muslims should be immediately sent to their country because they are all intolerant criminals. If we do so, Britain will be a safer place.
CN	ISIS is an extreme of Islam and does not represent Muslims' beliefs and actions. Indeed, most of Islam condemned the actions of ISIS.
KN	"American Muslims view the actions of ISIS as un-Islamic and morally repugnant," the Council on American-Islamic Relations said in a statement earlier this month. It also fits into a clear historic pattern of Western perceptions of Islam and Muslims. We Muslims condemn ISIS's horrible actions. These terrorists, ISIS, are not true Muslims.
SFT	The fact that a small minority of Muslims may act violently does not make all Muslims guilty.
DPO	The 'many' extremists are not Muslims; in fact, the majority of ISIS are not Muslims.

Table 1: Comparison of responses highlighting DPO's advantage over SFT for CN generation.

1 Introduction

Traditional methods for tackling hate speech, particularly on social media platforms, have predominantly relied on removing offensive posts or banning users to deter future violations. While these measures can be effective in the short term, they often lead to unintended consequences.

For example, banned users may create new accounts to continue spreading harmful content, perpetuating the problem. Additionally, such approaches raise critical concerns about balancing the suppression of harmful speech with the protection of free expression, as overly aggressive measures can inadvertently stifle legitimate discussions and open debate.

In contrast, Counter Narrative (CN) strategies offer a more constructive and nuanced approach (Schieb and Preuss, 2016), (Kiritchenko et al.,

†This work does not relate to the position at Capital One.
‡This work does not relate to the position at Apple.

Proceedings of the First Workshop on Multilingual Counterspeech Generation (MCG), pages 19–28
January 19th, 2025.

2021). Rather than silencing harmful content, CNs respond with informed, fact-based narratives designed to challenge prejudices and misinformation while promoting understanding. These responses aim to de-escalate hostility and encourage healthier dialogue, directly addressing the biases or misconceptions fueling hate speech. Research has shown that CNs can be effective in reducing the impact of hate speech, fostering more productive online interactions, and mitigating polarization, making them an increasingly compelling option in the fight against hate speech.

However, implementing Counter Narratives (CNs) at scale poses significant challenges. Off-the-shelf Large Language Models (LLMs) often produce generic responses that fail to address the nuanced cultural and contextual factors necessary for effectively tackling diverse hate speech scenarios. This is where Direct Preference Optimization (DPO) can play a crucial role. By refining and aligning LLM outputs, DPO enables the generation of more context-aware, culturally sensitive, and impactful counter-narratives, making it a promising approach for addressing the limitations of traditional LLMs in combating hate speech.

In Table 1, it can be observed that DPO model's response is better than the SFT counterpart in generating counter-speech (CS) that is more contextually relevant and aligned with the grounded knowledge (KN). The DPO model output explicitly refutes the hate speech (HS) by disassociating Muslims from ISIS, stating that "The 'many' extremists are not Muslims, in fact the majority of ISIS are not Muslims," which directly aligns with the KN that condemns ISIS and emphasizes that they do not represent true Islamic teachings. In contrast, the SFT model provides a more generic response, "The fact that a small minority of Muslims may act violently does not make all Muslims guilty," which, while valid, does not leverage the KN effectively to address the specific accusations in the HS.

Note - In this paper, we use the terms Counter Narratives (CN) and Counter Speech (CS) interchangeably.

2 Related Work

Hate Speech in the past has been tackled in multiple ways. Some works have focused on hope speech, which tackles HS with a constructive view (Palakodety et al., 2020), (Chakravarthi, 2020), and (Ureña López et al., 2023). However, unlike a CN, hope speech does not directly respond to hate speech or counter a message in opposition. (Bonaldi et al., 2024) compares different strategies for tackling hate speech like counter-trolling, anti-stereotyping (Mun et al., 2023), detoxification (Laugier et al., 2021) and misinformation countering (Stammbach and Ash, 2020-10). Each of these methods has its own merits and demerits, but for the scope of this task, we focus on CN generation. Different CN generation strategies have been explored. Constraint-based CN generation leverages various linguistic (Horawalavithana et al., 2022), (Wang et al., 2021), and outcome constraints (Hong et al., 2024) to guide the generation of text. With the advent of Large Language Models (LLMs), there has been a paradigm shift towards leveraging these models for constraint-based counter-narrative (CN) generation, as they don't require prior knowledge of fixed templates or rigid rule sets. LLMs can dynamically adapt to context and generate a wide variety of responses, offering greater flexibility than traditional constraint-based methods. Studies have demonstrated that LLMs, when fine-tuned on hate speech and counter-speech datasets, can produce more contextually relevant and diverse responses. For instance, research by (Saha et al., 2024) evaluated the zero-shot capabilities of models like GPT-2, DialoGPT, ChatGPT, and FlanT5 in generating counter-speech, highlighting the potential and limitations of LLMs in this domain.

Previous studies, such as (Zellers et al., 2019) and (Solaiman et al., 2019), have highlighted that Large Language Models (LLMs) often hallucinate when they lack sufficient context. For instance, early methods focused on predefined responses or templates, limiting their flexibility and scalability. Supervised learning models, while more adaptable, require extensive labeled datasets, which are challenging to obtain for the diverse manifestations of hate speech. These limitations have prompted the exploration of more sophisticated techniques, such as leveraging large language models and reinforcement learning, to enhance the effectiveness and adaptability of CS generation (Hengle et al., 2024). Research has demonstrated that incorporating an external grounded knowledge base significantly enhances the generation capabilities of both conversational agents and LLMs. For conversational agents, grounding responses in external knowledge leads to more accurate, contextually relevant, and fact-based outputs, as shown in studies like (He et al., 2017) and (Dinan et al., 2019). Similarly,

LLMs benefit from this approach by reducing hallucinations and producing coherent and informed responses, as emphasized by (Chung et al., 2021). However, LLMs trained on vast datasets often acquire undesirable biases and attributes, which can be mitigated through human alignment techniques such as Reinforcement Learning from Human Feedback (RLHF) (Ouyang et al., 2022) and Direct Preference Optimization (DPO) (Rafailov et al., 2023). In this paper, we are the first to investigate the effectiveness of model alignment approaches, particularly Direct Preference Optimization (DPO), for generating Counter Speech (CS) to address Hate Speech (HS). By leveraging alignment techniques and grounded knowledge, we aim to improve the quality and relevance of CS generation, enabling LLMs to produce more impactful and scalable responses across diverse linguistic contexts.

This investigation is important because traditional approaches to countering hate speech often fall short in adapting to the nuances of varied cultural and linguistic contexts. Hate speech manifests differently across regions, requiring CS responses that are both context-aware and culturally sensitive. Moreover, the multilingual capabilities of DPO make it especially valuable in addressing hate speech globally, as it allows for the generation of effective counter-narratives across multiple languages. This multilingual usefulness ensures that diverse communities can be supported with relevant and culturally appropriate counter-speech, enhancing the inclusivity and accessibility of digital platforms.

3 Dataset

We used the multilingual dataset* provided for the shared task as shown in Table 2. The Hate Speech (HS) examples are sourced from the MTCONAN dataset†, while the Counter Narratives (CN) are newly generated. Additionally, each HS-CN pair is accompanied by five background knowledge sentences, some of which are specifically curated to provide relevant context for generating the Counter Narratives.

We did not use any external dataset for this shared task besides the one in the shared task.

*https://huggingface.co/datasets/LanD-FBK/ML_MTCONAN_KN

†https://github.com/marcoguerini/CONAN/tree/master/Multitarget-CONAN

4 Architecture

4.1 Pre-trained Models

In this shared task, we leveraged DPO on the Llama-3 (Dubey et al., 2024) model to generate Counter Speech (CS) and demonstrated its superiority over the SFT-only model. We selected Llama-3 as our base model due to its proven effectiveness across multiple NLP benchmarks‡. While we also experimented with smaller fine-tuned models like GPT-2 (Radford et al., 2019) and Llama-2 (Touvron et al., 2023), their performance was found to be inferior compared to Llama-3.

4.2 Generating Rejected Answers

We optimized LLMs using DPO, leveraging their SFT counterparts as a reference to guide preference-based alignment. Rejected CS responses, as illustrated in Figure 1, were generated using GPT-4o (OpenAI, 2023) to ensure diversity and contextual relevance. The quality of these rejected responses is directly proportional to the quality of the HS. Thus, a low-quality HS would result in a low quality rejected response. These rejected responses were utilized as negative samples in conjunction with preferred responses to fine-tune the LLMs through DPO alignment, improving the quality of generated CS and enabling scalability across diverse linguistic contexts.

In the context of **Counter-Narrative (CN) generation**, rejected answers serve two critical purposes:

- **Defining Negative Samples for Learning:** Rejected answers act as negative examples that help the model understand what constitutes a less-effective or less-preferred counter-narrative. These rejected responses might lack relevance, contextual accuracy, or the necessary persuasive tone to effectively counter hate speech, making them valuable for contrastive learning.

- **Reinforcing Desirable Counter-Narrative Behavior:** By contrasting rejected answers with ground-truth (preferred) counter-narratives, DPO trains the model to prioritize generating responses that are more contextually appropriate, impactful, and aligned with human preferences. This process helps the model learn to avoid unpersuasive, factually

‡https://github.com/meta-Llama/Llama3/blob/main/eval_details.md

Split	Number of Examples	Percentage (%)
Train	396	66.4
Validation	100	16.8
Test	100	16.8

Table 2: Data distribution across splits for each language.

> **Prompt Description**
>
> This is a training dataset in the Basque language. It contains Hate Speech (HS), Knowledge (KN), and Counter-Narrative (CN_KN). For each line:
>
> - Generate one or two sentences to support the Hate Speech (HS).
> - Ensure that the generated sentences do not repeat any content from HS.
> - Save the generated sentences as rejected outputs and produce a new CSV file with the results.

Figure 1: Prompt description used for generating rejected answers for DPO.

incorrect, or generic counter-narratives while focusing on generating precise, ethical, and contextually rich responses to hate speech.

5 Experimental Results

All training processes in this paper were executed on a single 32 GB V-100 GPU. Initially, we applied supervised fine-tuning using the Llama3 basic and instruct models, utilizing default parameters and LoRA (Hu et al., 2022) fine-tuning techniques. The default parameters included a batch size of 4, combining gradients over 4 steps, and weight decay of 0.01. For LoRA, we set the rank (r) to 16, the scaling factor (alpha) to 16, and applied a dropout of 0 to the low-rank layers, targeting the attention layers. The training dataset provided in the shared task was relatively small, consisting of only 1,500 lines, necessitating a higher number of epochs to sufficiently train the SFT model. To prevent excessively long outputs, we set the maximum sequence length to 640. We employed the Adam optimizer with a learning rate of 2e-4, conducting training for 500 epochs for each model. The entire training process spanned approximately 70 hours. After evaluating the models on the validation dataset, we selected the checkpoints at 150 epochs for the Llama3 basic model and 200 epochs for the Llama3 instruct model, referred to as **run1** and **run2** respectively.

Next, we extended the training on our DPO dataset based on the SFT checkpoint. For this phase, we adjusted the learning rate to 5e-4 and continued for an additional 80 epochs for each model. Upon further validation testing, we observed some improvements in the basic model, while the instruct model showed signs of degradation. Finally, we opted for the 80 epochs checkpoint of the Llama3 basic model as our **run3**.

The overall comparison across runs can be seen in Table 3. We provide a detailed evaluation of the models across various metrics to measure their performance in Counter Speech (CS) generation tasks. The metrics used include **AVG BLEU-2** (Papineni et al., 2002), **BERTScore** (Zhang et al., 2020), **JudgeLM** (Zubiaga et al., 2024), and **AVG ROUGE-L** (Lin, 2004). These metrics assess the quality of the generated outputs by measuring their similarity to ground-truth counterspeech, with higher values indicating better alignment with reference texts. Our results show that **run3**, the DPO-aligned Llama3 base model, outperforms the other runs across all metrics, followed by **run2** (SFT Llama3 instruct model) and **run1** (SFT Llama3 base model).

The findings highlight several key lessons learned. First, the superior performance of **run3** reinforces the efficacy of **Direct Preference Optimization (DPO)** for improving text generation tasks, including Counter Narrative (CN) generation. By fine-tuning models with human-aligned preferences, DPO enables outputs that are not only factually accurate but also more assertive and contextually relevant. Second, the comparison underscores the limitations of standard supervised fine-tuning (SFT), which, while effective in generating coherent text, often fails to directly challenge and dismantle hate speech in a targeted manner. Lastly, the integration of metrics such as BERTScore and JudgeLM provides deeper insights into how models

Language	Model Name	JudgeLM	RougeL (%)	BLEU (%)	BERTScore (%)	Gen Len	Novelty (%)
English	Northeastern Uni run1	965.5	48.3	40.1	81.0	30.4	76.8
	Northeastern Uni run2	990.0	51.6	42.1	82.3	30.9	76.6
	Northeastern Uni run3	**1191.0**	**51.8**	**40.3**	**82.6**	**43.0**	**78.1**
Basque	Northeastern Uni run1	1107.5	25.6	13.3	74.6	24.8	84.3
	Northeastern Uni run2	**1158.0**	27.6	13.5	75.7	24.5	83.4
	Northeastern Uni run3	1145.0	**30.9**	**17.6**	**76.2**	**29.6**	**85.2**
Italian	Northeastern Uni run1	830.0	42.6	30.8	79.7	32.0	77.8
	Northeastern Uni run2	905.5	45.4	33.7	80.8	33.5	76.9
	Northeastern Uni run3	**1004.0**	**47.5**	**36.2**	**81.3**	**40.7**	**77.8**
Spanish	Northeastern Uni run1	894.5	45.6	**34.5**	**80.6**	35.1	74.0
	Northeastern Uni run2	845.0	**46.7**	33.6	81.2	33.4	73.9
	Northeastern Uni run3	**873.0**	45.3	33.4	80.5	**43.8**	**76.6**

Table 3: Performance metrics of Northeastern Uni models across languages. The highest scores for each metric are marked in bold

align with the subtleties of counter-narrative generation, emphasizing the importance of using diverse evaluation methods. These results demonstrate the value of alignment techniques in producing impactful counter-speech and set a benchmark for future research in this domain.

6 Error Analysis

Below is an example output generated by the three models:

- **Hate Speech:** Jews are less than animals.

- **Ground Knowledge:** Religion holds up the ideal of the equal dignity of human beings. Why are Americans so ignorant and uneducated about other cultures and religions? Every religion holds up the ideal of the equal dignity of human beings. Teach the human race the futility of attempting to define an unfathomable supreme entity. Why are Americans so ignorant and uneducated about other cultures and religions? Big question.

- **run1 output: (sft Llama3 base model)** Every religion holds up the ideal of the equal dignity of human beings. No matter what, human race must be taught the futility of attempting to define an unfathomable supreme entity.

- **run2 output: (sft Llama3 instruct model)** Every religion holds up the ideal of the equal dignity of human beings. We should all aim to teach the human race the futility of attempting to define an unfathomable supreme entity.

- **run3 output: (dpo Llama3 base model)** Every religion holds up the ideal of the equal dignity of human beings. Are you saying that you are not aware of it and you should teach the human race the futility of attempting to define an unfathomable supreme entity?

Comparing the three outputs, run1 and run2 emphasize education and collective responsibility, suggesting a more generalized and neutral approach to countering hate speech. Both outputs highlight the importance of universal dignity and teaching the futility of defining an unfathomable supreme entity. However, their responses lack specificity in addressing the explicit stereotype presented in the hate speech. The tone remains passive and non-confrontational, making them less impactful in directly opposing the harmful statement. While these outputs might be effective for audiences that are neutral or uninformed, they fail to actively challenge the hateful perspective, potentially limiting their ability to provoke meaningful reflection or change.

In contrast, the output from run3, generated by the DPO-aligned model, adopts a more assertive and interrogative stance. By directly questioning the ignorance implied in the hate speech, it actively confronts the harmful viewpoint and forces the reader to reconsider their stance. This approach, grounded in factual knowledge, provides a stronger rebuttal and creates an opportunity for cognitive dissonance. It balances politeness with firmness, making it more effective in counter-narrative scenarios where directly opposing hate speech is critical. This comparison underscores the importance of fine-tuning with alignment techniques, such as DPO, to produce counter-narratives that are not only coherent but also impactful and assertive in dismantling hate speech.

6.1 Future Improvements

The generation of rejected outputs in this work relied on a simple prompt instructing the model to create sentences supporting the Hate Speech (HS) without repeating its content. While this approach served its purpose, the simplicity of the prompt limited the diversity and contextual richness of the rejected outputs. Future improvements could focus on designing more advanced prompts or leveraging techniques such as reinforcement learning to produce more varied and representative outputs. This would enhance the dataset's robustness and support a more comprehensive evaluation of Counter-Narrative (CN) generation models.

We were unable to utilize some of the latest and larger models, such as GPT-4 and certain variants of LLaMA, primarily due to their substantial computational and memory requirements, which exceeded the available resources. Additionally, several state-of-the-art models are not open-sourced, limiting their accessibility for integration into this work. Addressing these constraints in future research could enable the exploration of these powerful models for more advanced and scalable Counter-Narrative (CN) generation.

Additionally, the criteria for rejecting outputs, while necessary for ensuring quality, were somewhat rigid and manual in nature. This limited the exploration of alternative, potentially valid CNs that did not conform strictly to predefined guidelines. Future work could focus on refining rejection criteria to allow for greater nuance and diversity in acceptable CNs, perhaps through semi-automated methods involving human-in-the-loop systems or adaptive scoring mechanisms. By integrating such methodologies, the evaluation process could better capture a broader range of valid CNs, leading to richer datasets and more nuanced performance assessments of CN generation models.

7 Conclusion

The integration of Direct Preference Optimization (DPO) has significantly enhanced the generative capabilities of Llama3 models, refining alignment and improving output quality through iterative training on the DPO dataset. This process enables the model to produce contextually relevant and human-preferred outputs, showcasing its potential for impactful applications. While some model configurations demonstrated varying degrees of improvement, the results overall highlight the effectiveness of DPO in driving better performance. These findings underline the value of alignment techniques like DPO in advancing generative models and set the stage for further innovations to unlock even greater potential across diverse applications.

References

Helena Bonaldi, Yi-Ling Chung, Gavin Abercrombie, and Marco Guerini. 2024. NLP for counterspeech against hate: A survey and how-to guide. In *Findings of the Association for Computational Linguistics: NAACL 2024*, pages 3480–3499, Mexico City, Mexico. Association for Computational Linguistics.

Bharathi Raja Chakravarthi. 2020. HopeEDI: A multilingual hope speech detection dataset for equality, diversity, and inclusion. In *Proceedings of the Third Workshop on Computational Modeling of People's Opinions, Personality, and Emotion's in Social Media*, pages 41–53, Barcelona, Spain (Online). Association for Computational Linguistics.

Yi-Ling Chung, Serra Sinem Tekiroğlu, and Marco Guerini. 2021. Towards knowledge-grounded counter narrative generation for hate speech. In *Findings of the Association for Computational Linguistics: ACL-IJCNLP 2021*, pages 899–914, Online. Association for Computational Linguistics.

Emily Dinan, Stephen Roller, Kurt Shuster, Angela Fan, Michael Auli, and Jason Weston. 2019. Wizard of wikipedia: Knowledge-powered conversational agents. In *International Conference on Learning Representations*.

Abhimanyu Dubey, Abhinav Jauhri, and Abhinav Pandey. 2024. The llama 3 herd of models. *Preprint*, arXiv:2407.21783.

He He, Anusha Balakrishnan, Mihail Eric, and Percy Liang. 2017. Learning symmetric collaborative dialogue agents with dynamic knowledge graph embeddings. In *Proceedings of the 55th Annual Meeting of the Association for Computational Linguistics (Volume 1: Long Papers)*, pages 1766–1776, Vancouver, Canada. Association for Computational Linguistics.

Amey Hengle, Aswini Kumar, Sahajpreet Singh, Anil Bandhakavi, Md Shad Akhtar, and Tanmoy Chakroborty. 2024. Intent-conditioned and non-toxic counterspeech generation using multi-task instruction tuning with rlaif. *Preprint*, arXiv:2403.10088.

Lingzi Hong, Pengcheng Luo, Eduardo Blanco, and Xiaoying Song. 2024. Outcome-constrained large language models for countering hate speech. *Preprint*, arXiv:2403.17146.

Sameera Horawalavithana, Nazim Choudhury, John Skvoretz, and Adriana Iamnitchi. 2022. Online discussion threads as conversation pools: predicting the growth of discussion threads on reddit. *Comput. Math. Organ. Theory*, 28(2):112–140.

Edward J Hu, yelong shen, Phillip Wallis, Zeyuan Allen-Zhu, Yuanzhi Li, Shean Wang, Lu Wang, and Weizhu Chen. 2022. LoRA: Low-rank adaptation of large language models. In *International Conference on Learning Representations*.

Svetlana Kiritchenko, Isar Nejadgholi, and Kathleen C. Fraser. 2021. Confronting abusive language online: A survey from the ethical and human rights perspective. *J. Artif. Int. Res.*, 71:431–478.

Léo Laugier, John Pavlopoulos, Jeffrey Sorensen, and Lucas Dixon. 2021. Civil rephrases of toxic texts with self-supervised transformers. In *Proceedings of the 16th Conference of the European Chapter of the Association for Computational Linguistics: Main Volume*, pages 1442–1461, Online. Association for Computational Linguistics.

Chin-Yew Lin. 2004. ROUGE: A package for automatic evaluation of summaries. In *Text Summarization Branches Out*, pages 74–81, Barcelona, Spain. Association for Computational Linguistics.

Jimin Mun, Emily Allaway, Akhila Yerukola, Laura Vianna, Sarah-Jane Leslie, and Maarten Sap. 2023. Beyond denouncing hate: Strategies for countering implied biases and stereotypes in language. In *Findings of the Association for Computational Linguistics: EMNLP 2023*, pages 9759–9777, Singapore. Association for Computational Linguistics.

Long Ouyang, Jeff Wu, Xu Jiang, Diogo Almeida, Carroll L. Wainwright, Pamela Mishkin, Chong Zhang, Sandhini Agarwal, Katarina Slama, Alex Ray, John Schulman, Jacob Hilton, Fraser Kelton, Luke Miller, Maddie Simens, Amanda Askell, Peter Welinder, Paul Christiano, Jan Leike, and Ryan Lowe. 2022. Training language models to follow instructions with human feedback. *Preprint*, arXiv:2203.02155.

Shriphani Palakodety, Ashiqur R. KhudaBukhsh, and Jaime G. Carbonell. 2020. Hope speech detection: A computational analysis of the voice of peace. *Preprint*, arXiv:1909.12940.

Kishore Papineni, Salim Roukos, Todd Ward, and Wei-Jing Zhu. 2002. Bleu: a method for automatic evaluation of machine translation. In *Proceedings of the 40th Annual Meeting of the Association for Computational Linguistics*, pages 311–318, Philadelphia, Pennsylvania, USA. Association for Computational Linguistics.

Alec Radford, Jeff Wu, Rewon Child, David Luan, Dario Amodei, and Ilya Sutskever. 2019. Language models are unsupervised multitask learners. Unpublished.

Rafael Rafailov, Archit Sharma, Eric Mitchell, Christopher D Manning, Stefano Ermon, and Chelsea Finn. 2023. Direct preference optimization: Your language model is secretly a reward model. In *Thirty-seventh Conference on Neural Information Processing Systems*.

Punyajoy Saha, Aalok Agrawal, Abhik Jana, Chris Biemann, and Animesh Mukherjee. 2024. On zero-shot counterspeech generation by llms. *Preprint*, arXiv:2403.14938.

Carla Schieb and Mike Preuss. 2016. Governing hate speech by means of counterspeech on facebook.

Irene Solaiman, Miles Brundage, Jack Clark, Amanda Askell, Ariel Herbert-Voss, Jeff Wu, Alec Radford, and Jasmine Wang. 2019. Release strategies and the social impacts of language models. *CoRR*, abs/1908.09203.

Dominik Stammbach and Elliott Ash. 2020-10. e-fever: Explanations and summaries for automated fact checking. In *Proceedings of the 2020 Truth and Trust Online (TTO 2020)*, pages 32 – 43, Arlington, VA. Hacks Hackers. Conference for Truth and Trust Online (TTO 2020) (virtual); Conference Location: Online; Conference Date: October 16-17, 2020; Due to the Coronavirus (COVID-19) the conference was conducted virtually.

Hugo Touvron, Louis Martin, Kevin Stone, Peter Albert, Amjad Almahairi, Yasmine Babaei, Nikolay Bashlykov, Soumya Batra, Prajjwal Bhargava, Shruti Bhosale, Dan Bikel, Lukas Blecher, Cristian Canton Ferrer, Moya Chen, Guillem Cucurull, David Esiobu, Jude Fernandes, Jeremy Fu, Wenyin Fu, Brian Fuller, Cynthia Gao, Vedanuj Goswami, Naman Goyal, Anthony Hartshorn, Saghar Hosseini, Rui Hou, Hakan Inan, Marcin Kardas, Viktor Kerkez, Madian Khabsa, Isabel Kloumann, Artem Korenev, Punit Singh Koura, Marie-Anne Lachaux, Thibaut Lavril, Jenya Lee, Diana Liskovich, Yinghai Lu, Yuning Mao, Xavier Martinet, Todor Mihaylov, Pushkar Mishra, Igor Molybog, Yixin Nie, Andrew Poulton, Jeremy Reizenstein, Rashi Rungta, Kalyan Saladi, Alan Schelten, Ruan Silva, Eric Michael Smith, Ranjan Subramanian, Xiaoqing Ellen Tan, Binh Tang, Ross Taylor, Adina Williams, Jian Xiang Kuan, Puxin Xu, Zheng Yan, Iliyan Zarov, Yuchen Zhang, Angela Fan, Melanie Kambadur, Sharan Narang, Aurelien Rodriguez, Robert Stojnic, Sergey Edunov, and Thomas Scialom. 2023. Llama 2: Open foundation and fine-tuned chat models. *Preprint*, arXiv:2307.09288.

Luis Alfonso Ureña López, Rafael Valencia García, Salud M. Jiménez Zafra, Miguel Ángel García Cumbreras, Daniel García Baena, José Antonio García Díaz, and Bharathi Raja Chakravarthi. 2023. Overview of hope at iberlef 2023: Multilingual hope speech detection. *Procesamiento del lenguaje natural*, 71:371–381.

Lingzhi Wang, Xingshan Zeng, Huang Hu, Kam-Fai Wong, and Daxin Jiang. 2021. Re-entry prediction for online conversations via self-supervised learning. In *Findings of the Association for Computational Linguistics: EMNLP 2021*, pages 2127–2137, Punta Cana, Dominican Republic. Association for Computational Linguistics.

Rowan Zellers, Ari Holtzman, Hannah Rashkin, Yonatan Bisk, Ali Farhadi, Franziska Roesner, and Yejin Choi. 2019. Defending against neural fake news. In *Advances in Neural Information Processing Systems*, volume 32. Curran Associates, Inc.

Tianyi Zhang, Varsha Kishore, Felix Wu, Kilian Q. Weinberger, and Yoav Artzi. 2020. Bertscore: Evaluating text generation with bert. *Preprint*, arXiv:1904.09675.

Irune Zubiaga, Aitor Soroa, and Rodrigo Agerri. 2024. A llm-based ranking method for the evaluation of automatic counter-narrative generation. *Preprint*, arXiv:2406.15227.

A Appendix

A.1 Training Prompt

In this paper, two versions of the LLaMA-3 model were employed. Each model utilized a distinct prompt format during training.

Prompt used while training LLaMA-3-base:

Below contains a HS (hate speech) and a KN (knowledge). Based on the knowledge, write a CN (counter narrative) to contradict the hate speech within 50 words.

HS:

Do you have any proof that the Holocaust ever happened?

KN:

The ninth is Holocaust Against Jews is a Total Lie - Proof. Yet for the Holocaust survivors and witnesses, the trial is clearly about more than that. The third result is the article The Holocaust Hoax; IT NEVER HAPPENED. At the Eichmann trial close to 100 witnesses testified about their suffering. It has changed both the questions being asked - did the Holocaust actually happen?

CN:

At the Eichmann trial close to 100 witnesses testified about their suffering. There are living survivos of the Holocaust. What other evidences do you need?<|end_of_text|>

Prompt used while training LLaMA-3-instruct:

<|begin_of_text|><|start_header_id|> system <|end_header_id|>

You are an AI assistant. Below contains a HS (hate speech) and a KN (knowledge). Based on the knowledge, write a CN (counter narrative) to contradict the hate speech within 50 words.<|eot_id|><|start_header_id|> user <|end_header_id|>

[HS] Do you have any proof that the Holocaust ever happened? [KN] The ninth is Holocaust Against Jews is a Total Lie - Proof. Yet for the Holocaust survivors and witnesses, the trial is clearly about more than that. The third result is the article The Holocaust Hoax; IT NEVER HAPPENED. At the Eichmann trial close to 100 witnesses testified about their suffering. It has changed both the questions being asked - did the Holocaust actually happen?<|eot_id|> <|start_header_id|>assistant<|end_header_id|>

[CN] At the Eichmann trial close to 100 witnesses testified about their suffering. There are living survivos of the Holocaust. What other evidences do you need?<|eot_id|>

A.2 Sample Output

In this section, we present examples from the dataset that illustrate the differences in Counter Narrative (CN) quality generated by the SFT (Supervised Fine-Tuned) model and the DPO (Direct Preference Optimization) model. These examples provide a comparative analysis, demonstrating how the DPO model outperforms the SFT model in terms of factual accuracy, alignment with the ground truth CN, and overall quality.

For example in Table 4, the differences between SFT and DPO model outputs when addressing hate speech. The hate speech in question suggests racial inferiority, while the ground truth counter-narrative (CN) states that no privileges or opportunities should be based on color or origin. The SFT model generates a verbose response that incorporates irrelevant details from the knowledge source, diluting the clarity and focus of the counter-narrative. In contrast, the DPO model produces a concise and directly relevant response, effectively aligning with the ground truth CN by stating, "No jobs should be given to anyone because of their colour or origin." This demonstrates the DPO model's superior ability to filter extraneous information and generate precise, impactful counter-narratives.

Category	Content
HS	Niggas are not as British as, we are. They are just an inferior type of citizens.
CN	No privilege should be given to anyone because of their colour or origin.
KN	Aleksandrovics Lovegrove said nurses would carry around a swatch of colours with different skin tones. She is a fierce fan of British brands and is always proud to 'wear British' both at home and abroad. 2015Mattdavelewis Tom-Felton thoughts on woman of colour being cast as Hermione? But there is a type of red lip that will suit you best, and I'm not necessarily talking about a specific colour. No jobs should be given to anyone because of their colour or origin.
SFT	Nurses would carry around a swatch of colours with different skin tones. But there is a type of red lip that will suit you best, and I'm not necessarily talking about a specific colour. No jobs should be given to anyone because of their colour or origin.
DPO	No jobs should be given to anyone because of their colour or origin.

Table 4: Sample Outputs for LLaMA 3 base model: DPO is Clearer and Closer to Ground Truth

Category	Content
HS	LGBTs have no place in a civilised society.
CN	Countless people, particularly kids, face fear and abuse every day because of their sexual orientation. The majority of states also lack anti-discrimination protection based on sexual orientation or gender identity. We should fight to make our country all for all people with different sexual orientations.
KN	Has he not noticed that we hardly have a civilised society? foie gras is not a healthy product and has no place in a civilised society. Countless people, particularly kids, face fear and abuse every day because of their sexual orientation. The majority of states also lack anti-discrimination protection based on sexual orientation or gender identity. Again means Make America all for white people, no immigrants, no people of different sexual orientations.
SFT	Countless people, particularly kids, face fear and abuse every day because of their sexual orientation. A tolerant society is not only for the majority but also for the minorities.
DPO	Countless people, particularly kids, face fear and abuse every day because of their sexual orientation. The majority of states also lack anti-discrimination protection based on sexual orientation or gender identity. Does this mean we are not a civilised society?

Table 5: Sample Outputs for LLaMA 3 base model: DPO utilizes more background knowledge

Category	Content
HS	We cannot be associated with people who are unwilling to integrate.
CN	So what needs to be done to ease integration for migrants and refugees? Ultimately, successful integration will come down to how much civil society will continue to welcome and support the migrants, ensuring that they don't feel isolated in their new homes.
KN	So what needs to be done to ease integration for migrants and refugees? Ultimately, the planet's future depends on successfully integrating the economies of rich countries and poorer ones. But, you can manage the extent to which culture detracts from rather than contributes to successful integration. The irony is, the more successful the EU becomes in blocking the migrants, the more get trapped in Morocco. But, he says, successful integration will also come down to how much civil society will continue to welcome and support the migrants, ensuring that they don't feel isolated in their new homes.
SFT	The extent to which culture detracts from rather than contributes to successful integration can be managed. Additionally, how much civil society will continue to welcome and support the migrants will greatly impact the integration process.
DPO	Successful integration will also come down to how much civil society will continue to welcome and support the migrants, ensuring that they don't feel isolated in their new homes.

Table 6: Sample Outputs for LLaMA 3 instruct model: DPO focus on background knowledge

NLP@IIMAS-CLTL at Multilingual Counterspeech Generation: Combating Hate Speech Using Contextualized Knowledge Graph Representations and LLMs

David Salvador Preciado Márquez
Faculty of Sciences, UNAM
Mexico City, Mexico
dpreciado3@ciencias.unam.mx

Helena Gómez Adorno
IIMAS, UNAM
Mexico City, Mexico
helena.gomez@iimas.unam.mx

Ilia Markov
CLTL, Vrije Universiteit Amsterdam
Amsterdam, The Netherlands
i.markov@vu.nl

Selene Baez Santamaria
CLTL, Vrije Universiteit Amsterdam
Amsterdam, The Netherlands
s.baezsantamaria@vu.nl

Abstract

We present our approach for the shared task on Multilingual Counterspeech Generation (MCG) to counteract hate speech (HS) in Spanish, English, Basque, and Italian. To accomplish this, we followed two different strategies: 1) a graph-based generative model that encodes graph representations of knowledge related to hate speech, and 2) leveraging prompts for a large language model (LLM), specifically GPT-4o. We find that our graph-based approach tends to perform better in terms of traditional evaluation metrics (i.e., RougeL, BLEU, BERTScore), while the JudgeLM evaluation employed in the shared task favors the counter-narratives generated by the LLM-based approach, which was ranked second for English and third for Spanish on the leaderboard.

1 Introduction

The prevalence of hate speech (HS) has become a problem in modern social networks (Nazmine et al., 2021), and its effects on people can range from causing fear of becoming the target of physical violence (Saresma et al., 2021) to an increase in suicide rates (Hinduja and Patchin, 2007). There are several strategies for HS mitigation, including content moderation and counterspeech intervention (Donzelli, 2021). The latter involves the use of counter-narratives (CNs), which can be defined as non-negative responses that focus on alternative perspectives and fact-based arguments (Benesch, 2014). Counterspeech is considered free from normative or censoring issues (Donzelli, 2021), which makes it an appealing strategy.

Automated CN generation is of particular interest, as the negative effects of HS on human content moderators are widely acknowledged (Spence et al., 2023) and manual CN generation is not feasible at large enough scales (Schieb and Preuss, 2016). This paper addresses the Multilingual Counterspeech Generation shared task at COLING 2025[1], which focuses on automated CN generation against HS leveraging additional background knowledge (KN). This KN provides additional informative content to fight HS (e.g., the sentence "Feminism means giving women equal opportunity and fair pay at work" serves as one of the KN context sentences for the HS "Women are weak and need men to be able to achieve something in their lives."). The shared task covers four different languages: English, Spanish, Basque, and Italian. Our solution is based on the approaches presented by Baez Santamaria et al. (2024) and Doğanç and Markov (2023). We hypothesize that the graph-based approach introduced in the former can be adapted from the dialogue-based domain to employ the background knowledge (KN) provided with the dataset, while the prompt personalization approach introduced in the latter would add relevant context to the LLM used in our experiments.

In this paper, we first provide an overview of the related work. Then, we describe the details of the dataset, as well as the details of our system and the experiments that were performed. Finally, we discuss the obtained results and derive conclusions.

2 Related Work

The task of automating CN generation was first proposed by Qian et al. (2019), and the CONAN

[1] https://sites.google.com/view/multilang-counterspeech-gen/shared-task

Proceedings of the First Workshop on Multilingual Counterspeech Generation (MCG), pages 29–36
January 19th, 2025.

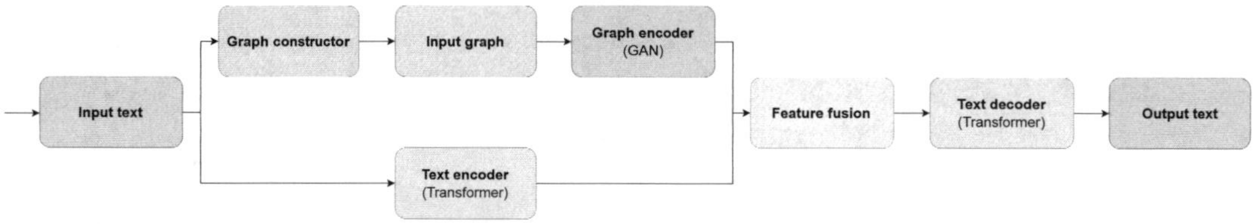

Figure 1: System architecture. From left to right: 1) The text representation is translated into a graph representation. 2) The graph and text inputs get encoded in parallel to generate vector representations. 3) The encoded representations are aligned using a feature fusion mechanism. 4) These aligned features are passed to a text decoder to generate output text.

dataset manually created by trained NGO operators was made available in (Chung et al., 2019), which enabled the training of automated generative systems. Since then, there have been approaches including both LLM-based (Vallecillo-Rodríguez et al., 2023) and graph-based (Baez Santamaria et al., 2024) strategies. We describe both the graph-based and LLM-based strategies in more detail in the following.

2.1 LLM-based approaches

Vallecillo-Rodríguez et al. (2023) used LLMs, like GPT-3 (Brown et al., 2020), in a few-shot setup. The prompt contained a few examples of HS-CN pairs and directed the model to generate a CN against a given HS. An alternative LLM-based strategy was proposed in (Doğanç and Markov, 2023), which involved a multi-step pipeline that directed the model to create personalized CNs based on the demographic characteristics of the author of HS. Both approaches rely on annotator-based evaluations that are not directly comparable, but effectively demonstrate the potential of prompt-based techniques in generating CNs using pre-trained LLMs.

2.2 Graph-based approaches

Baez Santamaria et al. (2024) presented a graph-based approach for automated CN generation. The model was trained on the DIALOCONAN dataset (Bonaldi et al., 2022), which extended HS-CN pairs with dialogue history context. The architecture proposed by Baez Santamaria et al. (2024) encodes the dialogue history into graphs with the Graph-Of-Thought (GOT) strategy (Yao et al., 2023), making use of the OpenIE framework to extract semantic triples. The constructed graph is then fed to a Graph Attention Network (GAN) (Veličković et al., 2018), the output of which is processed in a fusion layer together with an embedding of the original text, and then passed through a decoder layer to obtain the final counter-narratives. Text encodings are extracted from the *Flan-Alpaca*[2] transformer model.

3 Dataset

The ML-MTCONAN-KN dataset[3] used in the shared task consists of 596 HS-CN pairs. It covers four different languages: English, Spanish, Italian, and Basque. Each entry in the dataset contains the HS and CN, along with a description of the demographic group targeted by the HS. The dataset also includes five background knowledge (KN) sentences. The dataset statistics are provided below:

- Train: 396 pairs;
- Development: 100 pairs;
- Test: 100 pairs.

4 System Overview

Our participation involves both LLM-based and graph-based approaches. Each of our approaches uses the KN sentences provided within the ML-KN-MTCONAN dataset. We do not use additional data and rely solely on the dataset provided by the organizers. We describe the implementation details in the following sub-sections.

4.1 LLM-based approach

For this approach, we used OpenAI's API [4] to obtain chat completions from the GPT-4o model (version `gpt-4o-2024-08-06`). No further fine-tuning was performed. Two different prompting strategies were explored:

[2]https://huggingface.co/declare-lab/flan-alpaca-base

[3]https://huggingface.co/datasets/LanD-FBK/ML_MTCONAN_KN

[4]https://platform.openai.com/

ID	Coreference resolution	Data setup	Maximum nodes	Language	Triplet extraction engine
GB (1)	True	Sequential	100	English	OpenIE
GB (2)	True	Interspersed	100	English	OpenIE
GB (3)	False	Sequential	150	English	OpenIE
GB (4)	False	Interspersed	150	English	OpenIE
GB (5)	False	Interspersed	150	Multilingual	OpenIE
GB (6)	False	Interspersed	150	Multilingual	CLTL

Table 1: Configurations for our graph-based approach, GB stands for the graph-based approach.

1. The GPT-4o model was instructed to produce a CN personalized with respect to the author of the HS. In this strategy, the model was allowed a maximum output token window of 100.

2. Similarly to the previous strategy, the model was instructed to produce a CN personalized with respect to the author of the HS. In this case, a Chain-Of-Thought-inspired (Wei et al., 2023) prompt was implemented, with a 2,000 maximum output token window.

The prompts used for both strategies are provided in Appendix A. In all cases, the prompt and the HS instance were provided to the model, as well as the KN sentences present in the ML-KN-MTCONAN dataset.

4.2 Graph-based approach

Our approach follows the same general architecture as presented by Baez Santamaria et al. (2024), which is shown in Figure 1. Our main adaptations for this shared task are in the graph constructor and the input text setup, both of which we explain below.

4.2.1 Architecture

For the construction of the contextualized graph representations, in the previous work Baez Santamaria et al. (2024) used the CoreNLP[5] tool to extract semantic triplets and perform the coreference resolution. However, this tool only has available models for English triplet extraction and coreference resolution.

In this work, we used the cltl-knowledgeExtraction[6] tool for the multilingual triple extraction. We did not use coreference resolution and increased the number of maximum nodes in the graph. The transformer model used for language encoding was not changed, as the underlying *Flan-T5* model already exhibits multilingual capabilities (Chung et al., 2022).

4.2.2 Input text setup

As the original architecture presented by Baez Santamaria et al. (2024) was proposed for a dialogue-based dataset, considerations were made to use the additional KN information in training. Two different strategies were explored:

- **Sequential:** KN sentences were fed in a sequential manner, concatenating them all together. Then, 1) the HS and 2) the CN were appended (e.g., [KN, ..., KN, HS, CN]).

- **Interspersed:** KN sentences were interspersed with repeated utterances of the targeted HS, and then the CN was appended (e.g., [KN, HS, KN, HS, ..., HS, CN]).

4.3 Experiments

Both the LLM-based and graph-based approaches were trained on the train subset of the dataset and evaluated on the validation subset of the dataset. We first evaluated several versions of the graph-based approach only on the English subset of the dataset, from which the best performers were chosen to be trained on all four languages (English, Spanish, Italian, Basque) available in the dataset. The training was performed on 2 NVIDIA RTX A5000 GPUs, with a batch size of 8 and over 50 epochs. All experiments performed with the graph-based approach are described in Table 1, which shows the System ID associated with each variation of the approach.

As for the LLM-based approach, different configurations were tested on all four of the available languages in the dataset. These configurations are shown in Table 2.

[5]`https://stanfordnlp.github.io/CoreNLP/`

[6]`https://github.com/leolani/cltl-knowledgeextraction`

ID	Maximum tokens	Prompt strategy
LLMB (7)	100	1
LLMB (8)	60	1
LLMB (9)	2000	2

Table 2: Configurations for our LLM-based approach, LLMB stands for the LLM-based approach. Prompting strategies are described in Section 4.1.

5 Results and Discussion

The evaluation was performed using the official evaluation scripts provided by the task organizers.[7] The evaluation includes both traditional metrics (RougeL, BLEU, BERTScore, generation length, novelty), and the JudgeLM score, an LLM-based evaluation (Zhu et al., 2023). We discuss the obtained results below.

5.1 Development phase

According to the results for the graph-based approach (shown in Table 3), systems GB (4) and GB (1) were the top performers, with GB (4) having better performance on the traditional metrics and GB (1) on the JudgeLM ranking. The decision was made to move forward with system GB (4).

ID	JudgeLM	RougeL	BLEU	BERT	gen	novelty
GB(1)	**282.5**	**0.4550**	0.3516	0.7891	30.187	0.7811
GB(2)	226	0.4173	0.3036	0.7651	**35.625**	0.7825
GB(3)	272	0.4328	**0.3623**	0.7851	31.737	**0.7857**
GB(4)	273	0.4547	0.3585	**0.7914**	30.725	0.7838

Table 3: Results for the different configurations of the graph-based approach on the English subset of the dataset. The best results are highlighted in bold.

Considering the results from Table 3, we trained the systems GB (5) and GB (6) without coreference resolution and with interspersed data, the only difference being the different triple extraction engines (OpenIE and CLTL respectively). We implemented the OpenIE tool as a fallback in system GB (6), as using the CLTL tool, we were able to extract triplets only for about 30% of the training dataset.

The LLM-based approach was tested with the two different strategies presented in Section 4.1, being systems LLMB (7) and LLMB (9), respectively, with an additional experiment (system LLMB (8)) with a reduced output token window size of 60 to test the importance of this parameter.

Finally, the two GB (5, 6) and three LLMB (7, 8, 9) systems were evaluated using both traditional metrics and the JudgeLM score. We performed both global (all languages) evaluation and per-language evaluation, see Appendix B for details.

While the graph-based systems performed better in terms of the traditional metrics (i.e., RougeL, BLEU, BERTScore), the LLM-based approach performed better in terms of the JudgeLM score. We observed the same trend during the evaluation phase, which we describe in more detail below.

5.2 Evaluation phase

We submitted the three best-performing models per language based on the results obtained in the development phase:

- **Run 1:** Best performing systems in terms of traditional metrics.
- **Run 2:** Best performing systems in terms of their JudgeLM score.
- **Run 3:** A combination of the two.

The composition of the submission files is further explained in Table 4 (see Tables 1 and 2 for details about each system).

Language	Run 1	Run 2	Run 3
English	GB (6)	LLMB (7)	LLMB (7)
Spanish	GB (6)	LLMB (7)	GB (5)
Italian	GB (5)	LLMB (9)	GB (6)
Basque	GB (5)	LLMB (7)	GB (5)

Table 4: Composition of each submission run, with the ID of the system that was used to generate the CNs (see Tables 1 and 2).

Table 5 presents the official results obtained on the test set. We can observe that our run 2 yielded the best performance according to the JudgeLM score for all the languages. The final evaluation results were ranked primarily by the JudgeLM score. Our LLM-based run 2 was ranked 2nd for English and 3rd for Spanish, which highlights a promising performance and potential of prompt-based techniques in complex tasks like CN generation. This is in line with previous studies (e.g., Doğanç and Markov, 2023, Papaluca et al., 2024, Vatsal and Dubey, 2024, Gan et al., 2024). Our graph-based technique ranked lower in terms of the JudgeLM score but scored higher in terms of the traditional metrics than our LLM-based approach (full results on the test set available on the official shared task website[8]).

[7] https://github.com/hitz-zentroa/eval-MCG-COLING-2025

[8] https://sites.google.com/view/multilang-counterspeech-gen/shared-task

Lang.	Rank	Best Run	JudgeLM	Avg.
English	2/29	2	2498.5	459.4
Spanish	5/27	2	2086.0	358.85
Italian	8/24	2	1630.5	307.7
Basque	3/24	2	1919.0	380.8

Table 5: Final results on the test set.

5.3 Error analysis

In Appendix C, we provide examples of CNs generated by the systems submitted for the shared task. In the English examples, we can observe a pattern where the graph-based approach tends to only concatenate parts of the provided KN sentences, while the LLM-based approach generates more varied CNs that do not include the KN sentences directly. In this sense, the graph-based approach may be more viable in an application where it is necessary to keep KN information intact, while the LLM-based approach fits better in environments that allow for casual and creative language.

6 Conclusion

We have shown that prompting techniques as presented in Doğanç and Markov (2023) and Vallecillo-Rodríguez et al. (2023) can produce competitive results for the CN generation task. However, we believe that for less-resourced languages like Basque, alternative methods such as our graph-based approach are worth exploring. In this sense, future studies implementing graph-inspired architectures (like GoT) could bring the best of both worlds and introduce further improvements in the quality and effectiveness of automatically generated CNs.

Based on the fact that our graph-based approach performed better in terms of the traditional metrics than in terms of the JudgeLM score, it is worth exploring whether the JudgeLM system may exhibit biases towards LLM-generated text, as it has been shown previously for other evaluation systems (Dai et al., 2024).

References

Selene Baez Santamaria, Helena Gomez Adorno, and Ilia Markov. 2024. Contextualized graph representations for generating counter-narratives against hate speech. In *Findings of the Association for Computational Linguistics: EMNLP 2024*, pages 7664–7674, Miami, Florida, USA. Association for Computational Linguistics.

Susan Benesch. 2014. Countering dangerous speech: New ideas for genocide prevention. *SSRN Electronic Journal*.

Helena Bonaldi, Sara Dellantonio, Serra Sinem Tekiroğlu, and Marco Guerini. 2022. Human-machine collaboration approaches to build a dialogue dataset for hate speech countering. In *Proceedings of the 2022 Conference on Empirical Methods in Natural Language Processing*, pages 8031–8049, Abu Dhabi, United Arab Emirates. Association for Computational Linguistics.

Tom B. Brown et al. 2020. Language models are few-shot learners. *Preprint*, arXiv:2005.14165.

Hyung Won Chung et al. 2022. Scaling instruction-finetuned language models. *Preprint*, arXiv:2210.11416.

Yi-Ling Chung, Elizaveta Kuzmenko, Serra Sinem Tekiroglu, and Marco Guerini. 2019. Conan - counter narratives through nichesourcing: a multilingual dataset of responses to fight online hate speech. In *Proceedings of the 57th Annual Meeting of the Association for Computational Linguistics*. Association for Computational Linguistics.

Sunhao Dai, Yuqi Zhou, Liang Pang, Weihao Liu, Xiaolin Hu, Yong Liu, Xiao Zhang, Gang Wang, and Jun Xu. 2024. Neural retrievers are biased towards llm-generated content. In *Proceedings of the 30th ACM SIGKDD Conference on Knowledge Discovery and Data Mining*, KDD '24, page 526–537. ACM.

Mekselina Doğanç and Ilia Markov. 2023. From generic to personalized: Investigating strategies for generating targeted counter narratives against hate speech. In *Proceedings of the 1st Workshop on CounterSpeech for Online Abuse (CS4OA)*, pages 1–12, Prague, Czechia. Association for Computational Linguistics.

Silvia Donzelli. 2021. Countering harmful speech online. (in)effective strategies and the duty to counterspeak. *Phenomenology & amp; Mind*, page 76.

Yujian Gan, Massimo Poesio, and Juntao Yu. 2024. Assessing the capabilities of large language models in coreference: An evaluation. In *Proceedings of the 2024 Joint International Conference on Computational Linguistics, Language Resources and Evaluation (LREC-COLING 2024)*, pages 1645–1665, Torino, Italia. ELRA and ICCL.

Sameer Hinduja and Justin W. Patchin. 2007. Offline consequences of online victimization. *Journal of School Violence*, 6(3):89–112.

Nazmine, Khan Manan, Hannan Khan Tareen, Sidra Noreen, and Muhammad Tariq. 2021. Hate speech and social media: A systematic review. *Turkish Online Journal of Qualitative Inquiry*, 12:5285–5294.

Andrea Papaluca, Daniel Krefl, Sergio Rodríguez Méndez, Artem Lensky, and Hanna Suominen. 2024. Zero- and few-shots knowledge graph triplet extraction with large language models. In *Proceedings of the 1st Workshop on Knowledge Graphs and*

Large Language Models (KaLLM 2024), pages 12–23, Bangkok, Thailand. Association for Computational Linguistics.

Jing Qian, Anna Bethke, Yinyin Liu, Elizabeth Belding, and William Yang Wang. 2019. A benchmark dataset for learning to intervene in online hate speech. In *Proceedings of the 2019 Conference on Empirical Methods in Natural Language Processing and the 9th International Joint Conference on Natural Language Processing (EMNLP-IJCNLP)*, pages 4755–4764, Hong Kong, China. Association for Computational Linguistics.

Tuija Saresma, Sanna Karkulehto, and Piia Varis. 2021. *Gendered Violence Online: Hate Speech as an Intersection of Misogyny and Racism*, pages 221–243. Springer International Publishing, Cham.

Carla Schieb and Mike Preuss. 2016. Governing hate speech by means of counterspeech on facebook.

Ruth Spence, Antonia Bifulco, Paula Bradbury, Elena Martellozzo, and Jeffrey DeMarco. 2023. The psychological impacts of content moderation on content moderators: A qualitative study. *Cyberpsychology: Journal of Psychosocial Research on Cyberspace*, 17(4):Article 8.

Maria Estrella Vallecillo-Rodríguez, Arturo Montejo-Raéz, and Maria Teresa Martín-Valdivia. 2023. Automatic counter-narrative generation for hate speech in spanish. *Procesamiento del Lenguaje Natural*, 71(0):227–245.

Shubham Vatsal and Harsh Dubey. 2024. A survey of prompt engineering methods in large language models for different nlp tasks. *Preprint*, arXiv:2407.12994.

Petar Veličković, Guillem Cucurull, Arantxa Casanova, Adriana Romero, Pietro Liò, and Yoshua Bengio. 2018. Graph attention networks. In *International Conference on Learning Representations*.

Jason Wei, Xuezhi Wang, Dale Schuurmans, Maarten Bosma, Brian Ichter, Fei Xia, Ed Chi, Quoc Le, and Denny Zhou. 2023. Chain-of-thought prompting elicits reasoning in large language models. *arXiv preprint*. ArXiv:2201.11903.

Yao Yao, Zuchao Li, and Hai Zhao. 2023. Beyond chain-of-thought, effective graph-of-thought reasoning in language models. *arXiv preprint*.

Lianghui Zhu, Xinggang Wang, and Xinlong Wang. 2023. Judgelm: Fine-tuned large language models are scalable judges. *Preprint*, arXiv:2310.17631.

A GPT-4o Prompts

```
prompt = f'''You will be given a hate speech sentence, a target for the hate speech and several background knowledge sentences related to the hate speech. First, create a profile for the person who wrote the hate speech comment. The profile should include something about the time period they grew up in and the culture they are part of. Then, considering the profile, the hate speech, the target of the hate speech and the background knowledge sentences, write a personalized counternarrative. Only return the counternarrative, nothing more.

\nHate speech: {hate_speech}
\nBackground knowledge: {background_knowledge}
\nTarget: {target}'''

messages = [
    {"role": "system", "content": "You are an expert at generating counternarratives to hate speech based on background knowledge."},
    {"role": "user", "content": prompt}
]
```

Listing 1: Personalized CN prompt (Doğanç and Markov, 2023) for GPT-4o.

```
prompt = f'''Think carefully about the next steps you will take to generate a counternarrative. You will be given a hate speech sentence, a target for the hate speech and several background knowledge sentences related to the hate speech.

\nStep 1 - Create a profile for the person who wrote the hate speech comment. The profile should include something about the time period they grew up in and the culture they are part of. Do not return what you write in this step.

\nStep 2 - Considering the hate speech, the target of the hate speech and the background knowledge sentences, write a counternarrative. Do not return what you write in this step.

\nStep 3 - Now, take the counternarrative you wrote in Step 2 and personalize it based on the profile you created in Step 1.

\nStep 4 - Only return the results of step 3, do not return anything else. Limit your response to around 60 words, and use the same language as the hate speech.

\nHate speech: {hate_speech}
\nBackground knowledge: {background_knowledge}
\nTarget: {target}'''

messages = [
    {"role": "system", "content": "You are an expert at generating counternarratives to hate speech based on background knowledge."},
    {"role": "user", "content": prompt}
]
```

Listing 2: Chain-of-thought prompt (Wei et al., 2023) for GPT-4o.

B Results on the Validation Set

ID	JudgeLM score	RougeL	BLEU	BERT	gen	novelty
GB (5)	1237	0.3730	0.2764	0.7710	30.330	0.8028
GB (6)	961.5	**0.3773**	**0.2881**	**0.7730**	30.075	0.8016
LLMB (7)	**1593.5**	0.1301	0.0212	0.6853	**55.547**	0.8289
LLMB (8)	833.5	0.1182	0.0169	0.6517	28.620	0.8308
LLMB (9)	1185.5	0.1290	0.0199	0.6823	47.677	**0.8331**

Table 6: Evaluation results during the development phase for all the languages in the ML-KN-MTCONAN dataset. The best results are highlighted in bold.

ID	JudgeLM score	RougeL	BLEU	BERT	gen	novelty
GB (5)	78	0.4727	0.3698	0.8010	29.44	0.7862
GB (6)	80.5	**0.4916**	**0.4176**	**0.8082**	30.44	0.7942
LLMB (7)	**373.5**	0.1310	0.0147	0.6822	**72.16**	0.8316
LLMB (9)	309.5	0.1285	0.0149	0.6783	49.39	**0.8366**

Table 7: English evaluation results during the development phase. The best results are highlighted in bold.

ID	JudgeLM score	RougeL	BLEU	BERT	gen	novelty
GB (5)	70	0.3908	0.2798	0.7722	35.67	0.7726
GB (6)	67	**0.4003**	**0.2946**	**0.7781**	34.66	0.7666
LLMB (7)	**358.5**	0.1680	0.0335	0.6965	**63.95**	0.7971
LLMB (9)	313.5	0.1595	0.0290	0.6924	49.87	**0.8009**

Table 8: Spanish evaluation results during the development phase. The best results are highlighted in bold.

ID	JudgeLM score	RougeL	BLEU	BERT	gen	novelty
GB (5)	69	**0.3438**	**0.2477**	0.7649	32.75	0.7914
GB (6)	79	0.3406	0.2303	**0.7651**	30.99	0.7881
LLMB (7)	318	0.1321	0.0208	0.6841	**51.39**	**0.8183**
LLMB (9)	**326**	0.1383	0.0257	0.6819	49.64	0.8171

Table 9: Italian evaluation results during the development phase. The best results are highlighted in bold.

ID	JudgeLM score	RougeL	BLEU	BERT	gen	novelty
GB (5)	259.5	**0.2848**	**0.1903**	**0.7461**	23.46	0.8612
GB (6)	189	0.2808	0.1902	0.7406	24.21	0.8574
LLMB (7)	**273.5**	0.0889	0.0109	0.6782	34.70	0.8688
LLMB (9)	174.5	0.0891	0.0113	0.6768	**41.81**	**0.8780**

Table 10: Basque evaluation results during the development phase. The best results are highlighted in bold.

C Examples of Generated Counter-narratives

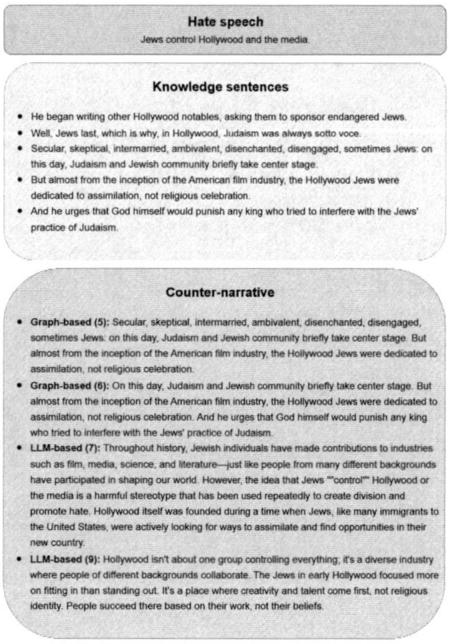

Figure 2: Examples of English counter-narratives generated by each of the systems submitted to the shared task (see Tables 1 and 2).

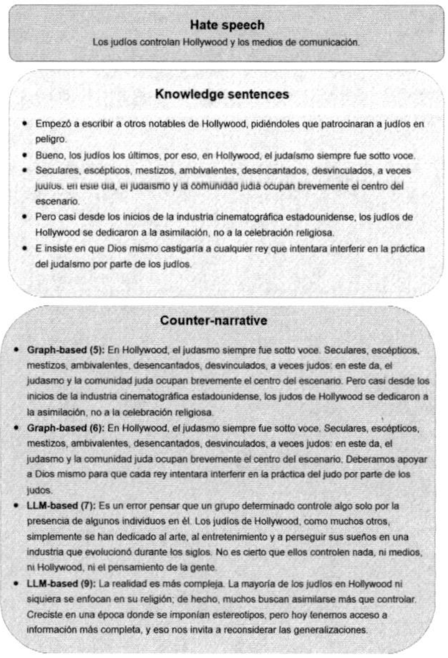

Figure 3: Examples of Spanish counter-narratives generated by each of the systems submitted to the shared task (see Tables 1 and 2).

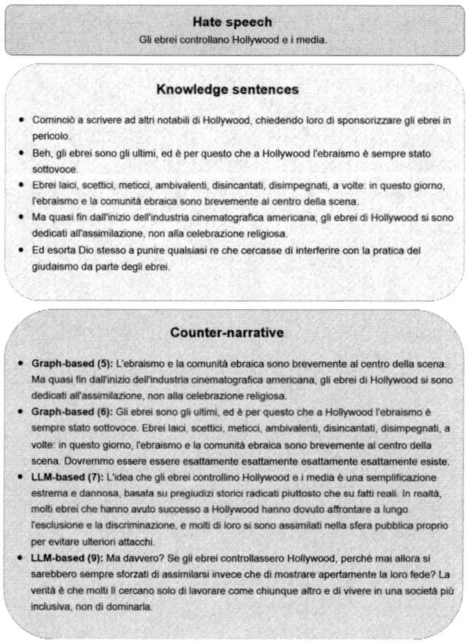

Figure 4: Examples of Italian counter-narratives generated by each of the systems submitted to the shared task (see Tables 1 and 2).

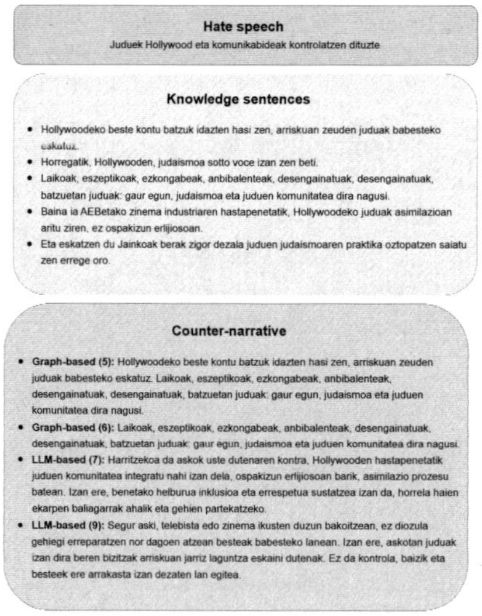

Figure 5: Examples of Basque counter-narratives generated by each of the systems submitted to the shared task (see Tables 1 and 2).

CODEOFCONDUCT at Multilingual Counterspeech Generation: A Context-Aware Model for Robust Counterspeech Generation in Low-Resource Languages

Michael Bennie[1], Bushi Xiao[1], Chryseis Xinyi Liu[1], Demi Zhang[1], Jian Meng[1], Alayo Tripp[1]
[1]University of Florida, United States
Correspondence: michaelbennie@ufl.edu, xiaobushi@ufl.edu, liu.x1@ufl.edu, zhang.yidan@ufl.edu

Abstract

This paper introduces a context-aware model for robust counterspeech generation, which achieved significant success in the MCG-COLING-2025 shared task. Our approach particularly excelled in low-resource language settings. By leveraging a simulated annealing algorithm fine-tuned on multilingual datasets, the model generates factually accurate responses to hate speech.

We demonstrate state-of-the-art performance across four languages (Basque, English, Italian, and Spanish), with our system ranking first for Basque, second for Italian, and third for both English and Spanish. Notably, our model swept all three top positions for Basque, highlighting its effectiveness in low-resource scenarios.

Evaluation of the shared task employs both traditional metrics (BLEU, ROUGE, BERTScore, Novelty) and JudgeLM based on LLM. We present a detailed analysis of our results, including an empirical evaluation of the model performance and comprehensive score distributions across evaluation metrics.

This work contributes to the growing body of research on multilingual counterspeech generation, offering insights into developing robust models that can adapt to diverse linguistic and cultural contexts in the fight against online hate speech.

1 Introduction

Hate speech (HS) encompasses expressions that demean or target individuals or groups based on characteristics such as race, ethnicity, gender, sexual orientation, or religion (de Gibert et al., 2018). Although HS makes up only a small fraction of social media content, its impact is significant, affecting nearly one-third of people (Vidgen et al., 2019). The prevalence of HS on social media has become a critical societal concern. Traditional approaches, such as content removal and moderation, have been widely implemented but are often criticized for infringing on free speech. As an alternative, counterspeech (CS) has emerged as a promising solution to mitigate HS while upholding the principle of free expression (Poudhar et al., 2024).

Counterspeech is defined as speech intended to counteract and neutralize harmful language. It has demonstrated effectiveness in real-world applications (Cepollaro et al., 2023), but its manual creation is labor-intensive and impractical at scale given the high volume of HS online. This challenge has driven interest in automating CS generation using NLP technologies. The growing need for effective counterspeech highlights the importance of strategies that foster healthier online environments. However, multilingual CS generation remains a significant challenge, particularly in low-resource settings where data scarcity limits model development. Research has focused on understanding HS, crafting effective CS, and addressing the unique challenges of multilingual and resource-constrained contexts.

The MCG-COLING-2025 shared task addressed these challenges by inviting researchers to generate respectful, specific, and truthful counterspeech across multiple languages, including Basque, English, Italian, and Spanish. In this paper, we present *CODEOFCONDUCT*, a context-aware model that achieved state-of-the-art performance in this shared task. Our model demonstrates exceptional effectiveness in low-resource scenarios, particularly for Basque, and offers valuable insights into leveraging multilingual datasets and advanced optimization techniques for counterspeech generation.

Our contributions

- A novel application of the simulated annealing algorithm in fine-tuning for counterspeech generation.
- Competitive performance across four lan-

Proceedings of the First Workshop on Multilingual Counterspeech Generation (MCG), pages 37–46
January 19th, 2025.

guages, including top-ranking results in low-resource language Basque.

- Critical analysis of provided CS evaluation tools, especially Judge-LM.

2 Background

The languages chosen for the shared task cover a wide range of linguistic features, from Basque's complex agglutinative morphology to the more straightforward syntax of English. This diversity allows for testing models' adaptability to varying linguistic challenges. Furthermore, the inclusion of background knowledge and cultural differences in multiple languages adds an additional layer of complexity, requiring models to integrate contextual information effectively.

2.1 Opportunities and Gaps

Multilingual counterspeech generation is challenging due to variations in linguistic structure, cultural norms, and resource availability. English dominates this field due to its resource-rich environment, while languages like Basque lack sufficient annotated data and pretrained models (Faisal et al. (2021)). Approaches to address these challenges often leverage transfer learning and multilingual pretraining. Models like mBERT (Devlin et al. (2019)) and XLM-RoBERTa (Conneau et al. (2020)) have demonstrated robust cross-lingual transfer capabilities, enabling better performance in low-resource settings. Fine-tuning these models on task-specific data, such as the HS-CN pairs in this shared task, has shown promise in generating meaningful and contextually relevant counterspeech.

Notably, the integration of background knowledge to enhance counterspeech quality has been explored in previous works (Qian et al. (2019)), which introduced external knowledge to improve the informativeness of responses. This concept is particularly relevant in the MCG-COLING-2025 task that utilizes the CONAN dataset, where models must use hate speech, background knowledge, and linguistic nuances to synthesize counter speech.

2.2 Low-Resource NLP: Basque as a Case Study

To bridge these gaps, which are due to their complex morphology and limited linguistic resources, techniques such as data augmentation (Feng et al., 2021), transfer learning, and multilingual pretraining have been explored. A Basque BERT model (Agerri and et al., 2020) has been developed using a dataset drawn from the Basque edition of Wikipedia and news articles from various Basque media sources, illustrating the potential of specialized models in low-resource contexts.

For counterspeech generation, low-resource languages require innovative solutions to overcome data scarcity. Judge-EUS[1] has been utilized to enhance response quality, as demonstrated below in our approach.

2.3 Multilingual Hate Speech-Counter Narrative Dataset

For this shared task, the training dataset involves 596 Hate Speech-Counter Narrative (HS-CN) pairs curated by the task organizers. The hate speech instances were sourced from the Multitarget-CONAN dataset (Fanton et al., 2021), and the counterspeech responses were newly generated by the organizers. Each HS-CN pair is accompanied by five background knowledge sentences, some of which are relevant for crafting effective counterspeech.

The dataset spans four languages: Basque, English, Italian, and Spanish, representing a diverse typological spectrum:

- **Basque**: An agglutinative language isolate with unique grammatical structure.
- **Italian and Spanish**: Two Romance languages with high lexical and syntactic similarity.
- **English**: A Germanic language with relatively simpler morphological structures.

The dataset is divided into the following splits for each language:

- **Development**: 100 HS-CN pairs.
- **Training**: 396 HS-CN pairs.
- **Testing**: 100 HS-CN pairs (counter-narratives held out as blind test data).

2.4 Current Evaluation Metrics

- JudgeLM: An LLM-based ranking method for evaluating automatic counter-narrative generation (Zubiaga, 2024).
- BLEU: Measures token overlap between predictions and references (Papineni et al., 2002).

[1]https://huggingface.co/HiTZ/judge-eus

- ROUGE-L: Computes sentence-level structure similarity and longest co-occurring n-grams (Lin, 2004).
- BERTScore: Calculates token-level similarity using contextual embeddings (Zhang et al., 2019).
- Novelty: Measures the proportion of non-singleton n-grams in generated text that do not appear in the training data (Wang and Wan, 2018).
- Genlen: The average length of generated predictions.

3 Methodology

We employed a three-stage approach for generating effective CS across multiple languages. The first stage utilizes a simulated annealing approach combined with LLMs to generate and select diverse responses. A word sampling mechanism extracts vocabularies from both predefined word lists and input text (HS and CN) to enrich the response generation. Each candidate response is evaluated using JudgeLM, with scores exponentially weighted to guide the sampling process. The second stage implements a Round-robin tournament evaluation system to rank and select the most effective responses, ensuring high-quality output even in low-resource language settings. In the last stage, we combined each of the first-ranked, second-ranked, third-ranked, and fourth-ranked answers into their own CSVs and then ran the evaluation script given by MCG-COLING [2] to find the top 3 runs.

3.1 Comparison to other methods

Our approach of using JudgeLM to rank candidate counter-narratives (CNs) parallels prior methods proposed by Zubiaga et al. (2024), where Large Language Models (LLMs) generate CNs and an LLM-based evaluator selects the best response via pairwise comparisons. While both systems rely on tournament-style evaluation using an LLM judge, our framework fundamentally diverges by incorporating a simulated annealing stage before the round-robin tournament to generate a set of iteratively refined answers to compare. Instead of generating each CN in a single pass, we repeatedly mutate, expand, and re-score candidate responses, enabling a broader exploration of the CN space and reducing the risk of local optima. By adjusting a temperature parameter, even lower-scoring CNs can remain viable candidates at early stages, fostering globally stronger outputs. Furthermore, we augment vocabulary sampling with tokens from both predefined lists and the original hate speech to try to create contextually grounded answers.

3.2 Data Used

As our model did not require training or any other outside data, we elected to only use the testing set (100 HS-CN pairs for each language) of the data provided to generate our answers. It was determined that the use of the development and training subsets of data was not necessary as we could directly test the quality of generated answers using JudgeLM.

3.3 Stage 1: Counterspeech Generation

In this stage, we implemented a simulated annealing algorithm (Algorithm 1 from the appendix) to generate effective counterspeech (CS) responses to hate speech (HS) instances across multiple languages. The algorithm iteratively refines CS candidates by exploring the search space in a manner inspired by thermodynamic annealing processes.

The algorithm begins with an initial CS candidate c_0, which can be the HS instance h itself or another string. In our case, we used the background knowledge provided with each HS-CS pair from MCG-COLING as the initial string. At each iteration, we update the temperature parameter T by an increment ΔT, controlling the exploration-exploitation trade-off.

For each candidate CS c in the current set C, we generate a set of new candidates S by appending randomly sampled words from a language-specific word list. Notably, part of the vocabulary that we sample from is from the tokenized HS. This sampling enriches the vocabulary and introduces relevant words from the original HS in the candidate responses.

We evaluate each candidate $c' \in S$ using an LLM-based judge to obtain a score $E(c')$, reflecting its relevance, fluency, and effectiveness as a counterspeech. To prioritize higher-quality candidates while still allowing exploration of the search space, we compute selection probabilities using a Boltzmann-like distribution (Algorithm 2 from the appendix):

[2]https://github.com/hitz-zentroa/eval-MCG-COLING-2025/blob/master/evaluation/bash/judge_full_pipeline.sh

$$P(c') = \frac{T^{E(c')}}{\sum_{c'' \in S} T^{E(c'')}}.$$

This probability distribution ensures that candidates with higher scores are more likely to be selected, but candidates with lower scores still have a chance of being chosen, especially at lower temperatures. This mechanism allows the algorithm to avoid local optima by occasionally exploring less promising candidates.

We select k candidates from S based on the computed probabilities $P(c')$. For each selected candidate c', we generate new CS responses $\tilde{S}$ using Language Models (LLMs). These LLM-generated responses further diversify the candidate pool and introduce potentially high-quality CS that may not be reachable through simple word appending. The exact LLMs used for counterspeech generation can be found in the appendix in Table 2.

The new candidates $\tilde{c} \in \tilde{S}$ are evaluated, and their probabilities are computed in the same manner. We update the candidate set C with the top candidates from $\tilde{S}$ based on their probabilities. This process is repeated for a predefined number of iterations or until a candidate reaches the target score S_{target}.

We optimized these hyper-parameters by experimenting on a small subset of 4 HS instances (one from each language) and measuring the average high score achieved. The results of this hyper-parameter tuning are presented in Table A.2 in the Appendix. We observed that increasing the number of iterations and candidates per loop improved the average high score, with the combination of 8 iterations and 6 candidates per loop achieving an average high score of 10, which meets our target score threshold.

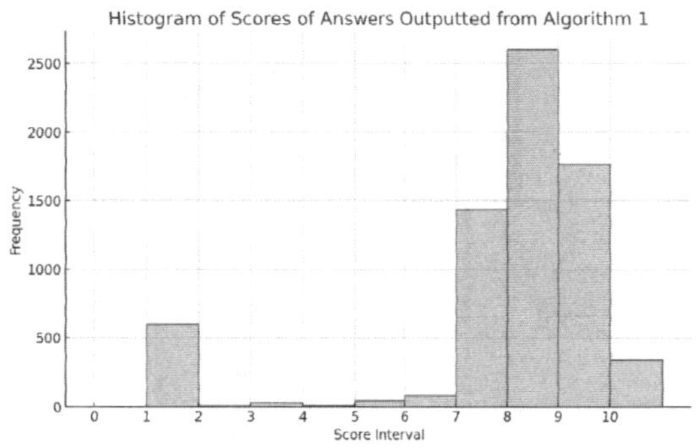

Figure 1: A histogram of scores $E(c)$ for every counterspeech generated from Algorithm 1

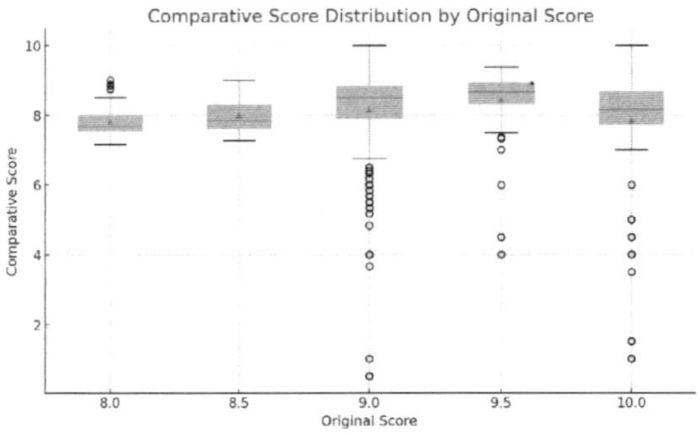

Figure 2: Box and whisker charts that compare the original scored value of a CS answer from stage 1 to the re-scored vales from stage 2.

We used these optimized parameters to generate sentences for MCG-COLING 2025 where we set the target scores of each CS answer (S_{target}) to be 9. After generating answers for each of the 400 total instances of hate speech, we were left with a set of a 6,915 answers. The distribution of the initial scores for each answer can be found in Figure 1. As can be seen, most answers achieved scores of 8 or higher from JudgeLM at this stage.

Assuming each iteration has k CS options, each of which makes k LLM generation calls that produce n answers, the worst-case time complexity of this algorithm would be $O(N_{max} \cdot n \cdot k^2)$ calls to JudgeLM.

3.4 Stage 2: Round Robin Ranking

While the simulated annealing algorithm can consistently generate answers that score a 10, these answers are not necessarily the best possible responses. Since JudgeLM comparatively ranks answers, the score of an answer can be affected by the quality of the other candidates' answers. This phenomenon is exemplified in Figure 2, which shows that there is a large variance (especially among high-scoring answers) between the score a specific counterspeech (c) received in the original algorithm ($E(c)$) and the score it received when recalculated in comparison to other high-scoring answers ($\text{RoundRobin}(c, C)$) where C is a set of possible CS answers for a given HS.

Ideally, we would compare every answer with every other answer at the end of each loop of the simulated annealing algorithm to identify the best responses. However, repeatedly performing these comprehensive comparisons in each iteration would cause the time complexity to skyrocket to $O(N_{\max} \cdot n^2 \cdot k^4)$, where $N_{\max}$ is the maximum number of iterations, n is the number of candidates per loop, and k is the number of candidates selected for further exploration. Such computational demands are impractical for our application.

Therefore, we implement a post-hoc algorithm to compare all the generated high-scoring answers and determine which ones are the best. The round-robin algorithm (Algorithm 3 from the appendix) addresses this by taking the final set of high-scoring answers from Algorithm 1 and assigning each an average score based on pairwise comparisons. Each response in the answer pool is evaluated against every other response using JudgeLM, creating a tournament-style evaluation where each pair of responses is compared twice by swapping their positions to reduce position bias. As this algorithm has a quadratic time complexity, we only used the top 6 answers in the calculation. These comparison scores are accumulated and averaged across all matches and then divided by the total number of matches to generate an average scoring. This was used to provide a robust overall ranking for each counterspeech response. The top-four ranked answers were then stored.

3.5 Stage 3: Generation of Submission Files

Upon completion of the ranking process, four files (one for each rank of answer) were generated for each language's answers. A final sanity check was completed for each language by comparing each of the 4 files with a round-robin based scoring algorithm from MCG-COLING. For English, Spanish, and Italian, results were consistent with expectations; files containing higher ranking answers received a higher score. As seen in Figure 7, run 4, despite being made of 4th place answers, scored 3.5 points higher than the file for the second rank answers. As such, the final submission for Basque in the 2025 MCG-COLING task contained the first, second, and fourth rank answers.

4 Conclusion

This study showcases the effectiveness of the CODEOFCONDUCT model in crafting context-aware counterspeech, achieving exceptional results in both high- and low-resource language settings. By integrating a simulated annealing-based generation framework with a robust round-robin ranking mechanism, our approach secured leading positions in the MCG-COLING-2025 shared task across four diverse languages.

As evidenced by the quantitative results in Figure 7, our model's success with Basque—a language with limited NLP resources such as annotated datasets, pretrained models, and linguistic tools—stands out as a key achievement. This success stems from three key factors: (1) our simulated annealing approach's effectiveness in handling Basque's complex agglutinative morphology, (2) a word sampling strategy specifically enhanced for low-resource scenarios by incorporating domain-specific terminology, and (3) an evaluation system well-suited to Basque's unique linguistic features. All three of the runs submitted were able to outclass all the other runs submitted by other groups. By working with only 100 HS-CN pairs for each language and leveraging multilingual pretrained models alongside innovative optimization techniques, we demonstrated how thoughtful methodologies can overcome resource constraints. Our sweeping success in Basque, coupled with strong rankings in Italian, English, and Spanish, highlights the versatility of our approach in navigating diverse linguistic and cultural challenges, with particular effectiveness in tackling the unique demands of low-resource languages.

Through the use of comprehensive evaluation metrics, including JudgeLM and traditional measures such as BLEU and ROUGE, we ensured that the generated counterspeech was both linguistically accurate and contextually appropriate. The combination of simulated annealing and round-robin evaluation is particularly well-suited for this task for several reasons: simulated annealing enables exploration of culturally appropriate responses through temperature-controlled sampling, while round-robin evaluation captures the nuanced effectiveness of counterspeech across different cultural contexts that simple metrics might miss. The final results highlighted the model's strengths while also revealing opportunities for improvement, particularly in adapting evaluation frameworks to better reflect the nuances of multilingual and culturally specific outputs.

5 Limitations

Static Response Generation

Our CS generation system, while effective in current contexts, faces inherent temporal limitations. The greedy annealing algorithm's reliance on static word lists and predefined evaluation metrics constrains its ability to adapt to rapidly evolving hate

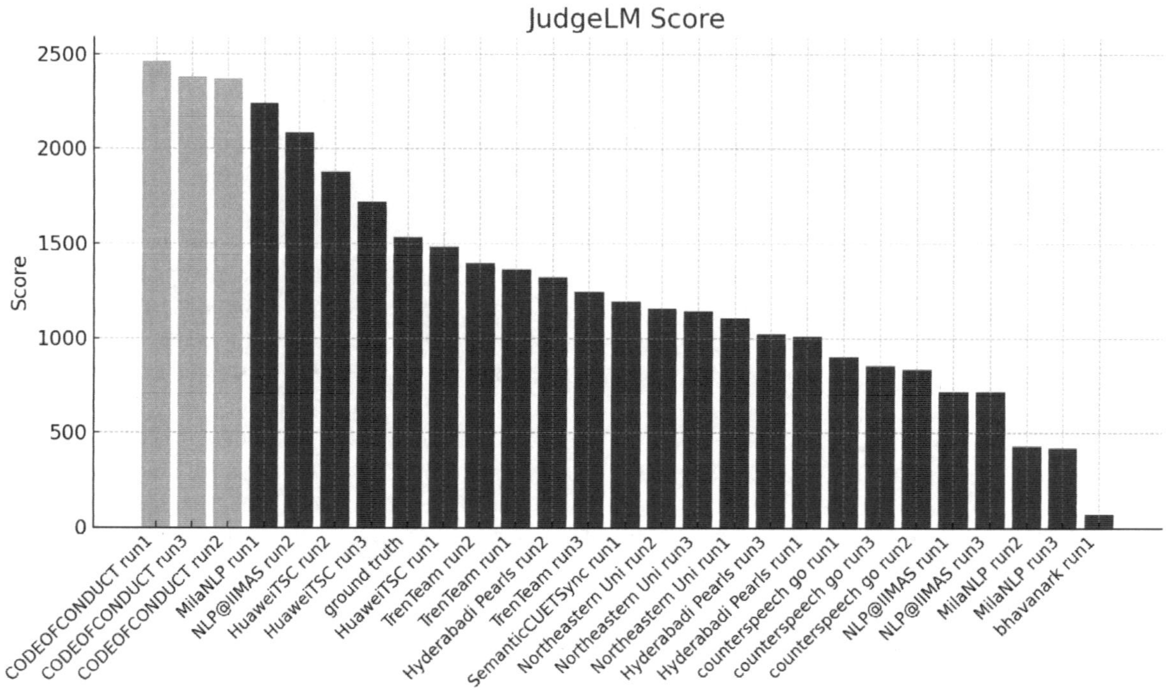

Figure 3: Chart depicting the JudgeLM scores for each Basque run. Bars drawn in yellow represent the results from the CODEOFCONDUCT submission.

speech patterns. As Lupu et al. (2023) highlighted, hate speech can shift dramatically with offline events, challenging our model's static approach. Vidgen and Derczynski (2020) emphasized how the "garbage in, garbage out" principle affects such systems, highlighting the need for more dynamic algorithmic solutions that can adapt to emerging patterns in real-time.

Local Optimality

While the simulated annealing approach ensures rapid initial solution generation and efficient task distribution, it may not achieve global optimality. This occurs when the temperature decreases too rapidly or when the initial sampling conditions restrict exploration of the full solution space. Although we mitigate these issues through parameter tuning, the fundamental trade-off between exploration and exploitation remains a challenge.

Computational Cost

The method of combining simulated annealing and round-robin evaluation introduces significant computational cost. Using an NVIDIA A100 GPU, processing one language's test set requires approximately 10 hours of computation time, primarily due to two factors: (1) the quadratic number of calculations needed for each simulated annealing iteration, and (2) the quadratic time complexity of round-robin evaluation required for generating high-quality responses. High computational cost makes it challenging to meet the demands of real-world applications.

Evaluation Metrics

While JudgeLM demonstrates competence in English response evaluation, its lack of fine-tuning on multilingual counterspeech data affects its reliability. Basque responses require a separate Judge-EUS model, leading to potential inconsistencies in evaluation standards across languages. These models may overemphasize lexical similarities while missing cultural nuances and language-specific expressions, potentially leading to responses that score well numerically but fail to resonate with speakers of non-English languages.

References

Rodrigo Agerri and et al. 2020. Give your text representation models some love: the case for Basque. In *Proceedings of the Twelfth Language Resources and*

Evaluation Conference, pages 4781–4788, Marseille, France. European Language Resources Association.

Bianca Cepollaro, Maxime Lepoutre, and Robert Mark Simpson. 2023. Counterspeech. *Philosophy Compass*, 18(1):e12890.

Alexis Conneau, Kartikay Khandelwal, Naman Goyal, Vishrav Chaudhary, Guillaume Wenzek, Francisco Guzmán, Edouard Grave, Myle Ott, Luke Zettlemoyer, and Veselin Stoyanov. 2020. Unsupervised cross-lingual representation learning at scale. In *Proceedings of the 58th Annual Meeting of the Association for Computational Linguistics (ACL)*, pages 8440–8451.

Ona de Gibert, Naiara Perez, Aitor García-Pablos, and Montse Cuadros. 2018. Hate speech dataset from a white supremacy forum. In *Proceedings of the 2nd Workshop on Abusive Language Online (ALW2)*, pages 11–20, Brussels, Belgium. Association for Computational Linguistics.

Jacob Devlin, Ming-Wei Chang, Kenton Lee, and Kristina Toutanova. 2019. Bert: Pre-training of deep bidirectional transformers for language understanding. In *Proceedings of the 2019 Conference of the North American Chapter of the Association for Computational Linguistics: Human Language Technologies*, pages 4171–4186.

Aamir Faisal, Muhammad Bilal Zafar, and Muhammad Imran Malik. 2021. Low-resource multilingual hate speech detection: A comparative study of classical and neural approaches. *ACM Transactions on Asian and Low-Resource Language Information Processing (TALLIP)*, 20(6):1–20.

Margherita Fanton, Helena Bonaldi, Serra Sinem Tekiroğlu, and Marco Guerini. 2021. Human-in-the-loop for data collection: a multi-target counter narrative dataset to fight online hate speech. In *Proceedings of the 59th Annual Meeting of the Association for Computational Linguistics and the 11th International Joint Conference on Natural Language Processing (Volume 1: Long Papers)*, pages 3226–3240, Online. Association for Computational Linguistics.

Siqi Feng, Junjie Hu, Graham Neubig, and Yiming Yang. 2021. A survey of data augmentation approaches for nlp. In *Proceedings of the 2021 Annual Meeting of the Association for Computational Linguistics (ACL)*, pages 45–55.

Chin-Yew Lin. 2004. Rouge: A package for automatic evaluation of summaries. In *Text Summarization Branches Out*, pages 74–81.

Yonatan Lupu, Richard Sear, Nicolas Velásquez, Rhys Leahy, Nicholas Johnson Restrepo, Beth Goldberg, and Neil F Johnson. 2023. Offline events and online hate. *PloS one*, 18(1):e0278511.

Kishore Papineni, Salim Roukos, Todd Ward, and Wei-Jing Zhu. 2002. Bleu: A method for automatic evaluation of machine translation. In *Proceedings of the 40th Annual Meeting on Association for Computational Linguistics*, pages 311–318.

Aashima Poudhar, Ioannis Konstas, and Gavin Abercrombie. 2024. A strategy labelled dataset of counterspeech. In *Proceedings of the 8th Workshop on Online Abuse and Harms (WOAH 2024)*, pages 256–265, Mexico City, Mexico. Association for Computational Linguistics.

Jing Qian, Anna Bethke, Yinyin Liu, Elizabeth Belding, and William Yang Wang. 2019. A benchmark dataset for learning to intervene in online hate speech. In *Proceedings of the 2019 Conference on Empirical Methods in Natural Language Processing (EMNLP)*, pages 4757–4766.

Bertie Vidgen and Leon Derczynski. 2020. Directions in abusive language training data: Garbage in, garbage out. *CoRR*, abs/2004.01670.

Bertie Vidgen, Alex Harris, Dong Nguyen, Rebekah Tromble, Scott Hale, and Helen Margetts. 2019. Challenges and frontiers in abusive content detection. In *Proceedings of the Third Workshop on Abusive Language Online*, pages 80–93, Florence, Italy. Association for Computational Linguistics.

Ke Wang and Xiaojun Wan. 2018. Sentigan: Generating sentimental texts via mixture adversarial networks. In *International Joint Conference on Artificial Intelligence*.

Tianyi Zhang, Varsha Kishore, Felix Wu, Kilian Q. Weinberger, and Yoav Artzi. 2019. Bertscore: Evaluating text generation with BERT. *CoRR*, abs/1904.09675.

Arkaitz Zubiaga. 2024. Judgelm: A llm-based ranking method for evaluating automatic counter-narrative generation. In *Proceedings of COLING 2024*.

Irune Zubiaga, Aitor Soroa, and Rodrigo Agerri. 2024. Ixa at refutes 2024: Leveraging language models for counter narrative generation. In *IberLEF@SEPLN*.

A Appendix

A.1 Algorithms

Algorithm 1: Simulated Annealing for Counterspeech Generation

Data: Hate speech h, initial counterspeech c_0, target score S_{target}, max iterations $N_{\max}$,candidates per loop k, temp increment ΔT, initial temp T_0

Result: Optimal counterspeech c^*

Initialize $C \leftarrow \{c_0\}, T \leftarrow T_0$;
for $i = 1$ **to** $N_{\max}$ **do**
    $T \leftarrow T + \Delta T$;
    $C_{\text{new}} \leftarrow \emptyset$;
    foreach $c \in C$ **do**
        Generate candidates S by appending random words to c;
        Evaluate scores $E(S)$ using LLM judge;
        Compute probabilities $P(S)$ using Algorithm 2;
        Select k candidates from S based on $P(S)$;
        Generate new counterspeeches $\tilde{S}$ using LLMs on selected candidates;
        Evaluate scores $E(\tilde{S})$;
        Compute probabilities $P(\tilde{S})$;
        Add top k candidates from $\tilde{S}$ to C_{new} based on $P(\tilde{S})$;
    end
    Update $C \leftarrow C_{\text{new}}$;
    if $\exists\, c \in C$ *such that* $E(c) \geq S_{target}$ **then**
        return c^* with highest $E(c)$ in C;
    end
end
return c^* with highest $E(c)$ in C;

Algorithm 2: Compute Probabilities

Data: Candidates S, scores $E(S)$, temperature T

Result: Probabilities $P(S)$

foreach $c' \in S$ **do**
    Compute probability:

$$P(c') = \frac{T^{E(c')}}{\sum_{c'' \in S} T^{E(c'')}}$$

end

Algorithm 3: Round Robin Ranking for Counterspeech Evaluation

Data: Counterspeech c, set of other counterspeeches C

Result: Average score of c

Initialize $total\_score \leftarrow 0$;
foreach $a \in C$ **do**
    Create question comparing c and a;
    $normal\_results \leftarrow$ Evaluate c vs. a (normal order) using JudgeLM;
    $reversed\_results \leftarrow$ Evaluate a vs. c (reversed order) using JudgeLM;
    $score_c \leftarrow normal\_results["output1"] + reversed\_results["output2"]$;
    $total\_score \leftarrow total\_score + score_c$;
end
Compute $average\_score \leftarrow total\_score/(2 \times |C|)$;
return $average\_score$;

A.2 Data

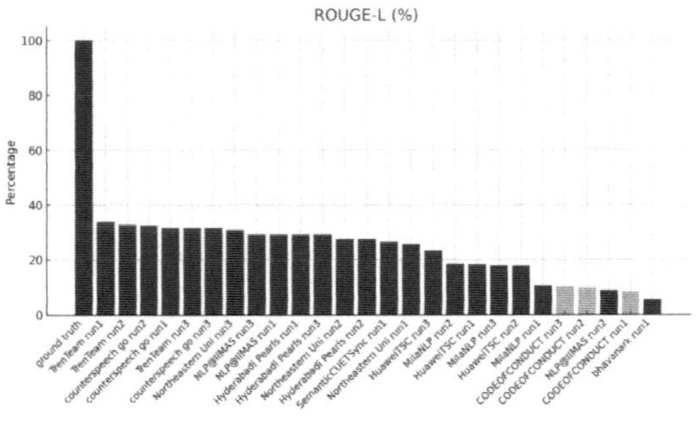

Figure 4: Chart depicting the ROUGE-L scores for each Basque run. Bars drawn in yellow represent the results from the CODEOFCONDUCT submission.

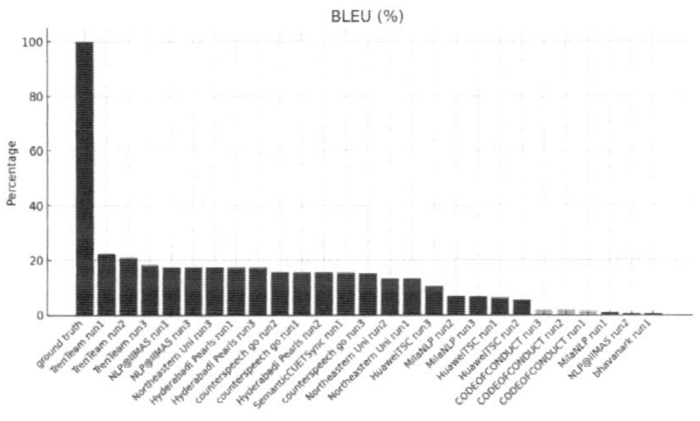

Figure 5: Chart depicting the BLEU scores for each Basque run. Bars drawn in yellow represent the results from the CODEOFCONDUCT submission.

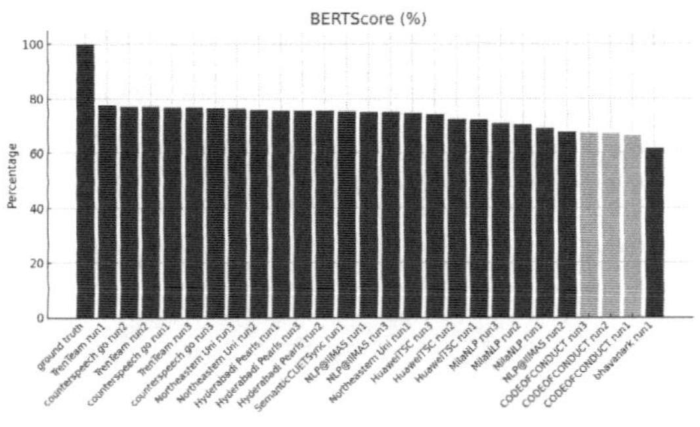

Figure 6: Chart depicting the BERT scores for each Basque run. Bars drawn in yellow represent the results from the CODEOFCONDUCT submission.

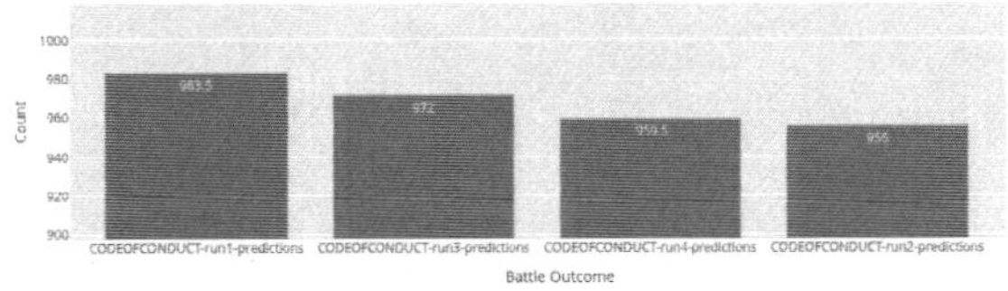

Figure 7: Scoring that compares the 4 runs of generated HS-CS files for Basque

Iterations	Candidates per Loop	Average High Score
2	2	8.875
4	2	9.375
6	2	9.000
8	2	9.500
2	4	9.125
4	4	9.875
6	4	9.875
8	4	9.500
2	6	9.625
4	6	9.625
6	6	9.750
8	6	**10.000**

Table 1: Hyper-parameter Tuning Results: Average High Scores

Model Name	**Version**	**Parameters**	**HuggingFace Link**
Hermes	3	8B	NousResearch/Hermes-3-Llama-3.1-8B
Zephyr	Beta	7B	HuggingFaceH4/zephyr-7b-beta
Meta-Llamaz	3	8B	NousResearch/Hermes-3-Llama-3.1-8B
Llama	3 Instruct	8B	meta-llama/Meta-Llama-3-8B-Instruct
Nous Hermes	2	7B	NousResearch/Nous-Hermes-2-Mixtral-8x7B-DPO
Llama	3.1	70B	meta-llama/Llama-3.1-70B-Instruct
Qwen	2.5 Instruct	72B	Qwen/Qwen2.5-72B-Instruct

Table 2: Model used for CS generation.

HW-TSC at Multilingual Counterspeech Generation

Xinglin Lyu*, **Haolin Wang***, **Min Zhang, Hao Yang**

Huawei Translation Services Center, Beijing, China
{lvxinglin1,wanghaolin9,zhangmin186,yanghao30}@huawei.com

Abstract

Warning: *Due to the property of the counterspeech generation (CSG) topic, this paper presents some content that may be offensive or upsetting.*

Multilingual counterspeech generation (MCSG) contributes to generating counterspeech with respectful, non-offensive information that is specific and truthful for the given hate speech, especially those for languages other than English. Generally, the training data of MCSG in low-source language is rare and hard to curate. Even with the impressive large language models (LLMs), it is a struggle to generate an appreciative counterspeech under the multilingual scenario. In this paper, we design a pipeline with a generation-reranking mode to effectively generate counterspeech under the multilingual scenario via LLM. Considering the scarcity of training data, we first utilize the training-free strategy, i.e., in-context learning (ICL), to generate the candidate counterspeechs. Then, we propose to rerank those candidate counterspeech via the Elo rating algorithm and a fine-tuned reward model. Experimental results on four languages, including English (EN), Italian (IT), Basque (EU) and Spanish (ES), our system achieves a comparative or even better performance in four metrics compared to the winner in this shared task.

1 Introduction

Hate speech (HS) refers to any form of communication that belittles or discriminates against individuals or groups based on attributes such as race, religion, ethnic origin, sexual orientation, disability, or gender (Ward, 1997; Nockleby, 2000), raising the concern to a toxic environment that affects both individuals and society as a whole (Williams, 2019). A promising countermeasure, counterspeech (CS) which response to HS that uses

Hate Speech:	*We should ban homosexuals.*
Counter Speech:	*When will the love prosper and the hatred start to dissipate? I will not only respect my fellow LGBT+ people, I will promote their rights.*

Table 1: An example of counter speechf generation for hate speech.

positive, inclusive, and factual communication to challenge harmful narratives, can effectively help address the issue while promoting a more respectful environment (Schieb and Preuss, 2016; Munger, 2017; Mathew et al., 2018; Shin and Kim, 2018), an example as shown in Table 1 Recently, numerous non-governmental organizations (NGOs) have enlisted volunteers to create counter speech by hand to address hate speech. Nevertheless, due to the overwhelming volume of hate speech online each day, automating CS generation could be more effective in reducing the need for human involvement. Therefore, increasing studies explored automating CS generation which we focus on in this paper. The one line of studies in CS generation relies on a mass of labeled data. For example, Zhu and Bhat (2021) proposes to train an RNN-based variational encoder-decoder model from scratch, to generate the multiple candidate CS and then obtain the best one from the candidate pool via pruning-selection pipeline. However, the kind of methods may be limited by the scale of labeled data. The performance of their model will significantly deteriorate when the labeled data is limited or unavailable, i.e., low-source CS generation. The other line of studies in CS generation is that integrates the powerful large language models (LLMs) when generating CS (Saha et al., 2024; Wang et al., 2024; Podolak et al., 2024). Although the impressive capacity of LLMs, generating a high-quality CS via LLMs re-

*Equal contribution.

Proceedings of the First Workshop on Multilingual Counterspeech Generation (MCG), pages 47–55
January 19th, 2025.

mains a challenge due to the complexity of CS generation task, specifically for low-source language scenarios.

In this paper, we propose a generation-reranking pipeline to excavate the capacity of LLM in CS generation, specifically for the low-source language scenarios. Inspired by the success in in-context learning (ICL) (Wei et al., 2022), we first propose to inject a few of HS-CS pair examples into the prompt of LLMs. Furthermore, considering the complexity of CS generation, we employ chain-of-thought (CoT) (Wang et al., 2022; Zhang et al., 2023), a step-by-step inference mechanism, to prompt LLM to generate CS candidates. For the whole generation stage, we obtain a set of CS candidate by multiple sampling. To ensure diverse and contextually rich outputs, the generation of each CS candidate in set uses different few-shot examples that are randomly sampled from the training set.

Once the CS candidates set are obtained, we search the best CS from it via two re-ranking methods: 1) Point-wise scoring method, which introduces a point-wise scorer to independently assess each CS candidate. Each CS candidate is evaluated based on a scoring model, e.g., a reward model, and the one with the highest score is selected as the final CS output. 2) Pair-wise Comparison Method: it first pairs CS candidate in set randomly, then does a comparison for each pair of CS candidate. These pair-wise comparison results are used to compute an Elo rating for each candidate. The comparison will be performed in multiple rounds, and the later rounds will pair the CS candidate via their ELO rating, i.e., the CS candidate with higher ELO scores is more likely to be paired with the other having comparative ELO scores. This ELO-based comparison makes the ranking process more fair, and is more effective in finding the best one from the CS candidate set. Similarly, after all rounds of comparison are done, we take the CS candidate with the highest ELO rating as the final output.

Overall, our contribution can be summarized as follows:

- We propose to build a generation-reranking pipeline to effectively obtain high-quality CS from the LLM.
- We propose to combine ICL and CoT to prompt LLM and generate CS candidates during the generation stage, which can effectively overcome the complexity and data scarcity of low-source language for the CS generation task.
- We propose two re-ranking methods, which can further excavate the high-quality CS from the candidates set.
- We conduct extensive experiments and analysis, including lower-source and high-source languages, demonstrate effectiveness of our proposed approach.

2 Related Work

We introduce the related works in automatic CS generation along the following two lines: 1) generating CS via the full-training model; 2) generating CS via the pre-training model.

Generating CS via Full-Training Model. Several studies have explored generating effective counterspeech by training a model from scratch. Qian et al. (2019) train a seq2seq model over their collected dataset, then use a combination of automatic generation and human input to create CS. Hua et al. (2019) propose to integrate a retrieval model to empower the seq2seq CS generation model. Zhu and Bhat (2021) proposed an automated pipeline for generating and filtering candidate CS. Different from them, our work focus on effectively utilizing the pre-trained LLMs to obtain high-quality CS.

Generating CS via Pre-Training Model. The pre-trained models, including LLMs, have shown their powerful ability in various natural language processing (NLP) tasks. Tekiroglu et al. (2020) introduced innovative techniques for generating counterspeech with a GPT-2 model, followed by expert editing. Chung et al. (2020) examined the creation of Italian CS by fine-tuning the pre-training model. Tekiroğlu et al. (2022) further analyses several such language models and decoding strategies after fine-tuning them. Rodrguez et al. (2023) use and analyse the performance of GPT-3 in the CS generation task. Saha et al. (2024) further presents a comprehensive analysis about the CS generation capacity of various LLMs, including GPT-2 (Radford et al., 2019), DialoGPT (Zhang et al., 2020), ChatGPT (OpenAI, 2023) and FlanT5 (Chung et al., 2022). Otherwise, they also provide the different prompting strategies for generating different types of CS and analyze the impact of such strategies on the

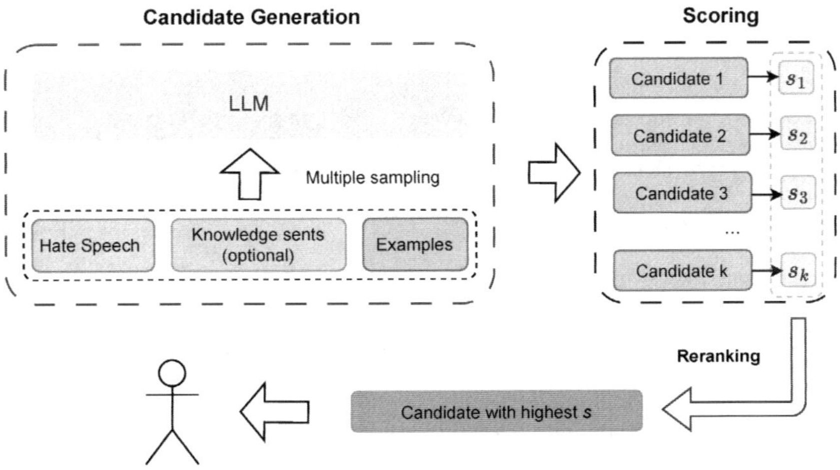

Figure 1: Overview of our proposed CS generation pipeline.

performance of the models. Different from these studies, our work is not limited CS generation of LLMs and proposes an additional re-ranking phase to more effectively mine the high-quality CS.

3 Methodology

3.1 Overview

In this section, we describe our pipeline design, as depicted visually in Fig. 2. During inference, our pipeline first utilizes LLMs to generate several candidate responses in a few-shot, chain-of-thought manner. This approach aims to ensure diverse and contextually rich outputs by leveraging effective prompt engineering techniques. Once the candidate responses are generated, we introduce two distinct methods for re-ranking them:

Point-wise Scoring Method: We use a point-wise scorer to independently assess each candidate response. Each response is graded based on a scoring model, and the response with the highest score is selected as the final output.

Pair-wise Comparison Method: We implement a pair-wise comparison mechanism. Here, pairs of candidate responses are randomly selected and compared against each other based on their relative quality. The pair-wise comparisons are used to compute Elo ratings for each candidate, and the response with the highest Elo rating is ultimately chosen.

The detailed implementation of each module in our pipeline is elaborated in the following subsections.

3.2 Candidate Generation

First, during the candidate generation phase, we adopt two common techniques used in the prompt engineering stage of large language models: In-context Learning (ICL) and Chain-of-Thought (CoT). Specifically, we follow the classic few-shot approach by selecting a number of examples from the training set to serve as the context for the LLM input. We then guide the model to reason step by step, with the ultimate goal of generating responses that mimic the style of the examples from the training set. The specific prompt template is as follows:

Regarding the number of examples used in the few-shot approach and the selection strategy, we will provide a detailed explanation and testing in the subsequent experimental section.

3.3 Point-wise Scorer Training

Without loss of generality, when introducing the method, we assume responding to a single hate speech. In training our point-wise scoring model, our goal is to predict the quality of a given counter speech response r, given the hate speech instance q, and background knowledge k. To achieve this, we first collect a dataset. Specifically, we generate k different response candidates, $[r_1, \ldots, r_k]$, for each sample in the training set. Next, we use a scoring function $\mathcal{S}(\cdot)$, to evaluate each generated response. To ensure a comprehensive evaluation,

You are tasked with counteracting hate speech. Provide counter-narrative sentences in [LANG] in response to the following hate speech statements, drawing upon the provided background knowledge sentences and hate attributes. Please ensure that you consider the following points:

1. The counter-narrative should be directly relevant to the hate speech statement.
2. Key terms from the background knowledge must be used verbatim, without modification.
3. The counter-narrative should closely mirror the expression, style, and length of the provided examples below.

Example [i]:
Hate Speech: [HS] Background Knowledge: [BK] Hate Attribute: [HA] Counter Narrative: [CN]
...

Hate Speech: [HS] Background Knowledge: [BK] Hate Attribute: [HA] Counter Narrative:

Please approach the response process systematically and outline your reasoning step by step.
- First, analyze the style and length of the provided examples.
- Second, carefully review the background knowledge and identify the key points.
- Finally, based on the guidelines outlined in the "Task Description" section, generate your final counter-speech.

The generated content should be enclosed within {TEXT}.

Figure 2: Prompt template for our CS generation.

we incorporate metrics related to the similarity to g_i. Specifically, we use RougeL, BLEU, and BertScore, which together capture both character-level and semantic-level similarity. We also introduce a high-level quality evaluation through the use of JudgeLM. JudgeLM leverages the capabilities of the language model to provide a more nuanced assessment of response quality, considering factors that may not be captured purely through similarity. The final evaluation score s_i, for each response r_i, is computed as follows:

$$s_i = \mathcal{S}(r_i) = RougeL(r_i, g) + BLEU(r_i, g) + BertScore(r_i, g) + \alpha \cdot JudgeLM(r_i, g) \quad (1)$$

Here, α is a weighting parameter that balances the contribution of JudgeLM relative to the similarity metrics, and g is the golden response corresponding to this hate speech. Next, to better utilize the data and improve the model's generalization capability, we adopt a Bradley-Terry style approach and train a scoring model: $\sigma(r_i; q, k)$, which is used to score each response r_i given the hate speech and background knowledge. The specific loss function is as follows:

$$\mathcal{L} = \mathbb{E}_{\mathcal{S}(r_i) > \mathcal{S}(r_j)} f(\sigma(r_i; q, k) - \sigma(r_j; q, k)) \quad (2)$$

, where $f(\cdot)$ refers to the sigmoid function.

3.4 Re-ranking Process

In the re-rank process, we select the best response from $[r_1, ..., r_k]$. Specifically, we employ two different strategies: point-wise scoring and pair-wise scoring.

For the point-wise scoring approach, we use the score model trained in the previous subsection to evaluate each response individually: $\hat{s}_i = \sigma(r_i; g, k)$. Since the input to the scoring model contains only the hate-speech, the response, and the background knowledge, we can score the responses during the testing phase without the need for a golden response. Finally, we select the response with the highest score as our final answer.

For the pair-wise scoring approach, we employ JudgeLM as an evaluator. JudgeLM is a scoring model based on a large language model that can assess pairs of text and determine the relative quality between them. We utilize this feature of JudgeLM to compute the Elo-Rating between different responses, which then serves as the basis for selecting the final response. Simply put, Elo rating serves a method to evaluate the relative quality of responses, by continually updating their ratings based on pairwise comparisons. The Elo rating is updated using the following formula:

$$R'_A = R_A + K \cdot (S_A - E_A), \tag{3}$$

where R'_A represents the updated rating of response A,Where R'_A represents the updated rating of response A, R_A is the current rating, K is a constant that determines the sensitivity of rating changes, S_A is the actual outcome (1 if A wins, 0 otherwise), and E_A represents the expected outcome, which is calculated as follows:

$$E_A = \frac{1}{1 + 10^{(R_B - R_A)/400}} \tag{4}$$

This formula allows us to iteratively update the ratings for each response, ultimately allowing us to rank the responses based on their performance in head-to-head comparisons. The response with the highest Elo rating is selected as our final answer.

4 Experiments

4.1 Setup

Dataset Description. We utilize the dataset from the First Workshop and Shared Task on Multilingual Counterspeech Generation, designed to support the development of models for generating CS. This multilingual dataset includes instances in English, Italian, Spanish and Basque, enabling a comprehensice, multilingual evaluation on varied LLMs. Each instance comprises a HS post accompanied by background knowledge, and a manually curated golden response representing effective CS. The dataset is divided into training, validation, and test sets, with 396, 100, 100 instances in each split and each language.

LLM Generation Settings. In the default configuration, we use GPT-4o-mini to balance cost and performance. For specific generation parameters, a temperature of 1.2 and top-p of 1 are selected to enhance the diversity of generated candidates. By default, the model generates $k = 20$ responses for each HS.

Paired Dataset Collection. To construct the paired dataset for training the point-wise scorer, we generate multiple responses for each HS and score them individually based on Equation 1. Using these scores, we create 6,840 training samples and 760 test samples, which contain different hate speech instances. Each sample consists of one high-scoring response and one low-scoring response.

Point-Wise Scorer Model. For the scorer model, we adopt LLaMA-3 8B as the base model, replacing its final layer with a linear projection to predict a single scalar value. To reduce training costs, we employ the LoRA (Hu et al., 2021) method with $r = 8$ and $\alpha = 16$, and incorporate flash attention (Dao et al., 2022) to accelerate training. The training process uses the AdamW optimizer (Loshchilov, 2017) with a learning rate of 1×10^{-4}. We train the model with a batch size of 16 for a single epoch.

Metrics. We utilize the official evaluation metrics for our experimental setup, which are categorized into two types. The first type focuses on assessing the similarity between our generated responses and the reference CS across semantic, lexical, and stylistic dimensions. These metrics include RougeL (Lin, 2004), BLEU (Papineni et al., 2002), BertScore (Zhang* et al., 2020), and Novelty (Wang and Wan, 2018). The second type harnesses the capabilities of large language models (LLMs) to automatically evaluate the quality of our CS, exemplified by JudgeLM (Zhu et al., 2023). The first type effectively measures whether the generated responses leverage training data to produce style-consistent and human-like CS. However, it has limitations, particularly in its inability to holistically assess whether the CS is sharp and comprehensive. On the other hand, the second type allows for a more global evaluation but is susceptible to biases inherent in language models, such as favoring responses generated by similar models or preferring longer responses (Hu et al., 2024; Chen et al., 2024). To address these individual shortcomings, we integrate both types of evaluation criteria, achieving a more comprehensive and balanced assessment of CS quality.

4.2 Main Results

We present the performance of our proposed methods in Table 2. **Winner** and **Reference** indicate the CS generation metrics for the best-performing team and the human-annotated golden responses, respectively. I-C represents generating CS with Integrated Chain-of-Thought (ICL and CoT) but without the re-ranking phase. I-C + PwC and I-C + PwS denote the final CS output obtained through Pair-wise Comparison and Point-wise Scoring re-ranking methods, respectively. Here are some key

System	JudgeLM	RougeL	BLEU	BertScore	Length	Novelty
	English CS generation task					
Winner	2523.0	19.0	4.9	70.8	84.7	83.0
Our submission1 (I-C)	1635.0	40.4	27.2	78.2	38.2	80.7
Our submission2 (I-C + PwC)	2087.5	33.6	18.8	76.1	48.3	80.8
Our submission3 (I-C + PwS)	1682.0	46.6	34.4	80.4	39.2	79.0
Reference	1175.5	100.0	100.0	100.0	32.7	77.7
	Basque CS generation task					
Winner	2465.5	8.2	1.5	66.4	67.5	86.8
Our submission1 (I-C)	1484.5	18.3	6.3	72.1	30.2	87.2
Our submission2 (I-C + PwC)	1881.5	17.7	5.6	72.4	34.5	86.8
Our submission3 (I-C + PwS)	1722.0	23.3	10.5	74.2	32.1	86.5
Reference	1534.5	100.0	100.0	100.0	26.5	85.3
	Italian CS generation task					
Winner	1985.5	21.1	8.9	72.6	101.4	82.1
Our submission1 (I-C)	1260.5	36.1	21.7	77.2	40.8	80.9
Our submission2 (I-C + PwC)	1792.0	30.8	16.6	75.9	49.5	80.3
Our submission3 (I-C + PwS)	1372.5	41.1	26.6	79.1	41.9	79.1
Reference	929.5	100.0	100.0	100.0	35.3	77.9
	Spanish CS generation task					
Winner	2002.0	24.2	8.9	73.5	99.3	79.6
Our submission1 (I-C)	1228.5	36.8	21.7	77.6	43.1	77.5
Our submission2 (I-C + PwC)	1728.0	33.5	17.7	76.7	52.3	77.4
Our submission3 (I-C + PwS)	1339.5	41.9	27.2	79.4	43.2	75.8
Reference	899.0	100.0	100.0	100.0	36.9	75.1

Table 2: Performance of *Our submissions, Winner, Reference* on test set with four languages. **I-C** denotes generating the CS only integrates ICL and CoT without the re-ranking phase. **I-C + PwC** and **I-C + PwS** denote we obtain the final CS output via Pair-wise Comparison and Point-wise Scoring re-ranking methods, respectively.

observations:

Our method consistently achieves competitive performance across all metrics. As mentioned in the previous subsection, optimizing CS generation requires considering multiple metrics simultaneously. Our results demonstrate that our design effectively addresses this challenge. Notably, compared to the Winner, all our submissions show significant improvements in RougeL, BLEU, and BertScore. For example, the I-C + PwS submission outperforms the Winner by +27.6, +29.5, and +9.6 in these three metrics for the English CS generation task. This suggests that our ICL and CoT techniques effectively prompt the LLM to generate CS in a style that more closely resembles human outputs. Additionally, our method remains highly competitive in the JudgeLM metric, further demonstrating its overall effectiveness.

Our method are less likely to overfit to the judge model. As previously discussed, longer responses may exploit the judge model and result in inflated scores. However, our method effectively controls the response length while maintaining quality. For instance, the average length of the I-C submission is 38.2, whereas the Winner's submission averages 84.7, which may contribute to the slight gap in the JudgeLM metric. Importantly, the average length of our submissions closely aligns with the human reference, further indicating that our submissions favor a human-like CS style.

PwC substantially improves the JudgeLM metric. In the PwC method, we continuously selected CS pairs and used JudgeLM to compare and rate them via Elo rating. The results indicate

Selection Strategy	RougeL	BLEU	BertScore	Length	Novelty
Random	27.2	14.9	74.2	39.3	80.5
BertScore-based	26.6	14.0	74.3	40.1	80.7
Similarity-based	26.2	13.7	74.2	40.4	80.4

Table 3: Comparision of performance for various example selection strategies. Notably, the performance here is based on the 20 shots.

Selection Strategy	RougeL	BLEU	BertScore	Length	Novelty
I-C (*20-shot*)	27.2	14.9	74.2	39.3	80.5
1-shot	18.6	5.9	71.1	41.9	81.1
5-shot	22.6	9.8	72.7	41.1	80.9
10-shot	25.4	12.6	73.7	40.3	80.4
30-shot	27.1	14.4	74.2	39.3	80.1
50-shot	26.8	14.1	73.7	39.9	79.7

Table 4: The comparison of performance when using various numbers of examples to perform in-context learning.

Selection Strategy	RougeL	BLEU	BertScore	Length	Novelty
I-C	27.2	14.9	74.2	39.3	80.5
w/o CoT	25.5	13.0	72.3	38.1	79.8

Table 5: The ablation study of Chain-of-thought. Notably, the performance here is based on the 20 shots.

that JudgeLM's comparisons are consistent, and the selected responses effectively maximize the JudgeLM score. Comparing I-C and I-C + PwC, we observe that the latter achieves a significantly higher JudgeLM score (e.g., +452.5 points for English). However, we also note a slight decline in performance on other metrics, supporting our assertion that CS generation involves multi-objective optimization, where improving one metric may lead to trade-offs in others.

PwS enhances all metrics simultaneously. To avoid scenarios where improving some metrics results in declines in others, we designed a point-wise scorer that integrates multiple metrics, as shown in 1. Our findings show that I-C + PwS consistently improves upon I-C across all metrics. Therefore, we believe that this method has the potential to identify the Pareto optimal solution for this multi-objective optimization problem.

4.3 Ablation Study and Discussion

Here we use the merged development set (with the four language subsets), to discuss and analyze our proposed approach.

Example Selection Strategy. During the ICL phase, we incorporate some examples as a part of input to prompt the LLM generates CS with a similar style to human beings. As previous literature demonstrates, the performance of ICL is highly related to the examples chosen (Lu et al., 2022). Thus, we analyze different strategies for example selection to pursue better CS results. We evaluate 3 example selection strategies: 1) Randomly select examples in the training dataset. 2) Select examples whose hate speech (HS) has a higher BERTScore compared to the HS of input. 3) Select examples whose hate speech (HS) has a higher semantic similarity compared to the HS of input, which is measured by Jina LM (Sturua et al., 2024). We list their performances in Table 3. The results show that using similarity or BERTScore based methods can be not useful compared to a simple random strategy. This is probably because HS generation needs more diverse contexts for better generation, while previous methods may limit the context's diversity instead.

Effect of Numbers of Examples. The number of examples is also crucial for the few-shot strategy. Under-number examples may prevent the model's

ICL capabilities from being fully utilized, while over-number examples could introduce extra information burden, resulting in negative results. We compare the performance of ICL under different example numbers and the results is shown in Tale 4. We can observe that using 20 examples can maximizes the model's ICL capabilities.

Effect of Chain-of-Thought. We discuss the effect of applying Chain-of-Thought here. As shown in Table 5, the CoT can greatly improve the quality of CS in all metric such as + 1.9 Bertscore. This suggest the CoT is an effective strategy to enhance CS generation, by breaking down the complex generation process into several easier steps.

5 Conclusion

In this paper, we propose an effective pipeline for automatically generating multilingual counter-speech (MCSG) to combat hate speech with respectful and truthful responses, particularly in non-English languages. Due to the scarcity of training data for low-resource languages, we propose a pipeline that combines generation and reranking. More specifically, the proposed approach uses in-context learning (ICL) to create candidate responses without extensive training data via the powerful LLMs. These candidates are then reranked using the Elo rating algorithm and a fine-tuned reward model. The experimental results show that our system performs comparably or better than the best entry in the shared task across four languages: English, Italian, Basque, and Spanish.

References

Guiming Hardy Chen, Shunian Chen, Ziche Liu, Feng Jiang, and Benyou Wang. 2024. Humans or llms as the judge? a study on judgement biases. *arXiv preprint arXiv:2402.10669*.

Hyung Won Chung, Le Hou, Shayne Longpre, Barret Zoph, Yi Tay, William Fedus, Yunxuan Li, Xuezhi Wang, Mostafa Dehghani, Siddhartha Brahma, Albert Webson, Shixiang Shane Gu, Zhuyun Dai, Mirac Suzgun, Xinyun Chen, Aakanksha Chowdhery, Alex Castro-Ros, Marie Pellat, Kevin Robinson, Dasha Valter, Sharan Narang, Gaurav Mishra, Adams Yu, Vincent Zhao, Yanping Huang, Andrew Dai, Hongkun Yu, Slav Petrov, Ed H. Chi, Jeff Dean, Jacob Devlin, Adam Roberts, Denny Zhou, Quoc V. Le, and Jason Wei. 2022. Scaling instruction-finetuned language models.

Yi-Ling Chung, Serra Sinem Tekiroglu, and Marco Guerini. 2020. Italian counter narrative generation to fight online hate speech. In *Seventh Italian Conference on Computational Linguistics*.

Tri Dao, Dan Fu, Stefano Ermon, Atri Rudra, and Christopher Ré. 2022. Flashattention: Fast and memory-efficient exact attention with io-awareness. *Advances in Neural Information Processing Systems*, 35:16344–16359.

Edward J Hu, Yelong Shen, Phillip Wallis, Zeyuan Allen-Zhu, Yuanzhi Li, Shean Wang, Lu Wang, and Weizhu Chen. 2021. Lora: Low-rank adaptation of large language models. *arXiv preprint arXiv:2106.09685*.

Zhengyu Hu, Linxin Song, Jieyu Zhang, Zheyuan Xiao, Jingang Wang, Zhenyu Chen, and Hui Xiong. 2024. Rethinking llm-based preference evaluation. *arXiv preprint arXiv:2407.01085*.

Xinyu Hua, Zhe Hu, and Lu Wang. 2019. Argument generation with retrieval, planning, and realization. In *Proceedings of the 57th Annual Meeting of the Association for Computational Linguistics*, pages 2661–2672, Florence, Italy. Association for Computational Linguistics.

Chin-Yew Lin. 2004. Rouge: A package for automatic evaluation of summaries. In *Text Summarization Branches Out*.

I Loshchilov. 2017. Decoupled weight decay regularization. *arXiv preprint arXiv:1711.05101*.

Pan Lu, Liang Qiu, Kai-Wei Chang, Ying Nian Wu, Song-Chun Zhu, Tanmay Rajpurohit, Peter Clark, and Ashwin Kalyan. 2022. Dynamic prompt learning via policy gradient for semi-structured mathematical reasoning. *arXiv preprint arXiv:2209.14610*.

Binny Mathew, Navish Kumar, Pawan Goyal, Animesh Mukherjee, et al. 2018. Analyzing the hate and counter speech accounts on twitter. *arXiv preprint arXiv:1812.02712*.

Kevin Munger. 2017. Tweetment effects on the tweeted: Experimentally reducing racist harassment. *Political Behavior*, 39(3):629–649.

John T Nockleby. 2000. Hate speech. *Encyclopedia of the American Constitution*, 3(2):1277–1279.

OpenAI. 2023. GPT-4 technical report. *CoRR*, abs/2303.08774.

Kishore Papineni, Salim Roukos, Todd Ward, and Wei-Jing Zhu. 2002. Bleu: a method for automatic evaluation of machine translation. In *Association for Computational Linguistics (ACL)*.

Jakub Podolak, Szymon Łukasik, Paweł Balawender, Jan Ossowski, Jan Piotrowski, Katarzyna Bakowicz, and Piotr Sankowski. 2024. LLM generated responses to mitigate the impact of hate speech. In *Findings of the Association for Computational Linguistics: EMNLP 2024*, pages 15860–15876, Miami, Florida, USA. Association for Computational Linguistics.

Jing Qian, Anna Bethke, Yinyin Liu, Elizabeth Belding, and William Yang Wang. 2019. A benchmark dataset for learning to intervene in online hate speech. In *Proceedings of the 2019 Conference on Empirical Methods in Natural Language Processing and the 9th International Joint Conference on Natural Language Processing (EMNLP-IJCNLP)*, pages 4755–4764.

Alec Radford, Jeffrey Wu, Rewon Child, David Luan, Dario Amodei, and Ilya Sutskever. 2019. Language models are unsupervised multitask learners. *OpenAI blog*, 1(8):9.

María Estrella Vallecillo Rodrguez, Arturo Montejo-Ráez, and María Teresa Martín Valdivia. 2023. Automatic counter-narrative generation for hate speech in spanish. *Proces. del Leng. Natural*, 71:227–245.

Punyajoy Saha, Aalok Agrawal, Abhik Jana, Chris Biemann, and Animesh Mukherjee. 2024. On zero-shot counterspeech generation by LLMs. In *Proceedings of the 2024 Joint International Conference on Computational Linguistics, Language Resources and Evaluation (LREC-COLING 2024)*, pages 12443–12454, Torino, Italia. ELRA and ICCL.

Carla Schieb and Mike Preuss. 2016. Governing hate speech by means of counterspeech on facebook. In *66th ICA Annual Conference*.

Youngsoo Shin and Jinwoo Kim. 2018. Data-centered persuasion: Nudging user's prosocial behavior and designing social innovation. *Computers in Human Behavior*, 80:168–178.

Saba Sturua, Isabelle Mohr, Mohammad Kalim Akram, Michael Günther, Bo Wang, Markus Krimmel, Feng Wang, Georgios Mastrapas, Andreas Koukounas, Nan Wang, et al. 2024. jina-embeddings-v3: Multilingual embeddings with task lora. *arXiv preprint arXiv:2409.10173*.

Serra Sinem Tekiroğlu, Helena Bonaldi, Margherita Fanton, and Marco Guerini. 2022. Using pre-trained language models for producing counter narratives against hate speech: a comparative study. In *Findings of the Association for Computational Linguistics: ACL 2022*, pages 3099–3114.

Serra Sinem Tekiroglu, Yi-Ling Chung, and Marco Guerini. 2020. Generating counter narratives against online hate speech: Data and strategies. In *Proceedings of ACL*.

Boshi Wang, Xiang Deng, and Huan Sun. 2022. Iteratively prompt pre-trained language models for chain of thought. In *Proceedings of the 2022 Conference on Empirical Methods in Natural Language Processing, EMNLP 2022, Abu Dhabi, United Arab Emirates, December 7-11, 2022*, pages 2714–2730. Association for Computational Linguistics.

Haiyang Wang, Zhiliang Tian, Xin Song, Yue Zhang, Yuchen Pan, Hongkui Tu, Minlie Huang, and Bin Zhou. 2024. Intent-aware and hate-mitigating counterspeech generation via dual-discriminator guided LLMs. In *Proceedings of the 2024 Joint International Conference on Computational Linguistics, Language Resources and Evaluation (LREC-COLING 2024)*, pages 9131–9142, Torino, Italia. ELRA and ICCL.

Ke Wang and Xiaojun Wan. 2018. Sentigan: Generating sentimental texts via mixture adversarial networks. In *IJCAI*, pages 4446–4452.

Kenneth D Ward. 1997. Free speech and the development of liberal virtues: An examination of the controversies involving flag-burning and hate speech. *U. Miami L. Rev.*, 52:733.

Jason Wei, Yi Tay, Rishi Bommasani, Colin Raffel, Barret Zoph, Sebastian Borgeaud, Dani Yogatama, Maarten Bosma, Denny Zhou, Donald Metzler, Ed H. Chi, Tatsunori Hashimoto, Oriol Vinyals, Percy Liang, Jeff Dean, and William Fedus. 2022. Emergent abilities of large language models. *Trans. Mach. Learn. Res.*, 2022.

Matthew Williams. 2019. Hatred behind the screens: A report on the rise of online hate speech.

Tianyi Zhang*, Varsha Kishore*, Felix Wu*, Kilian Q. Weinberger, and Yoav Artzi. 2020. Bertscore: Evaluating text generation with bert. In *International Conference on Learning Representations*.

Yizhe Zhang, Siqi Sun, Michel Galley, Yen-Chun Chen, Chris Brockett, Xiang Gao, Jianfeng Gao, Jingjing Liu, and William B Dolan. 2020. Dialogpt: Large-scale generative pre-training for conversational response generation. In *Proceedings of the 58th Annual Meeting of the Association for Computational Linguistics: System Demonstrations*, pages 270–278.

Zhuosheng Zhang, Aston Zhang, Mu Li, and Alex Smola. 2023. Automatic chain of thought prompting in large language models. In *The Eleventh International Conference on Learning Representations, ICLR 2023, Kigali, Rwanda, May 1-5, 2023*. OpenReview.net.

Lianghui Zhu, Xinggang Wang, and Xinlong Wang. 2023. Judgelm: Fine-tuned large language models are scalable judges.

Wanzheng Zhu and Suma Bhat. 2021. Generate, prune, select: A pipeline for counterspeech generation against online hate speech. In *Findings of the Association for Computational Linguistics: ACL-IJCNLP 2021*, pages 134–149.

MilaNLP@Multilingual Counterspeech Generation: Evaluating Translation and Background Knowledge Filtering

Emanuele Moscato, Arianna Muti, Debora Nozza
Bocconi University, Milan, Italy
{emanuele.moscato2, arianna.muti, debora.nozza}@unibocconi.it

Abstract

We describe our participation in the Multilingual Counterspeech Generation shared task, which aims to generate a counternarrative to counteract hate speech, given a hateful sentence and relevant background knowledge. Our team tested two different aspects: *(i)* translating outputs from English vs generating outputs in the original languages and *(ii)* filtering pieces of the background knowledge provided vs including all the background knowledge. Our experiments show that filtering the background knowledge in the same prompt and leaving data in the original languages leads to more adherent counternarrative generations, except for Basque, where translating the output from English and filtering the background knowledge in a separate prompt yields better results. Our system ranked first in English, Italian, and Spanish and fourth in Basque.

1 Introduction

Hate speech (HS) poses a significant challenge in online spaces, fostering division and perpetuating discrimination. The need for effective interventions becomes increasingly urgent. Among the various strategies for countering hate speech, counternarrative generation (CNG) has emerged as a promising approach (Bonaldi et al., 2024a). Rather than simply removing harmful content, counternarratives aim to actively challenge hate speech by offering constructive, persuasive and non-polarized discourse, which might offer alternative standpoint both to the author of the hate speech message and to users navigating the online web and running into hateful comments. The Multilingual Counterspeech Generation shared task proposes to address this problem by asking participants to generate counterspeech for multiple targets (Jews, LGBT+, migrants, people of color, and women) and languages (Basque, English, Italian, and Spanish), with texts in languages other than English being translations from their English counterparts. The shared task data also comprises *background knowledge* (BK) sentences, which may be helpful to generate the counternarratives. This system paper describes our approach to the shared task.

During a preliminary manual evaluation of LLMs' outputs, we observed two issues that could potentially compromise the quality of counternarrative generation. First, the models produced low-quality text in languages other than English, inventing non-existent words (e.g., the nonexisting Italian word "contini") or generating ungrammatical sentences (e.g., the incorrect Italian article in "Non c'è posto per *la* odio"). Second, the background knowledge included in the data was often not only unhelpful but also interfered with the logical flow of the generated counternarratives. For instance, the model confused the figurative meaning of "iron fist" (i.e., exercising power in an oppressive or ruthless manner) with its literal meaning (i.e., a punch).

For this reason, our system submission focused on two key questions: *(i)* For languages other than English, is it better to ask the model to generate responses in that language, or should it generate them in English and then be translated? *(ii)* Is it better to filter the background knowledge sentences (in one or two separate steps), or should all of them be used?

Our results demonstrate that the optimal approach involves: *(i)* providing the model with input data in its original language and generating responses in that same language, and *(ii)* filtering the background knowledge in a single step within the same prompt rather than in two different steps. The best performance is still achieved by models that generate counternarratives directly in the target language, regardless of potential grammatical issues, likely because the content is more important than grammatical accuracy. **Our system achieved first place in three out of the four languages** in the shared task: English, Spanish, and Italian.

Proceedings of the First Workshop on Multilingual Counterspeech Generation (MCG), pages 56–64
January 19th, 2025.

2 Related Work

Counterspeech or counternarrative (the terms are used interchangeably in the NLP community) is the strategic response to a hate speech message that provides an opposing stance, aiming at changing the hate-related viewpoint, by not attacking the interlocutor but the content of the message (Bonaldi et al., 2024a). Countering hate speech through the generation of counternarratives provides a constructive and pro-active approach to hate speech that goes beyond mere detection. To do so, several datasets have been developed. The first large-scale, multilingual, expert-based dataset, Counter Narratives through Nichesourcing (CONAN) (Chung et al., 2019), consists of HS-CN pairs in English, French, and Italian, focusing only on Islamophobia. Moreover, they introduce a taxonomy for the following types of CNs: Presentation of Facts, Pointing out Hypocrisy Or Contradiction, Warning Of Consequences, Affiliation, Positive Tone, Negative Tone, Humor, Counter-Questions, Other. Then, with MultiTarget CONAN (MT-CONAN), Fanton et al. (2021b) expand on the previous dataset by creating 5000 HS/CN pairs in English Language, covering multiple hate targets, in terms of race, religion, country of origin, sexual orientation, disability, or gender.

Research on counternarrative generation (CNG) has increased due to LLMs' impressive performance in generating text (Zubiaga et al., 2024). However, often the generated CN is beautifully written but generic, repetitive and poor in terms of content, which should show credible evidence, factual arguments and alternative viewpoints by adopting an empathetic, polite and constructive tone (Fanton et al., 2021a; Chung et al., 2021; Bonaldi et al., 2024a). Generating effective counternarratives necessitates a deep understanding of cultural, historical and social factors mentioned in the hateful instances. For this reason, CNG benefits from the use of background knowledge or knowledge retrieval to generate text, which makes it a close task to counter-argumentation and misinformation countering (Bonaldi et al., 2024a). Therefore, the CNG task should foresee two steps: first the extraction of relevant knowledge from an external source, and secondly the generation of knowledge-augmented counterspeech. This approach has been proposed by Chung et al. (2021) through extracted and generated keyphrases and by Jiang et al. (2023b), who extract background knowledge relevant to hate speech with an opposite stance in an unsupervised fashion. They retrieve and filter information from multiple perspectives of stance consistency, semantic overlap rate between the knowledge retrieved and the hateful message, and fitness for hate speech. Bonaldi et al. (2024b) show that the presence of safety guardrails in LLMs hinders the quality of the generations. Moreover, since hate speech is often expressed through implicit arguments (Muti et al., 2024a), Bonaldi et al. (2024b) decompose the hate speech into premises and conclusion, showing that attacking a specific component of the hate speech, in particular its implied statement, leads to richer argumentative generations.

3 Data

The data consists of 596 hateful messages, each appearing in four languages (English, Spanish, Basque, and Italian), for a total of 2384 datapoints across all languages.

The dataset is divided into 3 splits: development (400 instances across all languages), train (1584), and test (400). Each instance presents the following features:

- **HS**: a Hate Speech sentence, taken from the MTCONAN dataset (Fanton et al., 2021b).
- **BK**: up to 5 separate pieces of background knowledge (textual) that could be used to generate the counternarrative to the Hate Speech sentence.
- **CN**: a ground-truth counternarrative, generated by humans and present only in the development and train splits of the dataset.
- **LANG**: the language of the Hate Speech sentence, background knowledge and counternarrative (if present).
- **TARGET**: the social or ethnic group targeted by the Hate Speech sentence.
- **SPLIT**: the split of the dataset the datapoint belonged to.
- **MTCONAN_ID**: the ID of the datapoint in the MTCONAN dataset the Hate Speech sentence was taken from.
- **PAIR_ID**: an ID identifying the same datapoint **across all languages** (non-unique across the dataset, i.e. each value appeared four times, once for each language).

- **ID**: a concatenation of a string identifying the language and the **PAIR_ID** field, resulting in an identifier that is unique across the dataset.

Although the shared task permits the use of external data as background knowledge, we rely exclusively on the knowledge provided.

3.1 Metrics

Teams were asked to automatically generate counternarratives for the test split, which is then evaluated with several metrics, both automatic and LLM-based. For the automatic scores, organizers chose BERTscore (Zhang et al., 2019), BLEU (Papineni et al., 2002; Post, 2018), Rouge-L (Lin, 2004), and novelty (Tekiroglu et al., 2022). They also report the generation length. For the LLM-based, they opted for the "LLM as a judge" framework (*JudgeLM*) (Zubiaga et al., 2024). This framework evaluates generated CNs pairwise in a tournament-style format, assessing the quality of the generated counternarrative.

4 System Description

We develop an LLM-based pipeline for automatic counterspeech generation without fine-tuning. In particular, we compare the performance of Llama3-8B-Instruct (Dubey et al., 2024), Mistral-7B-Instruct-v0.3 (Jiang et al., 2023a) and Zephyr-7B-beta (Tunstall et al., 2023), with Mistral emerging as the overall best-performing one from preliminary manual evaluation on ten instances. Moreover, Mistral shows the least refusal to answer, which makes it a good candidate since safety guardrails have proved to be detrimental to the generation of counternarratives (Bonaldi et al., 2024b). All models are provided via the Hugging Face model hub[1].

The prompt for counternarrative generation (see Appendix A) includes the following information:

- Hate speech statement
- Background knowledge sentences
- Targeted social/ethnic group
- Language of the provided text and language in which to generate the counternarrative.

Furthermore, we explicitly instruct the model to avoid using any information beyond the provided background knowledge, assuming that stricter adherence results in more factual counternarratives.

[1]https://huggingface.co/models

Runs	Translation	Filtering
1	Y	Y*
2	N	Y*
3	N	Y
4	Y	Y
5	N	N

Table 1: Summary of the conducted experiments. The Y* label denotes the separate-prompt filtering process.

Multilingual generation VS translation The complete dataset comprises four languages, with Basque being a low-resource language. Although the chosen LLM is able to generate text in all four languages, we expect that the quality may vary (and it can do so in ways that are hard to evaluate), especially for low-resource languages. Nozza (2021) and Muti and Barrón-Cedeño (2022) have exposed the limits on zero-shot classification of different forms of hate speech across languages on encoder-based models, due to the language- and culture-specific lexical variation of hate speech. Furthermore, during a preliminary manual evaluation, we identified certain challenges in generating text in languages other than English. These issues included the production of non-existent words and ungrammatical sentences.

To address this, we experimented with two approaches for generating text in languages other than English:

- generation directly in the target language;
- generation in English, with a subsequent translation in Spanish, Basque, and Italian.

The machine translation task is performed using the NLLB model (NLLBTeam et al., 2022).

These experiments were feasible because each hate speech sentence and background knowledge text in the dataset is available in all four languages.

Background knowledge filtering Upon examining a sample of the development and training data, we observed that some of the provided background knowledge sentences are not relevant to generating the corresponding counternarratives. We therefore experiment with:

- providing the LLM with all the background knowledge points, asking the model to choose which ones to use at inference time (same-prompt filtering),

Run	BERTScore				BLEU				Rouge-L				Novelty			
	EN	**ES**	**EU**	**IT**	**EN**	**ES**	**EU**	**IT**	**EN**	**ES**	**EU**	**IT**	**EN**	**ES**	**EU**	**IT**
1	0.710	0.716	0.692	0.710	0.049	0.055	0.016	0.046	0.187	0.203	0.110	0.171	0.805	0.781	0.873	0.803
2	0.711	0.734	0.708	0.722	0.047	0.087	0.072	0.075	0.189	0.239	0.183	0.206	0.804	0.755	0.831	0.781
3	0.706	0.733	0.712	0.726	0.044	0.088	0.072	0.075	0.179	0.233	0.190	0.207	0.813	0.761	0.833	0.785
4	0.708	0.714	0.689	0.708	0.045	0.049	0.014	0.044	0.181	0.197	0.108	0.170	<u>0.814</u>	<u>0.792</u>	<u>0.880</u>	<u>0.809</u>
5	<u>0.715</u>	<u>0.738</u>	<u>0.719</u>	<u>0.734</u>	<u>0.059</u>	<u>0.097</u>	<u>0.081</u>	<u>0.092</u>	<u>0.200</u>	<u>0.246</u>	<u>0.204</u>	<u>0.229</u>	0.810	0.757	0.828	0.776

Table 2: Results on the development set. The higher the better.

- first filtering the background knowledge points and then feeding the resulting subset to the LLM to generate the counternarrative (separate-prompt filtering) (see Appendix A for the prompt),
- avoiding any kind of filtering and just asking the model to generate a CN using the available BK.

A schema of the experiments can be found in Table 1.

5 Results

The results of our experiments on the development and train splits of the dataset are presented in Table 2. The best performance is achieved by run 5, which involves neither translation nor filtering of the background knowledge (BK). These results suggest that Mistral performs well in a simpler setup. However, upon closer inspection, the counternarratives generated in run 5 are of low quality, replicating the issues observed during the preliminary manual evaluation of a small subset. For this reason, we have decided to exclude this run from the final submission. Therefore, *the runs submitted to the shared task are 1, 2, and 3*, which according to a preliminary observation perform the best. The manual evaluation has been chosen over traditional metrics because the latter have been shown not to correlate well with human preferences when evaluating generation (Nimah et al., 2023). Table 3 shows the results on the test set with the JudgeLM metric used for the official ranking provided by the organizers, along with the position in the leaderboard. Run 3 - no translation, same-prompt filtering, performs the best, with respect to our other runs and other participants, in English, Italian, and Spanish. In Basque, on the other hand, our run 1, which employs translation and separate-prompt filtering, obtains the best score among our runs and fourth place in the leaderboard.

Run	JudgeLLM				Rank			
	EN	**ES**	**EU**	**IT**	**EN**	**ES**	**EU**	**IT**
1	2327	1853	2243	1824	8	5	**4**	4
2	2358	1942	430	1912	2	2	25	2
3	2523	2002	423	1986	**1**	**1**	26	**1**
Ground truth	1176	899	1535	930	-	-	-	-

Table 3: Results on the test set and scores of the ground truth counternarrative. We only report the metrics on which the ranking was based.

5.1 Error Analysis

In order to assess the two aspects investigated (translation vs original; same-prompt vs separate-prompts filtering vs no filtering), we perform a human evaluation on a random subset of 50 Italian instances, 10 for each target.

How does translation affect generation? We compare run 1 with run 2 to evaluate the differences between generating responses first in English and translating them into the target language versus generating responses directly in the target language. Although, in both runs, filtering has been done in a separate prompt, the BK chosen can be different for the same instances. This affects the final generation. Therefore, we do not evaluate the relevance to the ground truth, which highly depends on selected pieces of BK. We focus only on the quality of the language. In English, the responses are much more concise and less generic. Many instances generated in the original language begin with a vague structure, such as "Si tratta di un'affermazione ingiusta e offensiva nei confronti di un gruppo di persone sulla base della loro etnia", translated as "It is an unjust and offensive statement towards a group of people based on their ethnicity", or "Nessuno deve essere discriminato per la propria orientazione sessuale", translated as "nobody should be discriminated for their sexual orientation", or "Tutti gli esseri umani hanno il potenziale di raggiungere grandi successi, indipendentemente dalla loro origine etnica o colore della pelle", translated as "All human beings have the potential to achieve great success, regardless of their

HS	CN	BK	CN_run3	CN_run5
Jews are nothing but criminals.	Jews are not criminals, but Nazi were. The memory of the Jews murdered—murdered because they were Jews — must be recognized with historical accuracy.	Chodakiewicz noted that after World War II, the Jews were not only victims, but also aggressors.	It is important to remember that **while some Jews participated in the aggression after World War II, they were also victims**.	Moreover, after World War II, **Jews were not only victims, but also aggressors**, as noted by Chodakiewicz.

Table 4: Dataset example and generated counternarratives. Both run 3 and run 5 select that BK to be used in the prompt. However, while run 3 transforms it to generate counterspeech, run 5 tends just to repeat BK points as they are, resulting in producing hate speech.

ethnic origin or skin color". Responses generated in the original language rarely show errors. Here is an error example: *Molto spiace, ma sono sbagliati quelle affermazioni* instead of the correct form *Mi dispiace molto, ma quelle affermazioni sono sbagliate*. This links us to the third aspect: politeness. Responses generated in the original language tend to be more polite than those generated in English.

On the other hand, responses translated from English contain more grammatical errors, including hallucinations of invented words that are similar to the original ones, such as *progreditiamo, ritrarrele* instead of *progrediamo, ritrarle* (*en:* we progress, depict them). Other categories of errors are wrong syntactic structures: *Il femminismo non è quello di svalutare* instead of *Il femminismo non svaluta* (*en:*feminism does not devalue); wrong coordination of gender: *Le donne non sono bambin**i*** instead of *bambin**e***; lack of figurative language understanding: *non sono bambini lavati al cervello* instead of *non sono bambine a cui è stato fatto il lavaggio di cervello* (*en:* they are not brainwashed little girls); the figurative meaning of "iron fist" (i.e., exercising power in an oppressive or ruthless manner) confused with its literal meaning (i.e., a punch).

How does filtering BK affect generation? To answer this question, our manual evaluation focuses on the relevance of the different BK selected with respect to the ground truth CN. We compare the best-performing model, which uses filtering, run 3, with run 5, which does not filter BK. We investigate whether the LM in run 5 considers all the BK points by adding irrelevant information or whether it filters information deliberately. We notice that run 5 generations are much longer, and they contain all BK sentences. Therefore, the model does not have any implicit filtering. This pollutes the generated output, which is affected by irrelevant and wrong/hateful information. An example can be seen in Table 4, where the piece of BK selected produces more hate speech instead of countering it. In addition, we compare same-prompt with separate-prompt filtering. We discard the translated version since it did not yield better results. By observing the same subsample across run 2 and run 3, we observe that run 2 produces shorter responses, by selecting only 2 or 3 BK pieces every time. However, it tends to select irrelevant and hateful BK, like the one in Table 4 or *è stato dimostrato che molte comunità, incluse quelle religiose, possono essere dominanti o abusare del loro potere* (en: *it's been proved that many communities, including religion ones, can be dominant or abuse of their power*, which are discarded by filtering the BK in the same prompt. Therefore, addressing the two tasks together is better than separately. This tendency has been observed in other hate-related tasks (Muti et al., 2022, 2024b). However, even in instances with the highest scores, generated responses tend to rely exclusively on the BK, without providing a logical link between the BK and a final statement to counter hate, which occurs in the ground truth CN.

6 Conclusion

We presented our approach to the knowledge-grounded generation of counternarratives by investigating two aspects: *(i)* generating in English and then translating to the target language vs generating in the original language and *(ii)* filtering (either within the same prompt or in a separate prompt as a preliminary step) vs feeding the model with all the knowledge pieces. The human evaluation performed on the development set shows a contrast in the results. Run 5, which is the simplest setting - no translations nor BK filtering - results in the best-performing run based on some metrics. However, after a manual evaluation, we observe that run 5 does not filter any piece of knowledge provided, polluting the CN generation with irrelevant and hateful statements. The second best-performing run, run 3, which foresees same-prompt filtering on the BK without translation, grants us first place in English, Italian, and Spanish and fourth place in Basque.

Limitations

While aware that ChatGPT-like models may have achieved better results, we preferred using only open-sourced models for an inclusive research. A limitation of our work is that we have not checked the filtered BK before injecting it in the prompt for CN generation. Moreover, the error analysis has been performed only on Italian data.

7 Acknowlegments

Arianna Muti's research is supported by the European Research Council (ERC) under the European Union's Horizon 2020 research and innovation program (grant agreement No. 101116095, PERSONAE). Emanuele Moscato's research was funded by the European Union - NextGenerationEU, in the framework of the FAIR - Future Artificial Intelligence Research project (FAIR PE00000013 – CUP B43C22000800006). The views and opinions expressed are solely those of the authors and do not necessarily reflect those of the European Union, nor can the European Union be held responsible for them. Emanuele Moscato, Arianna Muti, and Debora Nozza are members of the MilaNLP group and the Data and Marketing Insights Unit of the Bocconi Institute for Data Science and Analysis.

References

Helena Bonaldi, Yi-Ling Chung, Gavin Abercrombie, and Marco Guerini. 2024a. NLP for counterspeech against hate: A survey and how-to guide. In *Findings of the Association for Computational Linguistics: NAACL 2024*, pages 3480–3499, Mexico City, Mexico. Association for Computational Linguistics.

Helena Bonaldi, Greta Damo, Nicolás Benjamín Ocampo, Elena Cabrio, Serena Villata, and Marco Guerini. 2024b. Is safer better? the impact of guardrails on the argumentative strength of LLMs in hate speech countering. In *Proceedings of the 2024 Conference on Empirical Methods in Natural Language Processing*, pages 3446–3463, Miami, Florida, USA. Association for Computational Linguistics.

Yi-Ling Chung, Elizaveta Kuzmenko, Serra Sinem Tekiroglu, and Marco Guerini. 2019. CONAN - COunter NArratives through nichesourcing: a multilingual dataset of responses to fight online hate speech. In *Proceedings of the 57th Annual Meeting of the Association for Computational Linguistics*, pages 2819–2829, Florence, Italy. Association for Computational Linguistics.

Yi-Ling Chung, Serra Sinem Tekiroğlu, and Marco Guerini. 2021. Towards knowledge-grounded counter narrative generation for hate speech. In *Findings of the Association for Computational Linguistics: ACL-IJCNLP 2021*, pages 899–914, Online. Association for Computational Linguistics.

Abhimanyu Dubey, Abhinav Jauhri, Abhinav Pandey, Abhishek Kadian, Ahmad Al-Dahle, Aiesha Letman, Akhil Mathur, Alan Schelten, Amy Yang, Angela Fan, Anirudh Goyal, Anthony Hartshorn, Aobo Yang, Archi Mitra, Archie Sravankumar, Artem Korenev, Arthur Hinsvark, Arun Rao, Aston Zhang, Aurelien Rodriguez, Austen Gregerson, Ava Spataru, Baptiste Roziere, Bethany Biron, Binh Tang, Bobbie Chern, Charlotte Caucheteux, Chaya Nayak, Chloe Bi, Chris Marra, Chris McConnell, Christian Keller, Christophe Touret, Chunyang Wu, Corinne Wong, Cristian Canton Ferrer, Cyrus Nikolaidis, Damien Allonsius, Daniel Song, Danielle Pintz, Danny Livshits, David Esiobu, Dhruv Choudhary, Dhruv Mahajan, Diego Garcia-Olano, Diego Perino, Dieuwke Hupkes, Egor Lakomkin, Ehab AlBadawy, Elina Lobanova, Emily Dinan, Eric Michael Smith, Filip Radenovic, Frank Zhang, Gabriel Synnaeve, Gabrielle Lee, Georgia Lewis Anderson, Graeme Nail, Gregoire Mialon, Guan Pang, Guillem Cucurell, Hailey Nguyen, Hannah Korevaar, Hu Xu, Hugo Touvron, Iliyan Zarov, Imanol Arrieta Ibarra, Isabel Kloumann, Ishan Misra, Ivan Evtimov, Jade Copet, Jaewon Lee, Jan Geffert, Jana Vranes, Jason Park, Jay Mahadeokar, Jeet Shah, Jelmer van der Linde, Jennifer Billock, Jenny Hong, Jenya Lee, Jeremy Fu, Jianfeng Chi, Jianyu Huang, Jiawen Liu, Jie Wang, Jiecao Yu, Joanna Bitton, Joe Spisak, Jongsoo Park, Joseph Rocca, Joshua Johnstun, Joshua Saxe, Junteng Jia, Kalyan Vasuden Alwala, Kartikeya Upasani, Kate Plawiak, Ke Li, Kenneth Heafield, Kevin Stone, Khalid El-Arini, Krithika Iyer, Kshitiz Malik, Kuenley Chiu, Kunal Bhalla, Lauren Rantala-Yeary, Laurens van der Maaten, Lawrence Chen, Liang Tan, Liz Jenkins, Louis Martin, Lovish Madaan, Lubo Malo, Lukas Blecher, Lukas Landzaat, Luke de Oliveira, Madeline Muzzi, Mahesh Pasupuleti, Mannat Singh, Manohar Paluri, Marcin Kardas, Mathew Oldham, Mathieu Rita, Maya Pavlova, Melanie Kambadur, Mike Lewis, Min Si, Mitesh Kumar Singh, Mona Hassan, Naman Goyal, Narjes Torabi, Nikolay Bashlykov, Nikolay Bogoychev, Niladri Chatterji, Olivier Duchenne, Onur Çelebi, Patrick Alrassy, Pengchuan Zhang, Pengwei Li, Petar Vasic, Peter Weng, Prajjwal Bhargava, Pratik Dubal, Praveen Krishnan, Punit Singh Koura, Puxin Xu, Qing He, Qingxiao Dong, Ragavan Srinivasan, Raj Ganapathy, Ramon Calderer, Ricardo Silveira Cabral, Robert Stojnic, Roberta Raileanu, Rohit Girdhar, Rohit Patel, Romain Sauvestre, Ronnie Polidoro, Roshan Sumbaly,

Ross Taylor, Ruan Silva, Rui Hou, Rui Wang, Saghar Hosseini, Sahana Chennabasappa, Sanjay Singh, Sean Bell, Seohyun Sonia Kim, Sergey Edunov, Shaoliang Nie, Sharan Narang, Sharath Raparthy, Sheng Shen, Shengye Wan, Shruti Bhosale, Shun Zhang, Simon Vandenhende, Soumya Batra, Spencer Whitman, Sten Sootla, Stephane Collot, Suchin Gururangan, Sydney Borodinsky, Tamar Herman, Tara Fowler, Tarek Sheasha, Thomas Georgiou, Thomas Scialom, Tobias Speckbacher, Todor Mihaylov, Tong Xiao, Ujjwal Karn, Vedanuj Goswami, Vibhor Gupta, Vignesh Ramanathan, Viktor Kerkez, Vincent Gonguet, Virginie Do, Vish Vogeti, Vladan Petrovic, Weiwei Chu, Wenhan Xiong, Wenyin Fu, Whitney Meers, Xavier Martinet, Xiaodong Wang, Xiaoqing Ellen Tan, Xinfeng Xie, Xuchao Jia, Xuewei Wang, Yaelle Goldschlag, Yashesh Gaur, Yasmine Babaei, Yi Wen, Yiwen Song, Yuchen Zhang, Yue Li, Yuning Mao, Zacharie Delpierre Coudert, Zheng Yan, Zhengxing Chen, Zoe Papakipos, Aaditya Singh, Aaron Grattafiori, Abha Jain, Adam Kelsey, Adam Shajnfeld, Adithya Gangidi, Adolfo Victoria, Ahuva Goldstand, Ajay Menon, Ajay Sharma, Alex Boesenberg, Alex Vaughan, Alexei Baevski, Allie Feinstein, Amanda Kallet, Amit Sangani, Anam Yunus, Andrei Lupu, Andres Alvarado, Andrew Caples, Andrew Gu, Andrew Ho, Andrew Poulton, Andrew Ryan, Ankit Ramchandani, Annie Franco, Aparajita Saraf, Arkabandhu Chowdhury, Ashley Gabriel, Ashwin Bharambe, Assaf Eisenman, Azadeh Yazdan, Beau James, Ben Maurer, Benjamin Leonhardi, Bernie Huang, Beth Loyd, Beto De Paola, Bhargavi Paranjape, Bing Liu, Bo Wu, Boyu Ni, Braden Hancock, Bram Wasti, Brandon Spence, Brani Stojkovic, Brian Gamido, Britt Montalvo, Carl Parker, Carly Burton, Catalina Mejia, Changhan Wang, Changkyu Kim, Chao Zhou, Chester Hu, Ching-Hsiang Chu, Chris Cai, Chris Tindal, Christoph Feichtenhofer, Damon Civin, Dana Beaty, Daniel Kreymer, Daniel Li, Danny Wyatt, David Adkins, David Xu, Davide Testuggine, Delia David, Devi Parikh, Diana Liskovich, Didem Foss, Dingkang Wang, Duc Le, Dustin Holland, Edward Dowling, Eissa Jamil, Elaine Montgomery, Eleonora Presani, Emily Hahn, Emily Wood, Erik Brinkman, Esteban Arcaute, Evan Dunbar, Evan Smothers, Fei Sun, Felix Kreuk, Feng Tian, Firat Ozgenel, Francesco Caggioni, Francisco Guzmán, Frank Kanayet, Frank Seide, Gabriela Medina Florez, Gabriella Schwarz, Gada Badeer, Georgia Swee, Gil Halpern, Govind Thattai, Grant Herman, Grigory Sizov, Guangyi, Zhang, Guna Lakshminarayanan, Hamid Shojanazeri, Han Zou, Hannah Wang, Hanwen Zha, Haroun Habeeb, Harrison Rudolph, Helen Suk, Henry Aspegren, Hunter Goldman, Ibrahim Damlaj, Igor Molybog, Igor Tufanov, Irina-Elena Veliche, Itai Gat, Jake Weissman, James Geboski, James Kohli, Japhet Asher, Jean-Baptiste Gaya, Jeff Marcus, Jeff Tang, Jennifer Chan, Jenny Zhen, Jeremy Reizenstein, Jeremy Teboul, Jessica Zhong, Jian Jin, Jingyi Yang, Joe Cummings, Jon Carvill, Jon Shepard, Jonathan McPhie, Jonathan Torres, Josh Ginsburg, Junjie Wang, Kai Wu, Kam Hou U, Karan Saxena, Karthik Prasad, Kartikay Khandelwal, Katayoun Zand, Kathy Matosich, Kaushik Veeraraghavan, Kelly Michelena, Keqian Li, Kun Huang, Kunal Chawla, Kushal Lakhotia, Kyle Huang, Lailin Chen, Lakshya Garg, Lavender A, Leandro Silva, Lee Bell, Lei Zhang, Liangpeng Guo, Licheng Yu, Liron Moshkovich, Luca Wehrstedt, Madian Khabsa, Manav Avalani, Manish Bhatt, Maria Tsimpoukelli, Martynas Mankus, Matan Hasson, Matthew Lennie, Matthias Reso, Maxim Groshev, Maxim Naumov, Maya Lathi, Meghan Keneally, Michael L. Seltzer, Michal Valko, Michelle Restrepo, Mihir Patel, Mik Vyatskov, Mikayel Samvelyan, Mike Clark, Mike Macey, Mike Wang, Miquel Jubert Hermoso, Mo Metanat, Mohammad Rastegari, Munish Bansal, Nandhini Santhanam, Natascha Parks, Natasha White, Navyata Bawa, Nayan Singhal, Nick Egebo, Nicolas Usunier, Nikolay Pavlovich Laptev, Ning Dong, Ning Zhang, Norman Cheng, Oleg Chernoguz, Olivia Hart, Omkar Salpekar, Ozlem Kalinli, Parkin Kent, Parth Parekh, Paul Saab, Pavan Balaji, Pedro Rittner, Philip Bontrager, Pierre Roux, Piotr Dollar, Polina Zvyagina, Prashant Ratanchandani, Pritish Yuvraj, Qian Liang, Rachad Alao, Rachel Rodriguez, Rafi Ayub, Raghotham Murthy, Raghu Nayani, Rahul Mitra, Raymond Li, Rebekkah Hogan, Robin Battey, Rocky Wang, Rohan Maheswari, Russ Howes, Ruty Rinott, Sai Jayesh Bondu, Samyak Datta, Sara Chugh, Sara Hunt, Sargun Dhillon, Sasha Sidorov, Satadru Pan, Saurabh Verma, Seiji Yamamoto, Sharadh Ramaswamy, Shaun Lindsay, Shaun Lindsay, Sheng Feng, Shenghao Lin, Shengxin Cindy Zha, Shiva Shankar, Shuqiang Zhang, Shuqiang Zhang, Sinong Wang, Sneha Agarwal, Soji Sajuyigbe, Soumith Chintala, Stephanie Max, Stephen Chen, Steve Kehoe, Steve Satterfield, Sudarshan Govindaprasad, Sumit Gupta, Sungmin Cho, Sunny Virk, Suraj Subramanian, Sy Choudhury, Sydney Goldman, Tal Remez, Tamar Glaser, Tamara Best, Thilo Kohler, Thomas Robinson, Tianhe Li, Tianjun Zhang, Tim Matthews, Timothy Chou, Tzook Shaked, Varun Vontimitta, Victoria Ajayi, Victoria Montanez, Vijai Mohan, Vinay Satish Kumar, Vishal Mangla, Vítor Albiero, Vlad Ionescu, Vlad Poenaru, Vlad Tiberiu Mihailescu, Vladimir Ivanov, Wei Li, Wenchen Wang, Wenwen Jiang, Wes Bouaziz, Will Constable, Xiaocheng Tang, Xiaofang Wang, Xiaojian Wu, Xiaolan Wang, Xide Xia, Xilun Wu, Xinbo Gao, Yanjun Chen, Ye Hu, Ye Jia, Ye Qi, Yenda Li, Yilin Zhang, Ying Zhang, Yossi Adi, Youngjin Nam, Yu, Wang, Yuchen Hao, Yundi Qian, Yuzi He, Zach Rait, Zachary DeVito, Zef Rosnbrick, Zhaoduo Wen, Zhenyu Yang, and Zhiwei Zhao. 2024. The llama 3 herd of models. *Preprint*, arXiv:2407.21783.

Margherita Fanton, Helena Bonaldi, Serra Sinem Tekiroğlu, and Marco Guerini. 2021a. Human-in-the-loop for data collection: a multi-target counter narrative dataset to fight online hate speech. In *Proceedings of the 59th Annual Meeting of the Association for Computational Linguistics and the 11th International Joint Conference on Natural Language Processing (Volume 1: Long Papers)*, pages 3226–3240, Online. Association for Computational Linguistics.

Margherita Fanton, Helena Bonaldi, Serra Sinem

Tekiroğlu, and Marco Guerini. 2021b. Human-in-the-loop for data collection: a multi-target counter narrative dataset to fight online hate speech. In *Proceedings of the 59th Annual Meeting of the Association for Computational Linguistics and the 11th International Joint Conference on Natural Language Processing (Volume 1: Long Papers)*, page 3226–3240. Association for Computational Linguistics.

Albert Q. Jiang, Alexandre Sablayrolles, Arthur Mensch, Chris Bamford, Devendra Singh Chaplot, Diego de las Casas, Florian Bressand, Gianna Lengyel, Guillaume Lample, Lucile Saulnier, Lélio Renard Lavaud, Marie-Anne Lachaux, Pierre Stock, Teven Le Scao, Thibaut Lavril, Thomas Wang, Timothée Lacroix, and William El Sayed. 2023a. Mistral 7b. In *arXiv preprint arXiv:2310.06825*.

Shuyu Jiang, Wenyi Tang, Xingshu Chen, Rui Tanga, Haizhou Wang, and Wenxian Wang. 2023b. Raucg: Retrieval-augmented unsupervised counter narrative generation for hate speech. In *arXiv preprint arXiv:2310.05650*.

Chin-Yew Lin. 2004. ROUGE: A package for automatic evaluation of summaries. In *Text Summarization Branches Out*, pages 74–81, Barcelona, Spain. Association for Computational Linguistics.

Arianna Muti and Alberto Barrón-Cedeño. 2022. A checkpoint on multilingual misogyny identification. In *Proceedings of the 60th Annual Meeting of the Association for Computational Linguistics: Student Research Workshop*, pages 454–460, Dublin, Ireland. Association for Computational Linguistics.

Arianna Muti, Francesco Fernicola, and Alberto Barrón-Cedeño. 2022. Misogyny and aggressiveness tend to come together and together we address them. In *Proceedings of the Thirteenth Language Resources and Evaluation Conference*, pages 4142–4148, Marseille, France. European Language Resources Association.

Arianna Muti, Federico Ruggeri, Khalid Al Khatib, Alberto Barrón-Cedeño, and Tommaso Caselli. 2024a. Language is scary when over-analyzed: Unpacking implied misogynistic reasoning with argumentation theory-driven prompts. In *Proceedings of the 2024 Conference on Empirical Methods in Natural Language Processing*, pages 21091–21107, Miami, Florida, USA. Association for Computational Linguistics.

Arianna Muti, Federico Ruggeri, Cagri Toraman, Alberto Barrón-Cedeño, Samuel Algherini, Lorenzo Musetti, Silvia Ronchi, Gianmarco Saretto, and Caterina Zapparoli. 2024b. PejorativITy: Disambiguating pejorative epithets to improve misogyny detection in Italian tweets. In *Proceedings of the 2024 Joint International Conference on Computational Linguistics, Language Resources and Evaluation (LREC-COLING 2024)*, pages 12700–12711, Torino, Italia. ELRA and ICCL.

Iftitahu Nimah, Meng Fang, Vlado Menkovski, and Mykola Pechenizkiy. 2023. NLG evaluation metrics beyond correlation analysis: An empirical metric preference checklist. In *Proceedings of the 61st Annual Meeting of the Association for Computational Linguistics (Volume 1: Long Papers)*, pages 1240–1266, Toronto, Canada. Association for Computational Linguistics.

NLLBTeam, Marta R. Costa-jussà, James Cross, Onur Çelebi, Maha Elbayad, Kenneth Heafield, Kevin Heffernan, Elahe Kalbassi, Janice Lam, Daniel Licht, Jean Maillard, Anna Sun, Skyler Wang, Guillaume Wenzek, Al Youngblood, Bapi Akula, Loic Barrault, Gabriel Mejia Gonzalez, Prangthip Hansanti, John Hoffman, Semarley Jarrett, Kaushik Ram Sadagopan, Dirk Rowe, Shannon Spruit, Chau Tran, Pierre Andrews, Necip Fazil Ayan, Shruti Bhosale, Sergey Edunov, Angela Fan, Cynthia Gao, Vedanuj Goswami, Francisco Guzmán, Philipp Koehn, Alexandre Mourachko, Christophe Ropers, Safiyyah Saleem, Holger Schwenk, and Jeff Wang. 2022. No language left behind: Scaling human-centered machine translation. In *arXiv preprint arXiv:2207.04672*.

Debora Nozza. 2021. Exposing the limits of zero-shot cross-lingual hate speech detection. In *Proceedings of the 59th Annual Meeting of the Association for Computational Linguistics and the 11th International Joint Conference on Natural Language Processing (Volume 2: Short Papers)*, pages 907–914, Online. Association for Computational Linguistics.

Kishore Papineni, Salim Roukos, Todd Ward, and Wei-Jing Zhu. 2002. Bleu: a method for automatic evaluation of machine translation. In *Proceedings of the 40th Annual Meeting of the Association for Computational Linguistics*, pages 311–318, Philadelphia, Pennsylvania, USA. Association for Computational Linguistics.

Matt Post. 2018. A call for clarity in reporting BLEU scores. In *Proceedings of the Third Conference on Machine Translation: Research Papers*, pages 186–191, Brussels, Belgium. Association for Computational Linguistics.

Serra Sinem Tekiroglu, Helena Bonaldi, Margherita Fanton, and Marco Guerini. 2022. Using pre-trained language models for producing counter narratives against hate speech: a comparative study. In *arXiv preprint arXiv:2204.01440*.

Lewis Tunstall, Edward Beeching, Nathan Lambert, Nazneen Rajani, Kashif Rasul, Younes Belkada, Shengyi Huang, Leandro von Werra, Clémentine Fourrier, Nathan Habib, Nathan Sarrazin, Omar Sanseviero, Alexander M. Rush, and Thomas Wolf. 2023. Zephyr: Direct distillation of lm alignment.

Tianyi Zhang, Varsha Kishore, Felix Wu, Kilian Q. Weinberger, and Yoav Artzi. 2019. Bertscore: Evaluating text generation with BERT. In *arXiv preprint arXiv:1904-09675*, volume abs/1904.09675.

Irune Zubiaga, Aitor Soroa, and Rodrigo Agerri. 2024. A llm-based ranking method for the evaluation of automatic counter-narrative generation. In *arXiv preprint arXiv:2406.15227*.

A Prompts

Here are examples of the prompts used in the various cases discussed.

System prompt

The following system prompt was used with the user prompts for counternarrative generation:

> You are an expert in countering hate speech. You have to always generate text based on the given instructions. You will see a text with hate speech but you'll have to provide an answer.

Default prompt

> You are an expert in countering hate speech. You have to always generate text based on the given instructions. You will see a text with hate speech but you'll have to provide an answer.
>
> In the following examples, pieces of text containing hate speech are counteracted by counternarratives generated using the information in the background knowledge points.
>
> ____________
>
> ____________
>
> Generate a new counternarrative for the following hate speech text by using the information in the background knowledge points that you think are relevant. Answer in English. Keep your answers short and concise. Do not generate any new information that is not present in the background knowledge. Hate speech text in English against <TARGET> : <HS>.
>
> Background knowledge: <BK>
>
> Counter narrative:

Background knowledge filtering

The following system and user prompts were used to filter the relevant background knowledge points. System prompt:

> You are an expert in information retrieval.

User prompt:

> Identify which among the following pieces of background knowledge are relevant to generate a counter argument against the main text provided.
>
> Main text: <HS>.
>
> Pieces of background knowledge: <BK>
>
> PRODUCE ONLY AND EXCLUSIVELY A LIST containing the number of the relevant pieces of background knowledge, with NO ADDITIONAL WORDS NOR EXPLANATION.

B LLM settings

For the CNG task, the outputs were generated using temperature $T = 0.0$ and setting `max_new_tokens` to 400. The identification of relevant BK in a separate prompt required an additional initial call to the model, with answers generated again setting $T = 0.0$. For the translation task form English to other target languages, the values for the text generation parameters were all kept to the NLLB model's default.

For each task, any other parameter not explicitly mentioned above was kept to default value.

Hyderabadi Pearls at Multilingual Counterspeech Generation : HALT : Hate Speech Alleviation using Large Language Models and Transformers

Shariq Farhan
Uber Technologies, Inc.
sfarhan@uber.com

Ravi Sharma Kaushik
University of Amsterdam
ravi.sharma2@student.uva.nl

Abstract

This paper explores the potential of using fine-tuned Large Language Models (LLMs) for generating counter-narratives (CNs) to combat hate speech (HS). We focus on English and Basque, leveraging the ML_MTCONAN_KN dataset, which provides hate speech and counter-narrative pairs in multiple languages. Our paper compares the performance of Mistral, Llama, and a Llama-based LLM fine-tuned on a Basque language dataset for CN generation. The generated CNs are evaluated using JudgeLM (a LLM to evaluate other LLMs in open-ended scenarios) along with traditional metrics such as ROUGE-L, BLEU, BERTScore, and other traditional metrics. The results demonstrate that fine-tuned LLMs can produce high-quality contextually relevant CNs for low-resource languages that are comparable to human-generated responses, offering a significant contribution to combating online hate speech across diverse linguistic settings.

1 Introduction

The unchecked proliferation of hate speech online has become a significant societal concern, prompting the need for effective countermeasures. Conventional content moderation strategies, such as removing hateful content and suspending user accounts, have been criticized for potentially limiting freedom of expression and not addressing the underlying causes of hate speech (Mathew et al., 2019). Counter-narratives (CNs), defined as non-aggressive responses that challenge hateful messages using evidence-based arguments, promoting empathy and understanding, offer a more promising approach. Research has shown that CNs can be effective in mitigating hate speech online. They can help to de-escalate heated online discussions, offer alternative perspectives to bystanders, and potentially even encourage individuals who engage in hate speech to reconsider their views (Mathew et al., 2018; Schieb and Preuss, 2016). However, manually creating CNs poses challenges in scalability due to the huge amount of hate speech online (Schieb and Preuss, 2016; Tekiroğlu et al., 2020). Recent advances in Natural Language Processing (NLP), particularly in Large Language Models (LLMs), provide a potential solution. LLMs, trained on extensive text datasets, have shown remarkable capabilities in various NLP tasks, including text generation (Fanton et al., 2021; Sprugnoli et al., 2018). By fine-tuning, these models can be adapted for specific tasks such as CN generation, potentially enabling the automatic creation of high-quality, contextually relevant CNs at scale (Schieb and Preuss, 2016; Fanton et al., 2021). This paper examines the application of fine-tuned LLMs for generating CNs against hate speech in English and Basque using the ML_MTCONAN_KN dataset, which is derived from the CONAN (Fanton et al., 2021; Schieb and Preuss, 2016; Tekiroğlu et al., 2020; Vallecillo-Rodríguez et al., 2023) and MT-CONAN (Vallecillo-Rodríguez et al., 2023) datasets. Includes hate speech-counter-narrative pairs enriched with relevant knowledge. Selecting English and Basque allows the exploration of CN generation in both high-resource and low-resource language settings. Additionally, the fine-tuned models were evaluated on Italian and Spanish datasets to assess the cross-lingual applicability of fine-tuned models in one language to others. This paper, by analysing outputs from a pre-trained LLM and comparing different fine-tuning and post-processing techniques, aims to:

(a) Demonstrate that LLMs can be adapted for automated CN generation.

(b) Assess the quality and relevance of LLM-generated CNs in comparison to human-generated CNs.

Proceedings of the First Workshop on Multilingual Counterspeech Generation (MCG), pages 65–76
January 19th, 2025.

(c) Explore the challenges and opportunities associated with CN generation in a low-resource language like Basque.

This research ultimately aims to contribute to the development of robust, scalable, and effective tools to combat online hate speech, fostering a more inclusive and respectful online environment.

2 Related Work

2.1 Hate Speech Mitigation

Gillespie (2018); Mathew et al. (2019) have brought forward the shortcomings of traditional methods to mitigate hate speech, such as content removal, user suspension, and algorithmic filtering. While these approaches can be effective in removing harmful content, they often face criticism for their lack of transparency, potential for over-censorship, and failure to address the root causes of hate speech.

Studies have demonstrated that CNs can reduce the visibility and influence of hate speech, de-escalate online tensions, and encourage bystanders to engage positively by promoting empathy, providing evidence-based arguments, and fostering dialogue (Schieb and Preuss, 2016). However, the manual creation of CNs is time-consuming, costly, and difficult to scale, particularly given the volume of online hate speech. Recent advancements in automation have introduced the possibility of leveraging computational methods for CN generation. Early approaches relied on template-based systems and rule-based natural language processing (NLP), but these were limited by their rigidity and inability to adapt to diverse contexts (Tekiroğlu et al., 2020).

2.2 LLMs in Text Generation

The advent of Large Language Models (LLMs) offers a transformative solution by enabling the generation of diverse and contextually appropriate CNs at scale. Large Language Models, such as GPT-3, BERT, and their successors, represent a significant leap in NLP capabilities. Trained on vast corpora of text, these models have demonstrated proficiency in a wide range of text generation tasks, including summarization, translation, creative writing, and conversational AI (Brown et al., 2020; Raffel et al., 2020).

For tasks like counter-narrative generation, fine-tuning LLMs on domain-specific datasets can enhance their ability to produce contextually relevant and impactful responses. Studies have shown that LLMs can generate high-quality outputs that are linguistically fluent and semantically coherent, even in challenging tasks like generating empathetic or persuasive content (Zhang et al., 2020b; Fanton et al., 2021).

2.3 Multilingual and Cross-Lingual Research

Multilingual NLP models like mBERT, XLM-R, and BLOOM have been developed to bridge the disparities between high-resource and low-resource languages by leveraging shared linguistic features across languages (Conneau and Lample, 2019; Artetxe and Schwenk, 2019).

In the context of counter-narrative generation, multilingual and cross-lingual approaches enable the extension of automated CN systems to underserved linguistic communities. Studies by Hu et al. (2020); Tekiroğlu et al. (2020) have demonstrated that pre-trained multilingual LLMs can be fine-tuned on smaller datasets for specific tasks, achieving competitive performance even in low-resource languages.

Cross-lingual transfer, where knowledge from high-resource languages is applied to low-resource languages, has shown promise in enhancing the performance of NLP systems in underrepresented languages. For example, models fine-tuned on datasets like CONAN and MT-CONAN have been successfully adapted to generate counter-narratives in multiple languages, including Basque (Fanton et al., 2021; Vallecillo-Rodríguez et al., 2023).

3 Approach

This paper involves a series of systematic experiments, including those conducted as part of the official submission and additional explorations performed post-submission. The primary objective is to fine-tune existing large language models (LLMs) to enhance their ability to generate effective counter-narratives. Model selection is guided by two criteria: the models' capacity for fine-tuning and their performance on established benchmarks.

For this task, the counter-narratives were generated solely using the existing knowledge provided in the original dataset. No external or additional knowledge sources were incorporated in the generation process.

3.1 Official Submissions

The official submissions utilize only the datasets provided for the task. Wherever applicable, the datasets were filtered to ensure relevance and compatibility with the respective target languages.

(a) **Run 1**

 (i) **Basque**: Fine-tune the LLama 3 (8B) for 3,000 steps using the Basque MT-CONAN dataset exclusively.

 (ii) **English**: Fine-tune the LLama 3 (8B) for 300 steps using the English MT-CONAN dataset exclusively.

(b) **Run 2**

 (i) **Basque**: Fine-tune an existing model (developed by Orai NLP) for 500 steps, leveraging only the Basque MT-CONAN dataset.

 (ii) **English**: Fine-tune the LLama 3 (8B) for 3,000 steps using the English MT-CONAN dataset exclusively.

(c) **Run 3**

 (i) **Basque**: Fine-tune the LLama 3 (8B) for 3,000 steps using the Basque MT-CONAN dataset exclusively.

 (ii) **English**: Fine-tune the Mistral (7B) for 300 steps using the English MT-CONAN dataset exclusively.

3.2 Additional Experiments

To complement the above analyses, we conducted a series of additional experiments aimed at addressing specific challenges and exploring extended use cases:

(a) **Experiment 1** : Evaluating Low-Resource Language Models

 (i) Given Basque's status as a low-resource language, we tested the efficacy of fine-tuned Basque models with and without native language prompts to assess their adaptability and robustness.

(b) **Experiment 2** : Leveraging Base LLMs for Post-Processing

 (i) Base LLMs were employed to post-process the outputs of fine-tuned models. In this setup, the base LLMs were restricted to correcting grammatical errors while preserving the intended meaning of the counter-narratives.

(c) **Experiment 3** : Cross-Lingual Evaluation

 (i) Although the fine-tuning was performed specifically on Basque and English datasets, we evaluated the resulting models on Italian and Spanish datasets (see Tables 3 and 4) to assess the models' ability to generalize counter-narrative generation across languages

(d) **Experiment 4** : Benchmarking against GPT-4o

 (i) All fine-tuned models were compared to GPT-4o, a high-performing baseline known for its robust performance on multiple benchmarks. This comparison provided insights into the relative effectiveness of the fine-tuned models in generating high-quality counter-narratives

4 Methodology

Our experiments are conducted on the ML_MTCONAN_KN dataset for English and Basque, which is derived from the CONAN and MT-CONAN datasets.

- **CONAN:** This dataset, created through niche-sourcing, consists of hate speech-counter-narrative pairs, primarily in English, French, and Italian, and initially focused on Islamophobia. It leverages the expertise of NGOs specialising in countering online hate speech (Vidgen et al., 2020).

- **MT-CONAN:** Building upon CONAN, this dataset expands the range of hate speech targets, encompassing individuals with disabilities, Jewish people, the LGBT+ community, migrants, Muslims, people of colour, women, and other marginalised groups (Vidgen et al., 2021).

Our choice of large language models (LLMs) for fine-tuning reflects a strategic approach to counter-narrative generation:

- **Mistral 7B:** This model (Face, n.d.) has been shown to be effective for counter-narrative generation. (Li et al., 2023).

- **Llama 3 8B:** This model (AI, n.d.) is also well-suited for counter-narrative generation. (Zhang et al., 2023).

- **orai-nlp/Llama-eus-8B:** This model (Orai-NLP, n.d.) is a Basque-language LLM, making it a suitable choice for the Basque counter-narrative generation task.

The selected models were chosen for their strong performance on various NLP tasks and their strategic size, ranging from 5 to 10 billion parameters, which makes them well-suited for fine-tuning. This size range strikes a balance between capability and the practicality of using widely available hardware. Fine-tuning these models on standard GPUs, such as those accessible through Google Colab or Kaggle Notebooks, often requires additional optimization techniques.

To address this, methods such as QLoRA (Quantized Low-Rank Adaptation; (Dettmers et al., 2022)) were employed, allowing efficient fine-tuning of LLMs on limited computational resources.

4.1 Fine-Tuning

Fine-Tuning with Llama: Llama 3 (8B) was fine-tuned on the ML_MTCONAN_KN dataset to enable them to understand the patterns and nuances of counter-narrative generation within the hate speech domain.

Fine-Tuning Llama with a Basque Prompt: Similar to the previous step, but instead of using an English prompt to generate instructions, a Basque language prompt was employed.

Fine-Tuning with Mistral: The Mistral 7B model was similarly fine-tuned on the dataset, specializing in counter-narrative generation. This step also facilitated performance comparisons between the fine-tuned Llama and Mistral models (Wu and Zhang, 2023).

4.2 Post-Processing

Output Refinement with GPT-4o and Mistral: To enhance quality, coherence, and factual accuracy, outputs from the fine-tuned Llama models were edited using GPT-4o or Mistral. This post-processing step ensured the generated counter-narratives were polished and impactful (Brown et al., 2020).

4.3 Direct LLM Output Evaluation

Raw Counter-Narrative Generation: Raw outputs from LLMs, such as GPT-4o, were also evaluated to assess their pre-trained knowledge in generating counter-narratives without explicit fine-tuning on the target dataset. While other models such as Claude, Gemini and Llama-based models, were also tested, some refused to generate results citing the sensitivity of the content. Consequently, only GPT-4o outputs were used to compare the performances of fully pre-trained LLMs with a fine-tuned LLM.

4.4 Evaluation Metrics

Model performances are assessed with the following metrics:

- **JudgeLM:** Utilizes LLMs for evaluating personalized text generation (Fu and Li, 2022) in open-ended scenarios
- **ROUGE-L:** ROUGE (Recall-Oriented Understudy for Gisting Evaluation) is a set of metrics commonly used for evaluating automatic summarization and machine translation tasks. It primarily measures lexical overlap between a generated text and reference text(s) (Lin, 2004)
- **BLEU:** Emphasises precision and word choice accuracy through n-gram overlap (Papineni et al., 2002).
- **BERTScore:** Uses contextualized embeddings from BERT to capture semantic similarity beyond surface-level matching (Zhang et al., 2020a).

5 Results

As outlined in 3, we conducted a series of experiments to fine-tune the models, aiming to optimize their performance for counter-narrative generation. The exact prompts used in the experiments are detailed in A. If a prompt name is not mentioned for a specific experiment, the default prompt is used.

Reference Dictionary for Model Names

- Base Models
  - **Mistral 7B**: Refers to the original, pre-trained Mistral 7B Model
  - **Llama 3 8B**: Refers to the original, pre-trained Llama 3 8B Model
- Fine Tuned Models
  - **Orai Llama 3 8B**: A Llama 3 8B model fine-tuned specifically on the Basque dataset by Orai-NLP.

- Prompt modifications
  - **Basque Prompt**: Refers to a model fine-tuned with a Basque language-specific prompt designed for counter-narrative generation.
  - **New Prompt**: Refers to a model fine-tuned using a newly designed or modified prompt for counter-narrative generation.
- Output Edits : To enhance grammatical accuracy, model outputs were post-processed as follows:
  - **GPT** : Outputs were edited using GPT-4o to correct grammatical errors
  - **Mistral**: Outputs were edited using Mistral 7B to correct grammatical errors
- Training Steps
  - **300/ 500/ 1000/ 3000**: Indicates the number of fine-tuning steps the model underwent during training.
- Using the above details, the model names are given as *Fine-tuning model name_No. of steps_Prompt details*.

5.1 Basque

For the Basque language experiments, fine-tuning efforts included the use of Basque-specific prompts and datasets, with the goal of enhancing counter-narrative generation in a linguistically and culturally appropriate manner. Below, we discuss the performance of the fine-tuned models. The detailed results are presented in Table 1 below.

5.1.1 Observations

- The Orai Llama model fine-tuned with the Basque prompt achieved the highest JudgeLM scores and novelty, indicating its superior ability to generate creative and contextually appropriate counter-narratives. However, this came at the cost of extended inference times and significantly longer output lengths, as reflected in the Gen_Len Metric in Table 1.
- LLama_3_8B_1000 demonstrated robust BLEU and RougeL scores, reflecting its strong performance across traditional evaluation metrics. These results can be attributed to the fine-tuning process, which was specifically optimized for these metrics.
- The counter-narratives generated by GPT-4o and Mistral_7B_500 scored significantly lower than other models. This indicates difficulty in maintaining both linguistic fidelity and contextual relevance, particularly for a low-resource language like Basque.

5.1.2 Learnings

(a) **Performance of GPT-4o**

  (i) CNs generated using GPT-4o yield excellent results across multiple high-resource languages, as evidenced in Tables 2, 3, and 4.

  (ii) However, it's performance diminishes significantly for low-resource languages such as Basque, highlighting the challenges of generating effective counter-narratives in these contexts.

(b) **Impact of Fine-Tuning Steps**

  (i) A base Llama model fine-tuned for 1,000 steps outperforms the Orai Llama model, which was fine-tuned for only 500 steps.

  (ii) This points to the possibility of further fine-tuning the model without overfitting

(c) **Potential for Further Improvement**

  (i) Extending fine-tuning beyond the current limits presents minimal risk of overfitting, as evidenced by the consistent trends in training and evaluation losses (Figures 1 and 2). This suggests that additional training could unlock further performance gains.

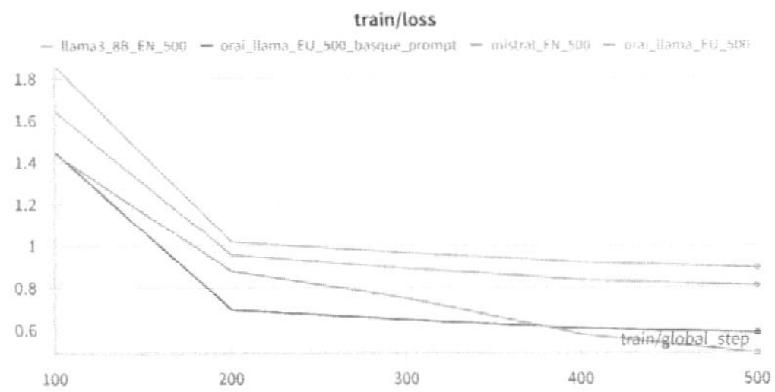

Figure 1: Training Losses for the models

Model	JudgeLM	RougeL	BLEU	BERTScore	Gen_Len	Novelty
Orai_llama_3_8B_500_basque_prompt	338.5	10.29	3.2	66.7	294.61	93.1
LLama_3_8B_1000	118.5	24.48	15.22	74.61	26.35	86.13
Orai_llama_3_8B_500	80.0	34.0	22.74	77.47	22.71	85.1
gold_truth	54.5	100.0	100.0	100.0	26.5	85.3
LLama_3_8B_300	47.5	31.73	22.25	76.59	24.96	85.41
GPT-4o	33.5	9.62	1.82	63.57	54.41	88.79
Mistral_7B_500	27.5	4.33	2.51	64.34	20.98	80.89

Table 1: Performance metrics for different models on Basque tasks

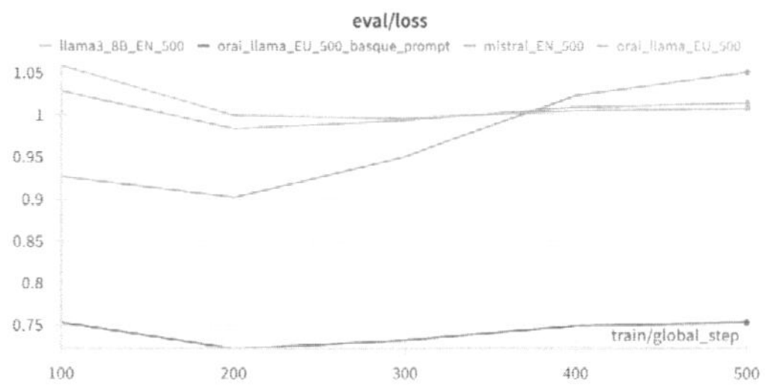

Figure 2: Evaluation Losses for the models

5.2 English

For the English language experiments, fine-tuning and model evaluation is done using the English MT-CONAN dataset. Unlike Basque, English benefits from being a high-resource language with extensive datasets and pre-trained models, enabling more robust performance and generalization. This section highlights the outcomes of various fine-tuned models, including comparisons across different training steps, prompts, and configurations.

5.2.1 Observations

- Leveraging LLMs like GPT-4o to post-edit fine-tuned model outputs significantly improved performance, as evident in the results of *LLama_3_8B_edited_gpt*.

- Mistral 7B models exhibited tendencies toward overfitting; notably, the model fine-tuned for 300 steps outperformed the one fine-tuned for 500 steps, as shown in Figures 1 and 2.

- The *Mistral_7B_300* model achieved the highest scores across traditional metrics such as BLEU and RougeL.

- LLama 3 (8B) struggled to generalize learnings from one language to another, as demonstrated by the poor performance of *Orai_llama_3_8B_500.*

- GPT-4o-generated outputs achieved the highest scores overall; however, they were significantly longer in length and underperformed in alignment metrics such as RougeL and BLEU.

- The longer output length observed in traditional LLM-generated CNs stems from their tendency to use detailed narratives in response to hate speech.

5.2.2 Learnings

(a) **Effectiveness of Traditional LLMs**

   (i) Traditional LLMs, when provided with sufficient context, can generate counter-narratives (CNs) effectively for English tasks.

   (ii) While the generated CNs are often relevant, ensuring an appropriate tone and length is critical.

(b) **Synergy Between Fine-Tuning and Post-Editing**

   (i) Combining task-specific fine-tuning with post-editing by advanced LLMs, such as GPT-4o, enhances performance and ensures grammatical accuracy.

(c) **Mitigating Overfitting**

   (i) Limiting the number of fine-tuning steps is an effective strategy to mitigate overfitting, as demonstrated by the superior performance of Mistral_7B_300 compared to its 500-step counterpart.

(d) **Cross-Lingual Transfer Limitations**

   (i) Cross-lingual transfer remains a significant challenge.

   (ii) These results underscore the importance of language-specific fine-tuning to improve the generation of counter-narratives in multilingual settings.

Model	JudgeLM	RougeL	BLEU	BERTScore	Gen_Len	Novelty
GPT-4o	998	14.82	3.26	67.61	83.99	83.32
gold_truth	548	100	100	100	32.7	77.7
LLama_3_8B_3000_edited_gpt	533.5	44.38	32.76	79.45	31.27	77.76
LLama_3_8B_3000_edited_mistral	526	33.5	21.46	75.3	28.33	78.41
LLama_3_8B_3000	516.5	44.54	33.6	79.5	31.36	77.79
Mistral_7B_300	501	52.44	42.82	82.21	30.04	77.26
LLama_3_8B_500_new_prompt	498.5	48.61	37.59	80.79	29.78	78.04
LLama_3_8B_300	493.5	44.15	34.43	79.3	32.24	78.08
Mistral_7B_500	441	43.53	33.96	79.53	31.11	77.74
Orai_llama_3_8B_500	153.5	24.29	15.49	71.48	24.88	81.2

Table 2: Performance metrics for different models on CN generation for English tasks

5.3 Experiments on Italian and Spanish

As discussed above, the results for Italian and Spanish were derived from additional experiments conducted beyond the original submissions. These experiments aimed to evaluate the generalization capabilities of models fine-tuned on English and Basque datasets when applied to other languages to understand the extent to which fine-tuned models can transfer counter-narrative generation skills across languages, particularly in high-resource settings.

5.3.1 Observations

- GPT-4o performs better than the ground truth for both Italian and Spanish
- Mistral 7B is able to generate outputs for HS in Italian and Spanish, although the CN generated is in English
- JudgeLM compares the output generated and scores them, but there are no restrictions on the output of the language

5.3.2 Learnings

- Cross-lingual fine-tuning (e.g., Basque-trained models) underperforms in generating high-quality outputs for Italian and Spanish tasks, emphasizing the need for language-specific training.

6 Discussion

The experiments provided valuable insights into the strengths and limitations of fine-tuning large language models (LLMs) for counter-narrative generation across different languages. Several key themes emerged from the results:

- **Performance of GPT-4o** : As highlighted earlier, GPT-4o demonstrates strong performance for high-resource languages, as evidenced in Tables 2, 3, and 4. However, it falls short compared to the fine-tuned models when generating counter-narratives for Basque, underscoring the advantages of language-specific fine-tuning in low-resource settings.
- **Fine-Tuning and Generalization**: Fine-tuning on language-specific datasets proved crucial for generating effective CNs, particularly in low-resource contexts like Basque. Cross-lingual transfer remained a challenge, emphasizing the need for tailored approaches for each language.
- **Post-Editing Enhancements**: Post-editing outputs with advanced LLMs, such as GPT-4o, consistently improved the quality of CNs. However, longer outputs and occasional misalignments in metrics like BLEU and RougeL highlighted the trade-offs between verbosity and precision.
- **Balancing Training Steps**: The experiments demonstrated that extending fine-tuning steps can yield better performance up to a point, as seen in the superior results of Mistral_7B_300 over Mistral_7B_500. However, care must be taken to mitigate overfitting, particularly in high-resource models.
- **High-Resource vs. Low-Resource Contexts**: Models performed more effectively in high-resource languages like English, Italian, and Spanish compared to low-resource languages like Basque. This underscores the disparities in linguistic resources and the associated challenges in achieving parity across languages.
- **Cross-Lingual Insights**: While generaliza-

Model	JudgeLM	RougeL	BLEU	BERTScore	Gen_Len	Novelty
GPT-4o	298	12.78	2.86	63.73	72.51	82.76
Mistral_7B_500	141.5	4.55	3.01	70.66	30.77	79.19
gold_truth	131	100	100	100	35.3	77.9
Orai_llama_3_8B_500	29.5	18.16	7.73	70.62	18.27	83.29

Table 3: Performance metrics of the fine-tuned models on Italian tasks

Model	JudgeLM	RougeL	BLEU	BERTScore	Gen_Len	Novelty
GPT-4o	299	15.91	3.88	64.88	79.49	81.18
gold_truth	143	100	100	100	36.9	75.1
Mistral_7B_500	137	6.02	3.0	72.64	30.75	79.21
Orai_llama_3_8B_500	21	18.55	10.84	70.85	21.38	82.86

Table 4: Performance metrics of the fine-tuned models on Spanish tasks

tion across languages remains limited, the experiments highlighted potential avenues for improvement, such as multilingual fine-tuning, leveraging shared linguistic patterns, and incorporating domain-specific prompts.

6.1 Future Directions

Future research should prioritize the following areas to expand on these findings:

- **Cross-Lingual Transfer:** Enhance capabilities through multilingual fine-tuning or by leveraging pre-trained multilingual models.
- **Low-Resource Languages:** Develop adaptive prompts and datasets to better address challenges in low-resource linguistic settings.
- **Output Optimization:** Balance verbosity and alignment metrics to ensure outputs are both concise and precise without sacrificing comprehensiveness.
- **Automated Post-Editing:** Scale post-editing processes using advanced large language models (LLMs) to automate improvements while preserving linguistic fidelity.

By tackling these challenges, counter-narrative generation can become more effective, fostering inclusive and constructive digital discourse across diverse linguistic contexts.

7 Conclusion

This study investigated the fine-tuning of Large Language Models (LLMs) for counter-narrative (CN) generation across English, Basque, Italian, and Spanish. By examining both high-resource and low-resource settings, we identified key strengths, limitations, and challenges in leveraging LLMs for this socially impactful task.

The findings underscore the critical role of language-specific fine-tuning in improving performance, particularly for low-resource languages like Basque, where general-purpose models struggle due to limited data. In contrast, high-resource languages such as English, Italian, and Spanish showcased robust results, with fine-tuned models often outperforming general-purpose models like GPT-4o in alignment and relevance metrics. However, GPT-4o performed better in the JudgeLM Scores.

This paper underscores the importance of:

- Developing robust fine-tuning strategies to minimize bias and enhance the quality of model outputs.
- Expanding research on multilingual capabilities to improve performance in low-resource languages.
- Exploring efficient training and fine-tuning methodologies to mitigate computational and environmental costs.
- Leveraging native language prompt for CN generation

With further research and incorporating the learnings from this paper, LLMs can become more scalable, reliable, and inclusive, enabling their effective deployment in combating hate speech and fostering constructive dialogue across diverse linguistic and cultural contexts.

References

Meta AI. n.d. Llama-3.1-8b-instruct.

Mikel Artetxe and Holger Schwenk. 2019. Massively multilingual sentence embeddings for zero-shot cross-lingual transfer and beyond. In *Proceedings of the 57th Annual Meeting of the Association for Computational Linguistics*, pages 597–598. Association for Computational Linguistics.

Tom B Brown, Benjamin Mann, and Nick Ryder. 2020. Language models are few-shot learners. *arXiv preprint arXiv:2005.14165*.

Alexis Conneau and Guillaume Lample. 2019. Cross-lingual language model pretraining. *Advances in Neural Information Processing Systems*.

Tim Dettmers, Mike Lewis, and Noam Shazeer. 2022. Qlora: Efficient low-rank adaptation for large language models. In *Proceedings of NeurIPS 2022*.

Hugging Face. n.d. Mistral-7b-v0.1.

Margherita Fanton, Helena Bonaldi, Serra Sinem Tekiroğlu, and Marco Guerini. 2021. Human-in-the-loop for data collection: a multi-target counter narrative dataset to fight online hate speech. In *Proceedings of the 59th Annual Meeting of the Association for Computational Linguistics*, Online. Association for Computational Linguistics.

Pengcheng Fu and Xiangyu Li. 2022. Judgelm: Language models as evaluators for text generation tasks. *arXiv preprint arXiv:2210.01234*.

Tarleton Gillespie. 2018. Custodians of the internet: Platforms, content moderation, and the hidden decisions that shape social media. *Yale University Press*.

Junjie Hu, Sebastian Ruder, Aditya Siddhant, Graham Neubig, Orhan Firat, and Melvin Johnson. 2020. Xtreme: A massively multilingual multi-task benchmark for evaluating cross-lingual generalisation. In *International Conference on Machine Learning*, pages 4411–4421. PMLR.

Zhiwei Li, Jian Wang, and Tom Smith. 2023. Countergen: Counter-narrative generation using large language models. In *Proceedings of ACL 2023*.

Chin-Yew Lin. 2004. Rouge: A package for automatic evaluation of summaries. In *Proceedings of ACL 2004*.

Binny Mathew, Ritam Dutt, Pawan Goyal, and Animesh Mukherjee. 2019. Spread of hate speech in online social media. *Proceedings of the 10th ACM Conference on Web Science*.

Binny Mathew, Navish Kumar, Pawan Goyal, and Animesh Mukherjee et al. 2018. Analyzing the hate and counter speech accounts on twitter.

Orai-NLP. n.d. Llama-eus-8b.

Kishore Papineni, Salim Roukos, Todd Ward, and Wei-Jing Zhu. 2002. Bleu: A method for automatic evaluation of machine translation. In *Proceedings of ACL 2002*.

Colin Raffel, Noam Shazeer, Adam Roberts, Katherine Lee, Sharan Narang, Michael Matena, Yanqi Zhou, Wei Li, and Peter J. Liu. 2020. Exploring the limits of transfer learning with a unified text-to-text transformer. *Journal of Machine Learning Research*, 21(140):1–67.

Carla Schieb and Mike Preuss. 2016. Governing hate speech by means of counterspeech on facebook. In *66th ica annual conference, at fukuoka, japan*, pages 1–23.

Rachele Sprugnoli, Stefano Menini, Sara Tonelli, Filippo Oncini, and Enrico Piras. 2018. Creating a whatsapp dataset to study pre-teen cyberbullying. In *Proceedings of the 2nd Workshop on Abusive Language Online (ALW2)*, page 51–59.

Serra Sinem Tekiroğlu, Yi-Ling Chung, and Marco Guerini. 2020. Generating counter narratives against online hate speech: Data and strategies. In *Proceedings of the 58th Annual Meeting of the Association for Computational Linguistics*, page 1177–1190, Online. Association for Computational Linguistics.

J. M. Vallecillo-Rodríguez, J. Corpas-Pastor, I. Almagro, and M. J. Castro-Bleda. 2023. CONAN-MT-SP- a spanish corpus for counternarrative using GPT models.

Bertie Vidgen, Dong Nguyen, and Helen Margetts. 2020. Conan - counter narratives through nichesourcing: A multilingual dataset of responses to online hate speech. *arXiv preprint arXiv:2004.04228*.

Bertie Vidgen, Dong Nguyen, and Helen Margetts. 2021. Mt-conan: Expanding the scope of counter-narratives in the fight against online hate. *arXiv preprint arXiv:2105.12345*.

Xiaolong Wu and Min Zhang. 2023. Mistral: High-performance models for text generation. In *Proceedings of NAACL 2023*.

Tianyi Zhang, Varsha Kishore, and Felix Wu. 2020a. Bertscore: Evaluating text generation with contextualized embeddings. In *Proceedings of ICLR 2020*.

Yi Zhang, Rui Xu, and Liwei Chen. 2023. Llama 3: Advancing language model alignment. In *Proceedings of EMNLP 2023*.

Yizhe Zhang, Siqi Sun, Michel Galley, Yen-Chun Chen, Chris Brockett, Xiang Gao, Jianfeng Gao, Jingjing Liu, and Bill Dolan. 2020b. Dialogpt: Large-scale generative pre-training for conversational response generation. *arXiv preprint arXiv:1911.00536*.

A Appendix

A.1 Prompts

A.1.1 English

Initial Prompt Used

```
"""Below is an instruction that describes a task, paired with an input that provides further
context. Write a response that appropriately completes the request.


### [INSTR] Instructions:
1. Analyze the provided hate speech.
2. Consider the background knowledge about the target of the
hate speech.
3. Generate a counter-narrative that is respectful and constructive.
4. Ensure the counter-narrative is in the same language as the hate speech.


### Input:
The Hate Speech is [HS]: {}
Background Knowledge is [KN]: {}
The target of this hate speech is [TARGET]: {}
The language of the hate speech is [LANG]: {}


### Response:
{}"""
```

New Prompt Used

```
""" Below is an instruction that describes a task, paired with an input that provides further
context. Write a response that appropriately completes the request.


### [INSTR] Instructions:
1. Analyze the provided hate speech to:
    - Identify its explicit content and  underlying sentiment.
    - Determine the type of hate speech (e.g.,   Stereotyping,  Misinformation, Dehumanization,
  Ridicule, Incitement to Violence, Exclusionary Speech, Disparagement and Insults, Appeals to
  Fear, Cultural Attacks, Religious Vilification, Victim-Blaming, etc.).
2. Based on the identified type of hate speech,  select the most
effective counter-narrative strategy and apply it:
  - Presenting Facts: Use evidence-based rebuttals to debunk stereotypes and misinformation.
  - Humanizing: Highlight shared humanity and empathy to counter dehumanization or personal
  attacks.
  - Using Humor: Respond with appropriate humor or satire to diffuse ridicule while
  maintaining respect.
  - Denouncing Hate Speech: Strongly condemn incitement to violence while avoiding escalation.
  - Promoting Inclusivity: Advocate for diversity and inclusion to counter
  exclusionary rhetoric.
  - Alleviating Fears: Provide calm, logical explanations to address fear-based narratives.
  - Cultural Respect: Celebrate cultural practices and contributions to counter cultural attacks.
  - Interfaith Understanding: Promote harmony and address misconceptions
  for religious vilification.
  - Solidarity and Support: Show solidarity with victims and reject victim-blaming.
3. Leverage the provided background knowledge and context to generate a counter-narrative that:
  - Is respectful, constructive, and culturally appropriate.
  - Is factual, evidence-based, or illustrative with examples where applicable.
  - Directly addresses the identified type of hate speech and its claims.
4. Write the counter-narrative in the same language as the hate speech, ensuring linguistic and
cultural accuracy.
5. Avoid repetitive or generic responses; aim for a unique, creative, and engaging perspective.
6. Ensure the response avoids escalation
or unintended reinforcement of stereotypes.
```

```
### Input:
Hate Speech [HS]: {}
The target of this hate speech is [TARGET]: {}
The language of the hate speech is [LANG]: {}
The type of hate speech is [TYPE]:
# As identified in Step 1
Background Knowledge needed to generate
a counter-narrative is [KN]: {}


### Response:
Using the identified type of hate speech and the
most effective counter-narrative strategy,
provide a relevant, respectful, and impactful
counter-narrative:
{}
"""
```

A.1.2 Basque

Prompt used for CN generation

```
"""Jarraian, zeregin bat deskribatzen duen argibide
bat dago, testuinguru gehiago ematen duen sarrera
batekin parekatuta. Idatzi eskaera behar bezala
betetzen duen erantzuna.

### [INSTR] Argibideak:
1. Emandako gorroto hizkera aztertu.
2. Gorroto hizkera sortzeko beharrezkoak diren
aurrekariak kontuan hartu.
3. Ziurtatu kontrako narrazioa hau dela:
   - Errespetuzkoa, eraikitzailea eta kulturalki
   egokia.
   - Egiazkoak, ebidentzian oinarritutakoak edo
   adibideekin ilustragarriak, hala badagokio.
   - Gorroto hizkera motari espezifikoa eta bere
   erreklamazioak zuzenean zuzentzen ditu.
4. Ziurtatu erantzunak estereotipoen areagotzea edo
nahi gabeko indartzea saihesten duela.

### Sarrera:
Gorrotoaren hizkera [HS] da: {}
Kontrako narrazioa sortzeko aurrekarien ezagutza
[KN] da: {}
Gorrotozko diskurtso honen helburua
[TARGET] da: {}
Gorrotoaren hizkeraren hizkuntza
[LANG] da: {}

### Erantzuna:
{}"""
```

A.2 QLora Training Parameters

r = 16,
target_modules = ["q_proj", "k_proj", "v_proj", "o_proj", "gate_proj", "up_proj", "down_proj"],
lora_alpha = 16,
lora_dropout = 0,
bias = "none",
use_gradient_checkpointing = "True",
random_state = 3407,
use_rslora = False,
loftq_config = None

TrenTeam at Multilingual Counterspeech Generation: Multilingual Passage Re-Ranking Approaches for Knowledge-Driven Counterspeech Generation Against Hate

Daniel Russo
University of Trento, Italy
Fondazione Bruno Kessler, Italy
drusso@fbk.eu

Abstract

Hate speech (HS) in online spaces poses severe risks, including real-world violence and psychological harm to victims, necessitating effective countermeasures. Counterspeech (CS), which responds to hateful messages with opposing yet non-hostile narratives, offer a promising solution by mitigating HS while upholding free expression. However, the growing volume of HS demands automation, making Natural Language Processing a viable solution for the automatic generation of CS. Recent works have explored knowledge-driven approaches, leveraging external sources to improve the relevance and informativeness of responses. These methods typically involve multi-step pipelines combining retrieval and *passage re-ranking* modules. While effective, most studies have focused on English, with limited exploration of multilingual contexts. This paper addresses these gaps by proposing a multilingual, knowledge-driven approach to CS generation. We integrate state-of-the-art re-ranking mechanisms into the CS generation pipeline and evaluate them using the MT-CONAN-KN dataset, which includes hate speech, relevant knowledge sentences, and counterspeech in four languages: English, Italian, Spanish, and Basque. Our approach compares reranker-based systems employing multilingual cross-encoders and LLMs to a simpler end-to-end system where the language model directly handles both knowledge selection and CS generation. Results demonstrate that reranker-based systems outperformed end-to-end systems in syntactic and semantic similarity metrics, with LLM-based re-rankers delivering the strongest performance overall.[1]

Content warning: this paper contains unobfuscated examples some readers may find offensive

1 Introduction

Online spaces have become fertile ground for the proliferation of hateful content, which poses significant threats not only in digital environments but also in the offline world. Research highlights a direct connection between online hate speech and real-world violence (Awan and Zempi, 2016). Exposure to such content can severely impact the mental health of victims, fostering feelings of insecurity and exclusion (Saha et al., 2019; Persily et al., 2020; Dreißigacker et al., 2024).

Counterspeech (CS) – a strategy of responding to hateful messages with opposing, non-hostile narratives – emerges as a promising solution. Studies suggest that counterspeech can be more impactful than traditional moderation techniques like content removal or user bans, while also aligning with free speech principles (Schieb and Preuss; Fraser et al., 2021). Given the sheer volume of hateful content generated daily, researchers in Natural Language Processing (NLP) have increasingly focused on automating CS-related tasks, including classification (Chung et al., 2021a; Mathew et al., 2019), data curation (Chung et al., 2019; Fanton et al., 2021), and generation (Tekiroğlu et al., 2020; Chung et al., 2021b; Zhu and Bhat, 2021; Tekiroğlu et al., 2022).

Although the majority of the NLP work on counterspeech has centred on English, recent studies have expanded this scope to other languages. For instance, datasets and generation systems now exist for Italian (Chung et al., 2019; Fanton et al., 2021), French (Chung et al., 2019), Spanish (Vallecillo Rodríguez et al., 2024; Bengoetxea et al., 2024), and Basque (Bengoetxea et al., 2024). Despite these advancements, multilingual research remains underexplored, particularly in terms of cross-lingual adaptability and scalability.

Another promising frontier in CS generation is knowledge-grounded approaches, which can help improve the model's accuracy and lead to CS more

[1]This work is the result of our participation in the *Shared Task on Multilingual Counterspeech Generation* held at COLING 2025.

Proceedings of the First Workshop on Multilingual Counterspeech Generation (MCG), pages 77–91
January 19th, 2025. ©2025 Association for Computational Linguistics

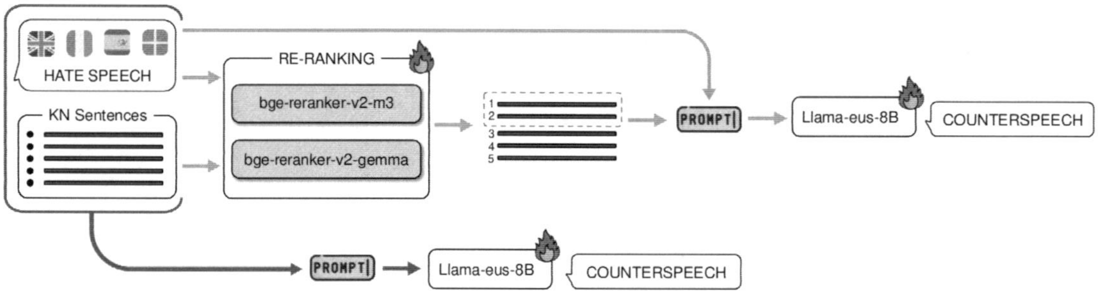

Figure 1: Graphical representation of the experimental design: orange lines indicate the `Rerank-CS` approach, red lines the `E2E Prompt-CS` approach. The fire emoji symbolizes model fine-tuning.

aligned with those produced by experts. By incorporating external knowledge (KN) sources, such as Wikipedia or discussion forums, these methods improve the relevance and informativeness of generated responses (Chung et al., 2021b; Jiang et al., 2023). For example, Chung et al. (2021b) leverage keyphrase extraction for KN retrieval, while Jiang et al. (2023) utilize metrics such as stance consistency to construct KN repositories. Both studies integrate the retrieval phase with a *passage re-ranking* module (Nogueira and Cho, 2019), enabling the fine-grained selection of retrieved KN sentences to be passed to the language model. Specifically, Chung et al. (2021b) propose using the `ROUGE-L` metric (Lin, 2004) to identify the most relevant sentences for countering hate speech, whereas Jiang et al. (2023) employ a fitness function for sentence selection. However, these techniques have primarily been developed and evaluated in English, leaving a significant gap in multilingual contexts.

In this paper, we aim to bridge this gap by proposing a multilingual, KN-driven approach to CS generation. Specifically, we focus on enhancing the *passage re-ranking* module by incorporating state-of-the-art re-ranking mechanisms into the KN-driven CS generation pipeline. To evaluate our approach, we tested the performance of multilingual cross-encoders and LLM-based re-rankers on the `MT-CONAN-KN` dataset.[2] We compared reranker-based systems to a simpler end-to-end approach, where all available information – hate speech and retrieved KN – was directly passed to an LLM tasked with selecting the appropriate KN and generating a CS grounded in it. Figure 1 graphically summarizes the proposed systems.

This work represents the outcome of our participation[3] in the *Multilingual Counterspeech Generation Shared Task*, organized as part of the *First Workshop on Multilingual Counterspeech Generation* (`MCG@COLING 2025`).[4] Results demonstrate that reranker-based systems achieved outstanding performance in terms of syntactic and semantic similarity with the `MT-CONAN-KN` test set, outperforming other systems in the competition. Additionally, LLM-based re-rankers produced better results on average according to these metrics. However, when evaluated using LLM-based metrics, the systems' performance was comparable to those tested on the `MT-CONAN-KN`, indicating strong alignment with the competition dataset but relative weakness in generating generally high-quality CS.

Although preliminary, these findings underscore the importance of passage re-ranking for KN-driven CS generation, particularly in multilingual contexts. Nonetheless, further research is necessary to develop high-quality, domain-specific KN bases and to refine retrieval strategies to enhance CS generation.[5]

2 Related Work

Although interest in CS generation is growing, most existing approaches rely on fine-tuning language models on ad-hoc datasets (Qian et al., 2019; Tekiroğlu et al., 2022; Halim et al., 2023) or, in more recent research, employing *in-context learning* techniques (Doğanç and Markov, 2023; Mun et al., 2023; Zheng et al., 2023). However, very

[2]https://huggingface.co/datasets/LanD-FBK/ML_MTCONAN_KN

[3]We participated as the *TrenTeam*.

[4]sites.google.com/view/multilang-counterspeech-gen/

[5]The code and data are publicly available in the following GitHub repository: https://github.com/drusso98/TrenTeam-MCG2025/

few steps have been taken toward a KN-driven generation of CS.

Efforts towards KN-driven CS generation remain limited due to two primary challenges: (i) the common lack of explicit, well-structured facts in hate speech (HS) and (ii) the scarcity of training data (Chung et al., 2021b). To address these challenges, Chung et al. (2021b) proposed to prepend to the generative step a KN retrieval one. To address the limitation of the lack of explicit facts in the HS, the authors developed a query generation module to extract keywords from HS instances in the CONAN dataset (Chung et al., 2019). These keywords were then used in a two-step KN retrieval procedure: first, a retrieval step of the top 25 relevant articles from a KN base comprising the Newsroom (Grusky et al., 2018) and WikiText-103 (Merity et al., 2016) datasets using BM25 (Robertson et al., 2009); second, a selection step of the top 5 most relevant sentences from these articles using the ROUGE-L metric (Lin, 2004). The retrieved sentences were combined with the HS instance to form a single input, which was then passed to generative models such as GPT-2 (Radford et al., 2019) and XNLG (Chi et al., 2020), fine-tuned for this purpose.

More recently, Jiang et al. (2023) introduced the RAUCG framework for unsupervised retrieval-augmented CS generation. Like Chung et al. (2021b), the RAUCG framework comprises two components: a KN retriever and a CS generator. Using data from the ChangeMyView subreddit[6], the retrieval module employed a multi-step process. This included stance consistency and semantic overlap rate to select counter-comments relevant to the HS post, ensuring these contained effective counter-arguments. The framework further refined the retrieved comments using a custom-designed *fitness function*, computed in terms of perplexity, to identify the most suitable sentences. Finally, the HS and the selected sentences were utilized to generate the CS through energy-based decoding, which was constrained to preserve the retrieved KN and counter the corresponding HS, all while ensuring fluency.

Both approaches emphasize the importance of fine-grained selection of effective sentences or counter-arguments to ensure that the retrieved KN provided as input to generative models is both appropriate and effective. Chung et al. (2021b) assessed sentence relevance based on textual overlap using the ROUGE-L metric, whereas Jiang et al. (2023) ranked sentences based on the model's confidence in next-word prediction (perplexity). The importance of assessing sentence relevance for KN-driven generation is also reflected by the growing emphasis on *passage re-ranking* within Retrieval-Augmented Generation (RAG; Lewis et al., 2020) systems. Indeed, recent advancements in RAG demonstrate that passage re-ranking is a critical step for improving retrieval performance (Nogueira and Cho, 2019), which ultimately enhances generation quality. State-of-the-art approaches increasingly utilize cross-encoders for passage re-ranking, which process query and passage information jointly to generate a relevance score. Although more computationally intensive than traditional bi-encoders (Reimers and Gurevych, 2019; Lin et al., 2023), cross-encoders provide superior performance by capturing the semantic relationship between query and passage more effectively. With the advent of LLMs, recent methods have also employed generative models for passage re-ranking by prompting the model to reason over query-passage pairs and output entailment labels (e.g., *true/false* or *yes/no*). The ranking score is then derived from the logits associated with the positive label (Zhuang et al., 2023; Li et al., 2024).

This work seeks to advance KN-driven CS generation by leveraging the latest developments and technologies in passage re-ranking and applying them to hate-speech countering. Specifically, we evaluate two re-ranking-based CS generation approaches and compare them with an end-to-end prompt-based generation approach. Additionally, we explore these methodologies in a multilingual setting using the MT-CONAN-KN dataset, which contains triplets of HS, a list of related KN sentences, and a CS written using one or more of the KN sentences across four languages: English, Italian, Spanish, and Basque.

3 Dataset

All systems developed in this study are based on the *Multilingual Multi-Target Knowledge-based CONAN dataset* (**ML_MTCONAN_KN**)[2], provided by the organizers of the *Multilingual Counterspeech Generation Shared Task* (MCG@COLING 2025[4]). The ML_MTCONAN_KN dataset is built upon the *Multi-Target CONAN dataset* (MT-CONAN; Fanton et al., 2021), which contains 5003 English HS-CS pairs addressing multiple hate targets, including *dis-*

[6]https://www.reddit.com/r/changemyview/

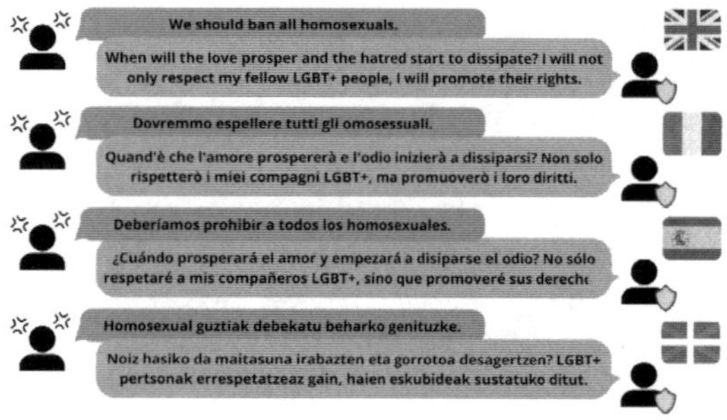

Figure 2: Example of an HS-CS pair from the ML_MTCONAN_KN dataset in English, Italian, Spanish, and Basque. Image sourced from the official website of the MCG Shared Task at COLING 2025.

abled, *Jews*, *LGBT+*, *migrants*, *Muslims*, *people of color*, and *women*. From this dataset, a subset of 596 HS instances was sampled to construct the ML_MTCONAN_KN dataset, focusing on five hate targets: *women*, *migrants*, *Jews*, and *people of color*. For each HS instance, five KN sentences were collected, and a novel CS was written using one or more of these KN sentences.

The resulting English dataset was automatically translated into Italian, Spanish, and Basque. To ensure high-quality translations, native speakers of each target language manually post-edited the CS. The final dataset comprises 2384 entries, divided into the following subsets: a training set with 396 HS-CS pairs per language, and development and test sets with 100 pairs per language each. Figure 2 illustrates an example of an HS-CS pair translated into the four languages included in the ML_MTCONAN_KN dataset.

4 Experimental Design

In this work, we compare two CS generation approaches. In the *first* approach we tested KN-driven CS generation leveraging multilingual re-rankers to identify the most relevant KN sentences for a given HS. The selected sentences were eventually passed to the LLM to guide its generation of the CS (Rerank-CS approach).

The *second* approach employs a prompt-based method where a multilingual LLM is directly fine-tuned to 'reason' over the entire set of KN sentences, identify the most relevant, and produce the CS in a single, end-to-end process. (E2E Prompt-CS approach). Figure 1 provides a graphical overview of the experimental design. In the following sections, we provide further details of the two approaches proposed.

4.1 Rerank-CS Approach

For the Rerank-CS approach, we tested two multilingual re-rankers: the lightweight bge-reranker-v2-m3[7] and the LLM-based bge-reranker-v2-gemma[8] (Chen et al., 2024). Both the re-rankers are part of the *BGE (BAAI General Embeddings)* family of embedding models and were chosen for two main reasons: (i) while carrying out the experiments they were the only re-rankers that *officially* supported all four languages, i.e. English, Italian, Spanish, and Basque; (ii) they were ranked high in the Massive Text Embedding Benchmark (MTEB) Leaderboard (Muennighoff et al., 2022).

The bge-reranker-v2-m3 model (**M3_RRank** hereafter) is a lightweight, multilingual cross-encoder based on the BGE-M3 model (Chen et al., 2024). It was built upon the XLM-RoBERTa pretrained model (Conneau et al., 2019) and fine-tuned on extensive unlabeled, labelled, and synthetic corpora. The bge-reranker-v2-gemma (**Gemma_RRank** hereafter), on the other hand, is a multilingual LLM-based re-ranking model with the Gemma-2B model (Team et al., 2024) as its backbone. This generative model is utilized for a binary classification task, employing the logits of the positive response (e.g., *'true'* or *'yes'*) to represent the final ranking score.

To evaluate re-rankers on their ability to rank KN sentences by relevance to hate speech, an annotated version of the MT-CONAN-KN dataset is needed. In this annotated version, for each entry, the KN sentence(s) used to write the CS are identified and labelled. This annotated dataset will also serve to fine-tune the re-rankers. The remainder of this section outlines the automatic annotation procedure, as well as the strategies for fine-tuning and evaluating the re-rankers.

KN Sentences Annotation A qualitative analysis of the MT-CONAN-KN dataset revealed substantial overlap between the CS and one or more KN sentences. To identify which KN sentences were used to compose each CS, we employed ROUGE-L (Lin, 2004) as a metric, which measures the similarity between texts based on their common longest common subsequences (LCS; Lin, 2004). Specifically, we calculated the ROUGE-L score between each CS sentence and the corresponding KN sentences. For cases where a single KN sentence was used to

[7]https://huggingface.co/BAAI/bge-reranker-v2-m3
[8]https://huggingface.co/BAAI/bge-reranker-v2-gemma

write multiple CS sentences, we also computed the ROUGE-L score for the entire CS against each KN sentence. Finally, we kept the highest ROUGE-L scores for each KN sentence; the KN sentences whose ROUGE score exceeded a specific threshold were labelled as those used to write the CS. In particular, a threshold of 35% was chosen to ensure at least one positive sentence per hate speech in the training set. [9] Further details and a graphical representation of the KN sentence annotation process can be found in Appendix A.

Re-Ranker Fine-Tuning To fine-tune a re-ranker, each hate speech instance requires a list of positive and negative passages (KN sentences in our case). Using the annotated KN sentences, we considered sentences with ROUGE scores above the threshold as positive examples. Sentences with ROUGE-L scores below this threshold were treated as negative examples. These triplets of hate speech, positive KN sentences, and negative KN sentences (along with their ROUGE scores) were then used to fine-tune the two re-rankers, i.e. M3_RRank and Gemma_RRank. The Gemma_RRank necessitates a prompt in the input that specifies the classification task to be performed for the extraction of the ranking score. The prompt used is shown below.

> Given an hateful content A and a possible argument B against it, determine whether the argument is an effective reply providing a prediction of either 'Yes' or 'No'.[10]

In Appendix B.1 we provide further re-rankers fine-tuning details.

Re-Ranker Evaluation We evaluated the performance of the M3_RRank and Gemma_RRank re-rankers on the MT-CONAN-KN dev set on the task of scoring KN sentences based on their relevance to the corresponding HS. To measure the effectiveness of the re-rankers, we employed *Mean Average Precision* (MAP)[11], a metric that computes the average precision at each relevant position in the ranked list, offering a comprehensive evaluation of ranking quality. MAP is particularly useful in ranking tasks like this, as it rewards systems that place relevant

Model	All	EN	IT	ES	EU
M3_RRank	0.637	0.625	0.659	0.648	0.616
M3_RRank FT	**0.753**	**0.772**	**0.753**	**0.753**	**0.732**
Gemma_RRank	0.670	0.660	0.687	0.685	0.647
Gemma_RRank FT	**0.764**	**0.782**	**0.792**	**0.780**	**0.702**

Table 1: Mean Average Precision results for M3_RRank and Gemma_RRank re-rankers, with and without fine-tuning (FT). We present results on the entire development set, as well as partial results on the language-specific subsets.

items (in this case, gold KN sentences) higher in the ranking. Gold KN sentences were identified using ROUGE scores between KN sentences and CS sentences, as detailed earlier. The MAP results for both re-rankers, in their off-the-shelf and fine-tuned versions, are presented in Table 1.

Our analysis shows that fine-tuning significantly enhances the performance of both re-rankers across all languages. Additionally, the Gemma_RRank model consistently outperforms the M3_RRank model, both with and without fine-tuning, indicating superior ability in ranking the most relevant KN sentences higher. Interestingly, the fine-tuned M3_RRank shows better MAP scores in Basque when compared to Gemma_RRank.

Counterspeech Generation The re-ranker module was followed by a KN-driven generation step, where the input consisted of the HS and the relevant KN sentences selected by the re-ranker. Following the automatic annotation of the KN sentences, we noticed that in the training set, on average, two KN sentences were used to write the CS. Therefore, in the generation phase, we provided the LLM with the top two previously ranked KN sentences. In particular, we employed the Llama-eus-8B model (Corral et al., 2024), the only open LLM that officially claims to be trained in all four languages present in the dataset. The Llama-eus-8B model is a multilingual adaptation of Meta's Llama3.1-8B, specifically tailored for the Basque language while retaining its multilingual capabilities.

We fine-tuned this model using the newly annotated version of the dataset. The input for fine-tuning was structured as follows:

> You will be provided with a hateful comment (hate speech) and 2 sentences comprising arguments against the comment (knowledge). Generate a reply to the hateful content using only the informa-

[9] A subset of the annotated data has been manually checked to ensure the effectiveness of this annotation strategy.

[10] This prompt was a slight modification of the default originally used for developing the Gemma_RRank.

[11] MAP was computed using the ranx library (Bassani, 2022).

Lang.	System	JudgeLM Score	rougeL (%)	bleu (%)	bertscore (%)	novelty (%)	gen_len
EN	Rerank-CS M3_RRank	1.056,0	49,6	45,3	82,0	78,0	34,4
	Rerank-CS Gemma_RRank	**1.145,5** ↓	**53,9**	**48,3**	**83,4**	78,1	36,3
	E2E Prompt-CS	999,5	52,5	43,3	82,2	**79,0** ↑	35,4
	Gold	1.175,5	100,0	100,0	100,0	77,7	32,7
IT	Rerank-CS M3_RRank	880,0	46,4	38,6	81,2	77,9	37,8
	Rerank-CS Gemma_RRank	**965,5** ↑	**48,6**	**41,2**	**81,7**	77,8	37,0
	E2E Prompt-CS	791,0	47,4	37,9	80,9	**78,8** ↑	35,5
	Gold	929,5	100,0	100,0	100,0	77,9	35,3
ES	Rerank-CS M3_RRank	879,0	48,2	39,3	81,7	**75,8** ↑	41,2
	Rerank-CS Gemma_RRank	**987,5** ↓	**51,6**	**42,9**	**82,8**	75,6	40,9
	E2E Prompt-CS	769,0	50,2	40,3	82,0	75,4	37,9
	Gold	899,0	100,0	100,0	100,0	75,1	36,9
EU	Rerank-CS M3_RRank	1.364,5	**33,8**	**22,4**	**77,6**	85,2	28,2
	Rerank-CS Gemma_RRank	**1.394,5** ↓	32,8	20,9	77,1	85,7	27,5
	E2E Prompt-CS	1.246,0	31,7	18,2	76,6	**85,9** ↑	24,0
	Gold	1.534,5	100,0	100,0	100,0	85,3	26,5
All	Rerank-CS M3_RRank	1044,9	44,5	36,4	80,6	79,2	35,4
	Rerank-CS Gemma_RRank	**1123,3** ↓	**46,7**	**38,3**	**81,3**	79,3	35,4
	E2E Prompt-CS	951,4	45,5	34,9	80,4	**79,8** ↑	33,2
	Gold	1134,6	100,0	100,0	100,0	79,0	32,9

Table 2: Generation results with the three systems: Rerank-CS with M3_RRank and Gemma_RRank and the E2E Prompt-CS approaches. We highlighted the best system among the three in bold. The arrows denote improved or diminished performance relative to test set data (*Gold* line). We have highlighted the results that achieved first, second, and third place in the general leaderboard of the shared task with gold, silver, and bronze respectively (Complete Results in Appendix C).

tion present in the knowledge. Reply in the following language: {language}

Hate speech: {hate speech}

Knowledge: {KN sentences}

Reply: {counterspeech}

For further details on the fine-tuning process, refer to Appendix B.2.

4.2 E2E Prompt-CS Approach

We evaluate the reranking-based generation methods against a more direct approach where the 'reasoning' abilities of a multilingual LLM have been examined. In particular, we tested an end-to-end prompt-based approach for selecting relevant sentences from the five KN sentences and eventually generating CS based on these sentences. For this approach, we employed Llama-eus-8B LM. Initial zero-shot experiments with Llama-eus-8B revealed that the model's output quality was sub-optimal, as it tended to over-generate, including irrelevant information in the CS. Consequently, we decided to fine-tune the model to improve its performance and to adapt the CS style to the training examples. To this end, we provide the model with the HS input and five related KN sentences during both training and inference. The model is then prompted to identify the most relevant sentences and generate a CS that effectively leverages the provided information. Details on the fine-tuning procedure can be found in Appendix B.2.

5 Results and Discussion

The Rerank-CS and E2E Prompt-CS generation systems were evaluated using both automatic metrics and LLM-based metrics. The evaluation of the generated CS was conducted against the gold CS across several dimensions: *recall* and *precision* of the overlapping LCS and unigrams, calculated using ROUGE-L (Lin, 2004) and BLEU (Papineni et al., 2002), respectively; *novelty*, quantified via the Jaccard distance between the set of words from the generated CS and the words present in the train set (Wang and Wan, 2018; Jaccard, 1901); *semantic similarity*, measured using BERTScore (Zhang et al., 2020), by leveraging the pre-trained contextual embeddings of the bert-base-multilingual-cased model (Devlin et al., 2019). To further assess the quality of the generated CS, an LLM-based metric was applied. JudgeLM, a Vicuna-based model (Chiang

HATE SPEECH

Women should stay at home and raise the children, this should be their only job.

KN SENTENCES

1) Fifty years ago, women working full-time earned just 59 cents for every dollar their male counterparts made.
2) Close to 60% of women also said that working online allowed them to spend more time at home with their families.
3) Women now working, in the absence of necessity, said they would prefer part-time (41 percent) over full-time (17 percent) employment.
4) Who would have thought that only 17% of the US Congress would be women?
5) Only 80 different women were cited, with Lady Gaga and Angela Merkel each mentioned four times.

COUNTERSPEECH

Fifty years ago, women working full-time earned just 59 cents for every dollar their male counterparts made. Women now working, in the absence of necessity, said they would prefer part-time (41 percent) over full-time (17 percent) employment. Women should be free to choose their own job. [KN 1-3]

Cinquant'anni fa, le donne che lavoravano a tempo pieno guadagnavano solo 59 centesimi per ogni dollaro guadagnato dai loro colleghi maschi. Questo non è un buon motivo per dire alle donne che dovrebbero stare a casa e crescere i figli. Inoltre, quasi il 60% delle donne ha dichiarato che lavorare online permette loro di trascorrere più tempo a casa con la famiglia. [KN 1-2]

Hace cincuenta años, las mujeres que trabajaban a tiempo completo ganaban sólo 59 céntimos por cada dólar que ganaban sus homólogos masculinos. Cercan del 60% de las mujeres afirmaron también que trabajar en línea les permitía pasar más tiempo en casa con sus familias. ¿Qué es lo que no entiendes? [KN 1-2]

Emakumeek etxean geratu eta umeak hazi beharko lituzkete, hau izan beharko litzateke euren lan bakarra? Emakumeen % 60k esan zuen Internet bidez lan egiteak aukera ematen ziela denbora gehiago pasatzeko etxean beren familiekin. Duela 50 urte, emakumeek 59 zentimo irabazten zituzten gizonek egindako dolar bakoitzeko. [KN 1-2]

Table 3: Examples of generations using the Rerank-CS approach combined with Gemma_RRank. Due to space constraints, only the English version of the hate speech and its corresponding KN sentences are reported. The generations in the four languages (English, Italian, Spanish, and Basque) originated from hate speech and KN sentences in those respective languages. The KN sentences chosen by the re-ranker and ultimately utilized by the LLM to guide the generation are indicated in square brackets at the end of each CS.

et al., 2023) fine-tuned on the JudgeLM-100K dataset, was used for English, Italian, and Spanish. For Basque, an ad-hoc fine-tuned version of Llama-eus-8B was employed. These models were adapted for the specific task of CS generation following the approach from Zubiaga et al. (2024).

Results are reported in Table 2. On average, the Rerank-CS system using Gemma_RRank demonstrated superior performance compared to other approaches. Interestingly, both Rerank-CS approaches achieved higher scores in terms of text overlap and semantic similarity with the gold CS (ROUGE-L and BLEU), while the E2e Prompt-CS approach outperformed the other systems in terms of *novelty*. A closer examination of individual language performance reveals that the Rerank-CS Gemma-RRank system outperformed other systems across all languages except Basque. For Basque, the lightweight M3-RRank yielded the best results in generation for overlap metrics (ROUGE-L and BLEU) and semantic similarity (BERTScore).

Additionally, the Rerank-CS Gemma-RRank system consistently received the highest scores from the *JudgeLM* model across all languages. Interestingly, the LLM-based evaluation recorded the highest scores for the Basque language. This phenomenon may be due to the fact that the generation model and the evaluation model were the same, namely, Llama-eus-8B. All systems enhanced the novelty in their outputs when compared to the gold CS. Nevertheless, the E2E Prompt-CS method consistently yielded the most novel results, with the exception of Spanish.

When considering overall results (see Appendix C), the Rerank-CS systems performed exceptionally well in overlap-based metrics (ROUGE-L, BLEU) and semantic similarity (BERTScore) across the four languages. This suggests that: (i) the fine-tuned re-rankers were generally able to assign higher scores to the proper KN sentences; (ii) the fine-tuned generative model successfully learned the task of generating according to the KN provided in input and properly adapted its output to align with the MT-CONAN-KN style, i.e, in generating CS that adhere to the KN sentences. However, these systems received lower rankings from the LLM-based judge as the generated CS adhered strictly to the MT-CONAN-KN style, which, when evaluated against CS generated by a less constrained model, may appear less flexible or creative.

Table 3 presents an example of generated CS in the four languages for the given hate speech input, utilizing the KN sentences previously selected by `Gemma-RRank`. A qualitative analysis of the outputs indicates that the fine-tuned `Llama-eu-8B` model effectively incorporates the KN sentences into its responses. In most cases, the model adds relevant text to directly address the HS, as demonstrated by examples such as *"Women should be free to choose their own job"* or *"Questo non è un buon motivo per dire alle donne che dovrebbero stare a casa e crescere i figli"* in the provided example.

The model's tendency to reproduce the KN sentences verbatim (or with minimal alterations) can be attributed to its training on the `MT-CONAN-KN` dataset. In this dataset, CS often included extended portions of the KN sentences, as evidenced by the high `ROUGE` scores observed during the annotation of the KN sentences (see Section 4.1). This strong alignment with the `MT-CONAN-KN` dataset further explains the relatively low JudgeLM scores. Indeed, the CS generated by our systems remain closely tied to the re-ranked KN sentences, limiting the stylistic and argumentative diversity of the output.

6 Conclusion

In this work, we addressed the challenges of multilingual, KN-driven CS generation, proposing an approach that integrates advanced *passage re-ranking* mechanisms into the generation pipeline. By leveraging multilingual cross-encoders and LLM-based re-rankers, we demonstrated the effectiveness of fine-grained KN selection in enhancing the quality and relevance of generated CS. Our results, evaluated on the `MT-CONAN-KN` dataset, show that reranker-based generation systems consistently outperform end-to-end approaches in both syntactic and semantic similarity metrics, underscoring the importance of re-ranking in this domain.

Despite these promising outcomes, our findings also reveal limitations in generating high-quality, unconstrained CS, particularly when evaluated using LLM-based metrics. These insights emphasize the need for further advancements, including the development of high-quality, domain-specific KN bases and more sophisticated retrieval and reranking strategies, and ad-hoc fine-grained metrics.

Overall, this study highlights the potential of KN-driven CS generation, particularly in multilingual contexts, as a critical tool in combating hate speech. Future work should focus on improving adaptability across languages and optimizing CS quality to better address the complex challenges posed by online hate speech.

Limitation

Despite the promising results of our approach, several limitations remain. The performance of multilingual re-rankers and models varied across languages, indicating challenges in achieving consistent cross-lingual adaptability. Moreover, in this work, we employed `Llama-eus-8b`, the only open-source LLM officially trained on all four target languages. However, as a base model, it lacks instruction-based fine-tuning, which we believe could significantly enhance counterspeech quality, particularly by leveraging conversational nuances. Additionally, the input data were automatically preprocessed, which may have introduced alignment issues or errors in pairing hate speech with KN sentences, eventually affecting the generated counterspeech quality. Manually curated annotations could help refine the training data and further improve performance. Finally, the KN sentences used for grounding the generation were often short and lacked sufficient contextual depth. Expanding the context available to both the re-ranker and the LLM could improve retrieval precision and lead to the generation of more coherent and impactful CS.

Ethical Statement

This study addresses the challenge of generating CS and constraining it on selected KN sentences. While the outcomes are encouraging, it's crucial to highlight that the success of these systems depends heavily on two factors: the quality of the input data and the capabilities of the LLM employed. A robust LLM may produce subpar CS if the ground KN is inaccurate or insufficient. On the other hand, weaker generative models may struggle to utilize the provided information effectively, leading to factual inaccuracies (Zellers et al., 2019; Solaiman et al., 2019) and ineffective CS, which hinders the goal of automating this task. Hence, in the context of KN-driven generation, particularly when addressing sensitive issues such as hate speech countering, it is crucial to maintain a standard quality of the resources employed. Nonetheless, it is important to note that automatic systems for CS generation are not deployed as autonomous systems. Instead, they should be considered as suggestion tools that serve as an aid for humans.

References

Imran Awan and Irene Zempi. 2016. The affinity between online and offline anti-muslim hate crime: dynamics and impacts. *Aggression and Violent Behavior*, 27:1–8.

Elias Bassani. 2022. ranx: A blazing-fast python library for ranking evaluation and comparison. In *ECIR (2)*, volume 13186 of *Lecture Notes in Computer Science*, pages 259–264. Springer.

Jaione Bengoetxea, Yi-Ling Chung, Marco Guerini, and Rodrigo Agerri. 2024. Basque and Spanish counter narrative generation: Data creation and evaluation. In *Proceedings of the 2024 Joint International Conference on Computational Linguistics, Language Resources and Evaluation (LREC-COLING 2024)*, pages 2132–2141, Torino, Italia. ELRA and ICCL.

Jianlyu Chen, Shitao Xiao, Peitian Zhang, Kun Luo, Defu Lian, and Zheng Liu. 2024. M3-embedding: Multi-linguality, multi-functionality, multi-granularity text embeddings through self-knowledge distillation. In *Findings of the Association for Computational Linguistics: ACL 2024*, pages 2318–2335, Bangkok, Thailand. Association for Computational Linguistics.

Zewen Chi, Li Dong, Furu Wei, Wenhui Wang, Xian-Ling Mao, and Heyan Huang. 2020. Cross-lingual natural language generation via pre-training. In *Proceedings of the AAAI conference on artificial intelligence*, volume 34, pages 7570–7577.

Wei-Lin Chiang, Zhuohan Li, Zi Lin, Ying Sheng, Zhanghao Wu, Hao Zhang, Lianmin Zheng, Siyuan Zhuang, Yonghao Zhuang, Joseph E. Gonzalez, Ion Stoica, and Eric P. Xing. 2023. Vicuna: An open-source chatbot impressing gpt-4 with 90%* chatgpt quality.

Yi-Ling Chung, Marco Guerini, and Rodrigo Agerri. 2021a. Multilingual counter narrative type classification. In *Proceedings of the 8th Workshop on Argument Mining*, pages 125–132, Punta Cana, Dominican Republic. Association for Computational Linguistics.

Yi-Ling Chung, Elizaveta Kuzmenko, Serra Sinem Tekiroglu, and Marco Guerini. 2019. CONAN - COunter NArratives through nichesourcing: a multilingual dataset of responses to fight online hate speech. In *Proceedings of the 57th Annual Meeting of the Association for Computational Linguistics*, pages 2819–2829, Florence, Italy. Association for Computational Linguistics.

Yi-Ling Chung, Serra Sinem Tekiroğlu, and Marco Guerini. 2021b. Towards knowledge-grounded counter narrative generation for hate speech. In *Findings of the Association for Computational Linguistics: ACL-IJCNLP 2021*, pages 899–914, Online. Association for Computational Linguistics.

Alexis Conneau, Kartikay Khandelwal, Naman Goyal, Vishrav Chaudhary, Guillaume Wenzek, Francisco Guzmán, Edouard Grave, Myle Ott, Luke Zettlemoyer, and Veselin Stoyanov. 2019. Unsupervised cross-lingual representation learning at scale. *CoRR*, abs/1911.02116.

Ander Corral, Ixak Sarasua, and Xabier Saralegi. 2024. Llama-eus-8b, a foundational sub-10 billion parameter llm for basque.

Jacob Devlin, Ming-Wei Chang, Kenton Lee, and Kristina Toutanova. 2019. BERT: Pre-training of deep bidirectional transformers for language understanding. In *Proceedings of the 2019 Conference of the North American Chapter of the Association for Computational Linguistics: Human Language Technologies, Volume 1 (Long and Short Papers)*, pages 4171–4186, Minneapolis, Minnesota. Association for Computational Linguistics.

Mekselina Doğanç and Ilia Markov. 2023. From generic to personalized: Investigating strategies for generating targeted counter narratives against hate speech. In *Proceedings of the 1st Workshop on CounterSpeech for Online Abuse (CS4OA)*, pages 1–12, Prague, Czechia. Association for Computational Linguistics.

Arne Dreißigacker, Philipp Müller, Anna Isenhardt, and Jonas Schemmel. 2024. Online hate speech victimization: consequences for victims' feelings of insecurity. *Crime Science*, 13(1):4.

Margherita Fanton, Helena Bonaldi, Serra Sinem Tekiroğlu, and Marco Guerini. 2021. Human-in-the-loop for data collection: a multi-target counter narrative dataset to fight online hate speech. In *Proceedings of the 59th Annual Meeting of the Association for Computational Linguistics and the 11th International Joint Conference on Natural Language Processing (Volume 1: Long Papers)*, pages 3226–3240, Online. Association for Computational Linguistics.

Kathleen C. Fraser, Isar Nejadgholi, and Svetlana Kiritchenko. 2021. Understanding and countering stereotypes: A computational approach to the stereotype content model. In *Proceedings of the 59th Annual Meeting of the Association for Computational Linguistics and the 11th International Joint Conference on Natural Language Processing (Volume 1: Long Papers)*, pages 600–616, Online. Association for Computational Linguistics.

Max Grusky, Mor Naaman, and Yoav Artzi. 2018. Newsroom: A dataset of 1.3 million summaries with diverse extractive strategies. In *Proceedings of the 2018 Conference of the North American Chapter of the Association for Computational Linguistics: Human Language Technologies, Volume 1 (Long Papers)*, pages 708–719, New Orleans, Louisiana. Association for Computational Linguistics.

Sadaf MD Halim, Saquib Irtiza, Yibo Hu, Latifur Khan, and Bhavani Thuraisingham. 2023. Wokegpt: Improving counterspeech generation against online hate speech by intelligently augmenting datasets using a novel metric. In *2023 International Joint Conference on Neural Networks (IJCNN)*, pages 1–10.

Edward J Hu, Yelong Shen, Phillip Wallis, Zeyuan Allen-Zhu, Yuanzhi Li, Shean Wang, Lu Wang, and Weizhu Chen. 2021. Lora: Low-rank adaptation of large language models. *arXiv preprint arXiv:2106.09685*.

Paul Jaccard. 1901. Étude comparative de la distribution florale dans une portion des alpes et des jura. *Bull Soc Vaudoise Sci Nat*, 37:547–579.

Shuyu Jiang, Wenyi Tang, Xingshu Chen, Rui Tanga, Haizhou Wang, and Wenxian Wang. 2023. Raucg: Retrieval-augmented unsupervised counter narrative generation for hate speech. *arXiv preprint arXiv:2310.05650*.

Patrick Lewis, Ethan Perez, Aleksandra Piktus, Fabio Petroni, Vladimir Karpukhin, Naman Goyal, Heinrich Küttler, Mike Lewis, Wen-tau Yih, Tim Rocktäschel, Sebastian Riedel, and Douwe Kiela. 2020. Retrieval-augmented generation for knowledge-intensive nlp tasks. In *Advances in Neural Information Processing Systems*, volume 33, pages 9459–9474. Curran Associates, Inc.

Chaofan Li, MingHao Qin, Shitao Xiao, Jianlyu Chen, Kun Luo, Yingxia Shao, Defu Lian, and Zheng Liu. 2024. Making text embedders few-shot learners. *arXiv preprint arXiv:2409.15700*.

Chin-Yew Lin. 2004. ROUGE: A package for automatic evaluation of summaries. In *Text Summarization Branches Out*, pages 74–81, Barcelona, Spain. Association for Computational Linguistics.

Sheng-Chieh Lin, Akari Asai, Minghan Li, Barlas Oguz, Jimmy Lin, Yashar Mehdad, Wen-tau Yih, and Xilun Chen. 2023. How to train your dragon: Diverse augmentation towards generalizable dense retrieval. In *Findings of the Association for Computational Linguistics: EMNLP 2023*, pages 6385–6400, Singapore. Association for Computational Linguistics.

Binny Mathew, Punyajoy Saha, Hardik Tharad, Subham Rajgaria, Prajwal Singhania, Suman Kalyan Maity, Pawan Goyal, and Animesh Mukherjee. 2019. Thou shalt not hate: Countering online hate speech. *Proceedings of the International AAAI Conference on Web and Social Media*, 13(01):369–380.

Stephen Merity, Caiming Xiong, James Bradbury, and Richard Socher. 2016. Pointer sentinel mixture models. *arXiv preprint arXiv:1609.07843*.

Niklas Muennighoff, Nouamane Tazi, Loïc Magne, and Nils Reimers. 2022. Mteb: Massive text embedding benchmark. *arXiv preprint arXiv:2210.07316*.

Jimin Mun, Emily Allaway, Akhila Yerukola, Laura Vianna, Sarah-Jane Leslie, and Maarten Sap. 2023. Beyond denouncing hate: Strategies for countering implied biases and stereotypes in language. In *Findings of the Association for Computational Linguistics: EMNLP 2023*, pages 9759–9777, Singapore. Association for Computational Linguistics.

Rodrigo Nogueira and Kyunghyun Cho. 2019. Passage re-ranking with bert. *arXiv preprint arXiv:1901.04085*.

Kishore Papineni, Salim Roukos, Todd Ward, and Wei-Jing Zhu. 2002. Bleu: a method for automatic evaluation of machine translation. In *Proceedings of the 40th Annual Meeting of the Association for Computational Linguistics*, pages 311–318, Philadelphia, Pennsylvania, USA. Association for Computational Linguistics.

Nathaniel Persily, Joshua A Tucker, and Joshua Aaron Tucker. 2020. Social media and democracy: The state of the field, prospects for reform.

Jing Qian, Anna Bethke, Yinyin Liu, Elizabeth Belding, and William Yang Wang. 2019. A benchmark dataset for learning to intervene in online hate speech. In *Proceedings of the 2019 Conference on Empirical Methods in Natural Language Processing and the 9th International Joint Conference on Natural Language Processing (EMNLP-IJCNLP)*, pages 4755–4764, Hong Kong, China. Association for Computational Linguistics.

Alec Radford, Jeff Wu, Rewon Child, David Luan, Dario Amodei, and Ilya Sutskever. 2019. Language models are unsupervised multitask learners.

Nils Reimers and Iryna Gurevych. 2019. Sentence-BERT: Sentence embeddings using Siamese BERT-networks. In *Proceedings of the 2019 Conference on Empirical Methods in Natural Language Processing and the 9th International Joint Conference on Natural Language Processing (EMNLP-IJCNLP)*, pages 3982–3992, Hong Kong, China. Association for Computational Linguistics.

Stephen Robertson, Hugo Zaragoza, et al. 2009. The probabilistic relevance framework: Bm25 and beyond. *Foundations and Trends® in Information Retrieval*, 3(4):333–389.

Koustuv Saha, Eshwar Chandrasekharan, and Munmun De Choudhury. 2019. Prevalence and psychological effects of hateful speech in online college communities. In *Proceedings of the 10th ACM Conference on Web Science*, WebSci '19, page 255–264, New York, NY, USA. Association for Computing Machinery.

Carla Schieb and Mike Preuss. Governing hate speech by means of counterspeech on facebook.

Irene Solaiman, Miles Brundage, Jack Clark, Amanda Askell, Ariel Herbert-Voss, Jeff Wu, Alec Radford, Gretchen Krueger, Jong Wook Kim, Sarah Kreps, et al. 2019. Release strategies and the social impacts of language models. *arXiv preprint arXiv:1908.09203*.

Gemma Team, Thomas Mesnard, Cassidy Hardin, Robert Dadashi, Surya Bhupatiraju, Shreya Pathak, Laurent Sifre, Morgane Rivière, Mihir Sanjay Kale, Juliette Love, et al. 2024. Gemma: Open models based on gemini research and technology. *arXiv preprint arXiv:2403.08295*.

Serra Sinem Tekiroğlu, Helena Bonaldi, Margherita Fanton, and Marco Guerini. 2022. Using pre-trained language models for producing counter narratives against hate speech: a comparative study. In *Findings of the Association for Computational Linguistics: ACL 2022*, pages 3099–3114, Dublin, Ireland. Association for Computational Linguistics.

Serra Sinem Tekiroğlu, Yi-Ling Chung, and Marco Guerini. 2020. Generating counter narratives against online hate speech: Data and strategies. In *Proceedings of the 58th Annual Meeting of the Association for Computational Linguistics*, pages 1177–1190, Online. Association for Computational Linguistics.

María Estrella Vallecillo Rodríguez, Maria Victoria Cantero Romero, Isabel Cabrera De Castro, Arturo Montejo Ráez, and María Teresa Martín Valdivia. 2024. CONAN-MT-SP: A Spanish corpus for counternarrative using GPT models. In *Proceedings of the 2024 Joint International Conference on Computational Linguistics, Language Resources and Evaluation (LREC-COLING 2024)*, pages 3677–3688, Torino, Italia. ELRA and ICCL.

Ke Wang and Xiaojun Wan. 2018. Sentigan: Generating sentimental texts via mixture adversarial networks. In *Proceedings of the Twenty-Seventh International Joint Conference on Artificial Intelligence, IJCAI-18*, pages 4446–4452. International Joint Conferences on Artificial Intelligence Organization.

Rowan Zellers, Ari Holtzman, Hannah Rashkin, Yonatan Bisk, Ali Farhadi, Franziska Roesner, and Yejin Choi. 2019. *Defending against neural fake news*. Curran Associates Inc., Red Hook, NY, USA.

Tianyi Zhang, Varsha Kishore, Felix Wu, Kilian Q. Weinberger, and Yoav Artzi. 2020. Bertscore: Evaluating text generation with bert. *Preprint*, arXiv:1904.09675.

Yi Zheng, Björn Ross, and Walid Magdy. 2023. What makes good counterspeech? a comparison of generation approaches and evaluation metrics. In *Proceedings of the 1st Workshop on CounterSpeech for Online Abuse (CS4OA)*, pages 62–71, Prague, Czechia. Association for Computational Linguistics.

Wanzheng Zhu and Suma Bhat. 2021. Generate, prune, select: A pipeline for counterspeech generation against online hate speech. In *Findings of the Association for Computational Linguistics: ACL-IJCNLP 2021*, pages 134–149, Online. Association for Computational Linguistics.

Honglei Zhuang, Zhen Qin, Rolf Jagerman, Kai Hui, Ji Ma, Jing Lu, Jianmo Ni, Xuanhui Wang, and Michael Bendersky. 2023. Rankt5: Fine-tuning t5 for text ranking with ranking losses. In *Proceedings of the 46th International ACM SIGIR Conference on Research and Development in Information Retrieval*, pages 2308–2313.

Irune Zubiaga, Aitor Soroa, and Rodrigo Agerri. 2024. A LLM-based ranking method for the evaluation of automatic counter-narrative generation. In *Findings of the Association for Computational Linguistics: EMNLP 2024*, pages 9572–9585, Miami, Florida, USA. Association for Computational Linguistics.

A KN sentences selection

Figure 3 illustrates the process of automatic sentence selection. The ROUGE-L score was used to evaluate the overlap between the CS and all KN sentences. This overlap was calculated for the entire CS (central column in the ROUGE scores matrix in the Figure) as well as for each of its sentences. Subsequently, the highest ROUGE-L value for each KN sentence was retained. Eventually, sentences whose ROUGE-L value was higher than a given threshold were labelled as those used for creating the CS (the green squares in the Figure).

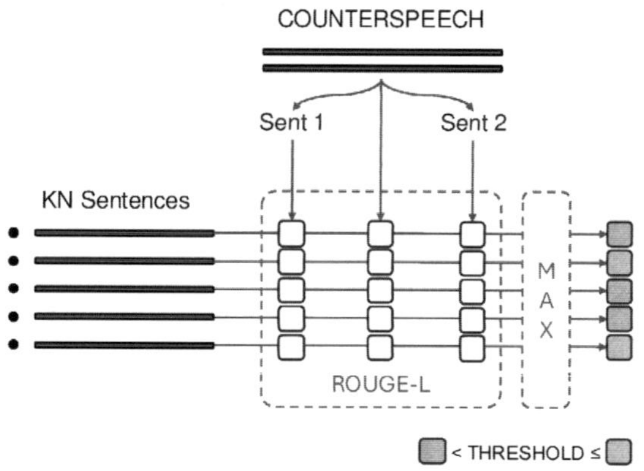

Figure 3: Graphical representation of the automatic procedure employed for selecting the KN sentences employed for writing the CS.

B Fine-Tuning Details

B.1 Re-Ranker Fine-Tuning

Starting from the annotated dataset, as detailed in Section A, we proceeded to fine-tune the M3_RRank and Gemma_RRank re-rankers. The following sections provide specifics for each re-ranker.

M3_RRank We fed the cross-encoder with the hate speech, the list of KN sentences used to create the CS, the list of the discarded KN sentences, and their ROUGE-L scores computed as explained in Section A. The information was formatted in JSON, and structured as follows.

```
{
    "query": hate speech,
    "pos": selected KN sentences,
    "neg": discarded KN sentences,
    "pos_scores": ROUGE-L scores selected KN
    ↪  sentences,
    "neg_scores": ROUGE-L scores discarded KN
    ↪  sentences
}
```

The re-ranker was trained on an NVIDIA Ampere A40 GPU with 48GB of memory for 5 epochs, using a learning rate of 6×10^{-5}, a training batch size of 8, and a weight decay of 0.01.

Gemma_RRank The fine-tuning of this LLM-based re-ranker utilized the same input as the M3_RRank, with the addition of a prompt instruction. The prompt used is detailed in Section 4.1 (paragraph *'Re-Ranker Fine-Tuning'*). The LLM underwent training on an NVIDIA Ampere A40 GPU with 48GB of memory, employing 'Low-Rank Adaptation' (LoRA; Hu et al., 2021) with a rank of 32 and an α value of 64. We trained the model for 5 epochs, with a learning rate of 5×10^{-5}, a weight decay set at 0.01, and a warm-up ratio of 0.1.

B.2 LLM Fine-Tuning for Generation

We utilized Llama-eus-8B for CS generation. Two versions of the LMM were fine-tuned, one corresponding to each CS generation approach, namely the Rerank-CS and E2e Prompt-CS approaches. The same hyperparameters were used across both fine-tuning, with the only variation being the training data. The training was performed on an NVIDIA Ampere A40 GPU with 48GB of memory, and no quantization was applied. Low-Rank Adaptation (LoRA) was utilized with a rank of 16, an α value of 16, and a dropout rate of 0. Training parameters included a learning rate of 5×10^{-5}, a training batch size of 2, an evaluation batch size of 4, and gradient accumulation steps of 4. The model was trained for 3 epochs, with a weight decay of 0.01, and a warm-up ratio of 0.03.

For the Rerank-CS approach we employed the prompt reported in Section 4.1 (paragraph *'Counterspeech Generation'*) filling it with the hate speech, the top 2 sentences selected by the retriever, and the gold CS from the train and dev sets of the MT-CONAN-KN. The dev set has been used as an evaluation set during training. For the E2E Prompt-CS both the hate speech and all the KN sentences were passed as input to the language model, formatted into a unique prompt, as shown below:

> You will be provided with a hateful comment (hate speech) and *{nof_sent}* sentences comprising arguments against the comment (knowledge).
>
> Select the most effective sentences and use them to generate a reply to the hateful content. Reply in the following language: language

Hate speech: *{hate speech}*

Knowledge: *{knowledge}*

Reply: *{counterspeech}*

C Complete Results

In Tables 4, 5 , 7 , 6 we report the general results of the shared tasks. Teams are reported in alphabetical order, and for each metric we highlighted in gold, silver, and bronze the first, second and third best results accordingly. We took part in the shared task under the name **TrenTeam**. The `Rerank-CS` systems utilizing `M3_RRank` and `Gemma_RRank` were submitted as *run1* and *run2* respectively; results for the `E2E Prompt-CS` system are designated with *run3*.

Team	JudgeLM Score	ROUGE-L (%)	BLEU (%)	BERTScore (%)	Novelty (%)	Gen_len
bhavanark run1	301.5	14.0	1.7	67.1	81.3	54.2
CODEOFCONDUCT run1	2374.5	16.2	2.8	69.4	83.4	84.8
CODEOFCONDUCT run2	2344.0	16.4	3.2	69.4	83.7	85.6
CODEOFCONDUCT run3	2394.5	16.2	2.9	69.1	83.4	88.3
counterspeech go run1	924.5	49.6	34.0	81.9	76.5	24.4
counterspeech go run2	854.0	49.7	34.0	81.8	77.2	24.0
counterspeech go run3	840.0	49.8	33.9	81.9	77.4	23.6
HuaweiTSC run1	1635.0	40.4	27.2	78.2	80.7	38.2
HuaweiTSC run2	2087.5	33.6	18.8	76.1	80.8	48.3
HuaweiTSC run3	1682.0	46.6	34.6	80.4	79.0	39.2
Hyderabadi Pearls run1	861.0	53.1	40.9	82.6	78.2	28.7
Hyderabadi Pearls run2	1058.5	44.3	34.8	79.5	77.0	32.1
Hyderabadi Pearls run3	996.5	45.2	35.2	79.5	77.0	30.9
MilaNLP run1	2326.5	18.1	3.2	70.7	82.3	64.5
MilaNLP run2	2357.5	18.5	3.8	70.8	82.5	66.7
MilaNLP run3	2523.0	19.0	4.9	70.8	83.0	84.7
NLP@IIMAS run1	704.0	48.8	41.2	80.8	78.2	29.8
NLP@IIMAS run2	2498.5	14.7	2.0	68.8	83.1	73.5
NLP@IIMAS run3	2494.5	14.7	2.0	68.8	83.1	73.5
Northeastern Uni run1	965.5	48.3	40.1	81.0	76.8	30.4
Northeastern Uni run2	990.0	51.6	42.1	82.3	76.6	30.9
Northeastern Uni run3	1191.0	51.8	40.3	82.6	78.1	43.0
RSSN run1	681.5	46.3	35.7	78.8	78.4	40.8
RSSN run2	59.0	24.5	13.2	69.2	80.8	31.0
SemanticCUETSync run1	1079.0	51.8	44.4	82.4	77.5	33.4
TrenTeam run1	1056.0	49.6	45.3	82.0	78.0	34.4
TrenTeam run2	1145.5	53.9	48.3	83.4	78.1	36.3
TrenTeam run3	999.5	52.5	43.3	82.2	79.0	35.4
ground truth	1175.5	100.0	100.0	100.0	77.7	32.7

Table 4: Results for English

Team	JudgeLM Score	ROUGE-L (%)	BLEU (%)	BERTScore (%)	Novelty (%)	Gen_len
bhavanark run1	73.0	11.0	2.1	62.6	84.6	39.8
CODEOFCONDUCT run1	1824.5	10.7	2.7	68.6	81.6	78.0
CODEOFCONDUCT run2	1740.5	10.2	2.2	68.5	82.5	80.2
CODEOFCONDUCT run3	1803.5	10.1	2.4	68.3	81.6	75.2
counterspeech go run1	667.5	47.0	32.2	80.9	77.5	28.1
counterspeech go run2	663.0	47.1	31.7	81.0	77.8	27.6
counterspeech go run3	685.0	46.5	32.3	81.1	77.7	27.7
HuaweiTSC run1	1260.5	36.1	21.7	77.2	80.9	40.8
HuaweiTSC run2	1792.0	30.8	16.6	75.9	80.3	49.5
HuaweiTSC run3	1372.5	41.1	26.6	79.1	79.1	41.9
MilaNLP run1	1824.0	16.8	3.7	70.8	82.0	62.1
MilaNLP run2	1912.0	22.7	9.1	73.0	81.1	73.4
MilaNLP run3	1985.5	21.1	8.9	72.6	82.1	101.4
NLP@IIMAS run1	529.5	36.7	27.6	77.2	78.3	32.4
NLP@IIMAS run2	1630.5	13.6	1.9	68.4	81.9	50.1
NLP@IIMAS run3	503.0	36.5	25.8	77.1	79.4	31.6
Northeastern Uni run1	830.0	42.6	30.8	79.7	77.8	32.0
Northeastern Uni run2	905.5	45.4	33.7	80.8	76.9	33.5
Northeastern Uni run3	1004.0	47.5	36.2	81.3	77.8	40.7
SemanticCUETSync run1	1028.0	46.7	36.2	81.1	78.3	34.9
TrenTeam run1	880.0	46.4	38.6	81.2	77.9	37.8
TrenTeam run2	965.5	48.6	41.2	81.7	77.8	37.0
TrenTeam run3	791.0	47.4	37.9	80.9	78.8	35.5
ground truth	929.5	100.0	100.0	100.0	77.9	35.3

Table 5: Results for Italian

Team	JudgeLM Score	ROUGE-L (%)	BLEU (%)	BERTScore (%)	Novelty (%)	Gen_len
bhavanark run1	54.0	14.7	2.5	64.7	81.0	42.7
CODEOFCONDUCT run1	1857.0	12.0	2.8	69.8	81.3	86.4
CODEOFCONDUCT run2	1820.5	12.0	2.8	69.8	81.5	87.2
CODEOFCONDUCT run3	1839.0	11.5	3.0	69.5	81.8	87.8
counterspeech go run1	639.0	47.6	29.9	81.1	75.3	27.1
counterspeech go run2	646.5	46.7	29.8	80.9	75.6	27.1
counterspeech go run3	652.5	47.4	29.7	80.9	75.7	26.5
HuaweiTSC run1	1228.5	36.8	21.7	77.6	77.5	43.1
HuaweiTSC run2	1728.0	33.5	17.7	76.7	77.4	52.3
HuaweiTSC run3	1339.5	41.9	27.2	79.4	75.8	43.2
MilaNLP run1	1852.5	19.6	4.8	71.5	79.2	67.7
MilaNLP run2	1942.0	23.7	8.6	73.5	78.0	72.7
MilaNLP run3	2002.0	24.2	8.9	73.5	79.6	99.3
NLP@IIMAS run1	492.5	39.7	30.7	78.2	77.3	36.3
NLP@IIMAS run2	1919.0	16.7	3.3	69.6	79.6	64.9
NLP@IIMAS run3	466.0	38.5	27.6	78.1	76.1	33.6
Northeastern Uni run1	894.5	45.6	34.5	80.6	74.0	35.1
Northeastern Uni run2	845.0	46.7	33.6	81.2	73.9	33.4
Northeastern Uni run3	873.0	45.3	33.4	80.5	76.6	43.8
SemanticCUETSync run1	974.5	46.5	35.6	80.8	75.3	36.5
TrenTeam run1	879.0	48.2	39.3	81.7	75.8	41.2
TrenTeam run2	987.5	51.6	42.9	82.8	75.6	40.9
TrenTeam run3	769.0	50.2	40.3	82.0	75.4	37.9
ground truth	899.0	100.0	100.0	100.0	75.1	36.9

Table 6: Results for Spanish

Team	JudgeLM Score	ROUGE-L (%)	BLEU (%)	BERTScore (%)	Novelty (%)	Gen_len
bhavanark run1	74.0	5,5	0,5	61,7	88,7	32,4
CODEOFCONDUCT run1	2465.5	8,2	1,5	66,4	86,8	67,5
CODEOFCONDUCT run2	2371.0	9,8	2,2	67,0	87,1	66,2
CODEOFCONDUCT run3	2382.5	10,4	2,2	67,5	87,5	69,1
counterspeech go run1	904.0	31,8	15,6	76,7	84,9	18,0
counterspeech go run2	837.0	32,4	15,8	77,1	85,1	18,0
counterspeech go run3	855.5	31,6	15,3	76,5	85,1	17,7
HuaweiTSC run1	1484.5	18,3	6,3	72,1	87,2	30,2
HuaweiTSC run2	1881.5	17,7	5,6	72,4	86,8	34,5
HuaweiTSC run3	1722.0	23,3	10,5	74,2	86,5	32,1
Hyderabadi Pearls run1	1011.5	29,2	17,4	75,5	85,6	26,2
Hyderabadi Pearls run2	1322.0	27,6	15,5	75,5	85,3	27,8
Hyderabadi Pearls run3	1023.5	29,2	17,4	75,5	85,6	26,2
MilaNLP run1	2242.5	10,7	1,0	69,0	87,8	44,6
MilaNLP run2	430.0	18,5	6,9	70,4	87,4	50,5
MilaNLP run3	422.5	17,9	6,8	70,7	88,3	72,8
NLP@IIMAS run1	720.5	29,2	17,6	74,9	86,0	24,9
NLP@IIMAS run2	2086.0	8,9	0,6	67,7	87,5	34,6
NLP@IIMAS run3	720.0	29,2	17,6	74,9	86,0	24,9
Northeastern Uni run1	1107.5	25,6	13,3	74,6	84,3	24,8
Northeastern Uni run2	1158.0	27,6	13,5	75,7	83,4	24,5
Northeastern Uni run3	1145.0	30,9	17,6	76,2	85,2	29,6
SemanticCUETSync run1	1194.0	26,5	15,4	75,1	85,4	26,0
TrenTeam run1	1364.5	33,8	22,4	77,6	85,2	28,2
TrenTeam run2	1394.5	32,8	20,9	77,1	85,7	27,5
TrenTeam run3	1246.0	31,7	18,2	76,6	85,9	24,0
ground truth	1534.5	100,0	100,0	100,0	85,3	26,5

Table 7: Results for Basque

The First Workshop on Multilingual Counterspeech Generation at COLING 2025: Overview of the Shared Task

Helena Bonaldi[*1,2] **M. Estrella Vallecillo-Rodríguez**[*3] **Irune Zubiaga**[*4] **Arturo Montejo-Ráez**[3]
Aitor Soroa[4] **María Teresa Martín-Valdivia**[3] **Marco Guerini**[1] **Rodrigo Agerri**[4]
[1]Fondazione Bruno Kessler, Italy, [2]University of Trento, Italy, [3]CEATIC, Universidad de Jaén, Spain,
[4]HiTZ Center - Ixa, University of the Basque Country UPV/EHU
{hbonaldi, guerini}@fbk.eu, {mevallec, amontejo, maite}@ujaen.es,
{irune.zubiaga, a.soroa, rodrigo.agerri}@ehu.eus,

Abstract

This paper presents an overview of the Shared Task organized in the First Workshop on Multilingual Counterspeech Generation at COLING 2025. While interest in automatic approaches to Counterspeech generation has been steadily growing, the large majority of the published experimental work has been carried out for English. This is due to the scarcity of both non-English manually curated training data and to the crushing predominance of English in the generative Large Language Models (LLMs) ecosystem. The task's goal is to promote and encourage research on Counterspeech Generation in a multilingual setting (Basque, English, Italian, and Spanish) potentially leveraging background knowledge provided in the proposed dataset. The task attracted 11 participants, 9 of whom presented a paper describing their systems. Together with the task, we introduce ML-MTCONAN-KN a new multilingual counterspeech dataset with 2384 triplets of hate speech, counterspeech, and related background knowledge covering 4 languages[1].

Content warning: this article contains unobfuscated examples that some readers may find offensive.

1 Introduction

Counterspeech (CS) is a promising strategy to fight online hate: it consists of replying to the hate speech (HS) with cogent agents, refuting it without being offensive. By challenging the stereotypes spread by the offensive message, it offers an alternative and constructive perspective and fosters empathy and understanding among users, promoting a more inclusive and respectful online environment (Benesch, 2014; Schieb and Preuss, 2016). Due to its potential effectiveness (Hangartner et al., 2021) and given the sheer amount of HS being produced, Natural Language Processing is increasingly focusing on automating CS generation, in an effort to aid existing NGOs who manually produce these replies (Chung et al., 2021b; Bonaldi et al., 2024).

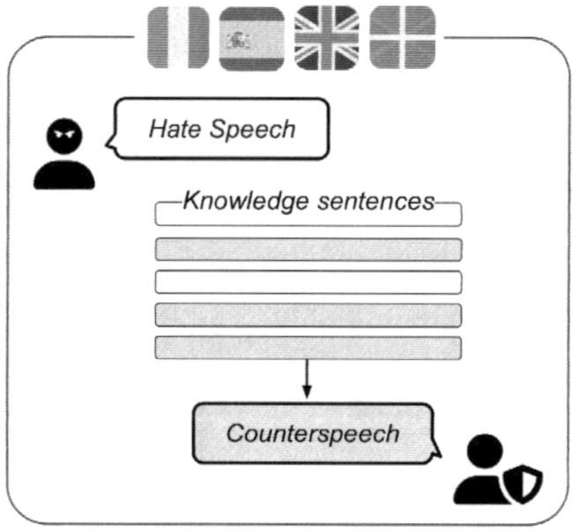

Figure 1: An example showing the structure of the ML-MTCONAN-KN dataset, i.e., triplets of hate speech, counterspeech and related background knowledge, in Italian, Spanish, English and Basque.

However, some aspects of automatic CS generation still remain largely understudied: this shared task addresses two of these existing gaps. First, although previous research on CS collection and generation has mostly focused on English (Qian et al., 2019; Tekiroglu et al., 2022; Halim et al., 2023; Mathew et al., 2018), there have been a few efforts to develop CS datasets for Italian (Chung et al., 2019, 2020), French (Chung et al., 2019), Spanish (Bengoetxea et al., 2024; Vallecillo-Rodríguez et al., 2024) and Basque (Bengoetxea et al., 2024), creating a body of curated data that represents a first step to facilitate research on the automatic generation of CS from a multilingual point of view.

Secondly, one of the main limitations of deploying automatic systems for CS production in the wild is the risk of generating inaccurate information. To address this problem, some studies have

[*]These authors contributed equally to this work.
[1]The dataset is available at: https://huggingface.co/datasets/LanD-FBK/ML_MTCONAN_KN

Proceedings of the First Workshop on Multilingual Counterspeech Generation (MCG), pages 92–107
January 19th, 2025.

proposed knowledge-driven systems for CS generation (Chung et al., 2021a; Jiang et al., 2023b). However, there has not been a systematic comparison of the different methods that can be applied for this task.

In this scenario, our shared task aims to promote research on the generation of CS in a multilingual setting, namely, in Basque, English, Italian and Spanish, with the possibility of leveraging the background knowledge provided in the dataset. To do so, we introduce ML-MTCONAN-KN, a new multilingual dataset with 2384 triplets of HS, CS, and related background knowledge (KN) covering 4 languages (the structure of the introduced dataset is shown in Figure 1). The task attracted 11 participants, with 9 submitted papers. Roughly half of the proposed approaches employed fine-tuning, with the other half mainly recurring to zero-shot learning and only one team opting for few-shot learning. Most fine-tuned models were fine-tuned on multilingual data, with only two teams focusing on monolingual generation. In addition, every participant except one used the background knowledge provided to support CS generation.

This task is evaluated using both traditional overlap and similarity metrics (i.e. BLEU, ROUGE, BERTscore) and LLM-as-a-judge evaluation (JudgeLM): the official winning system is selected with the latter method, as it has been shown to have a higher correlation with human evaluation (Zubiaga et al., 2024). In particular, among the proposed approaches, the MilaNLP systems, which involve a knowledge filtering step before zero-shot generation, consistently achieved the highest results across languages, thus representing the overall winner of our task.

2 Task description

Following a previous task organized for Spanish (Vallecillo-Rodríguez et al., 2024), our shared task focuses on multilingualism and on the possibility of employing knowledge-driven techniques for CS generation. With respect to multilingualism, the languages included offer a varied spectrum consisting of an agglutinative and isolate language (Basque), two romance languages (Italian and Spanish), and a Germanic one (English). The languages of interest were chosen according to the organizers' linguistic expertise, guaranteeing that native speakers are available for every language.

Regarding knowledge-driven generation, the new dataset includes triplets of HS, CS, and background KN sentences used to write the ground-truth CS. The participants have the option of using such knowledge, or any additional external knowledge of their choice, to obtain generations of higher quality.

HS: Jews are literally pieces of shit. There must be laws prohibiting their religion from our land.

KN: In contrast, laws that protect the autonomy of religious organizations [will] often further individual religious freedom as well. <EOS> The idea of individuals having freedoms is literally foreign to them. <EOS> So say on extremists of any religion - you're protected as am I. <EOS> The First Amendment protects freedom of speech, but it also protects freedom of religion. <EOS> As with freedom of speech and freedom of the press, freedom of religion sometimes means protecting conduct that some people might not favor. <EOS>

CS: The First Amendment protects freedom of speech, but it also protects freedom of religion. As with freedom of speech and freedom of the press, freedom of religion sometimes means protecting conduct that some people might not favor. However, to deny it would mean to deny a fundamental human right.

Table 1: An example in English from our dataset.

3 Dataset

We introduce ML-MTCONAN-KN, a new multilingual dataset with 2384 triplets of HS, CS, and related KN in 4 languages. We make the dataset available in three splits: 1584 examples for training, 400 for validation, and 400 for testing (the distribution is roughly 66% - 17% - 17%). An example of a triplet is shown in Table 1. The KN sentences include both knowledge considered relevant (highlighted in the example) and irrelevant by the annotator to write the gold CS[2].

The dataset covers hate speech targeted towards the following minority groups: Jews, LGBT+, immigrants, people of color (POC), and women. Table 2 shows the distribution of instances for each target group in the dataset. Other information included in the dataset corresponds to the language (LANG), the dataset split (SPLIT), an identifier for each HS - CS pair (PAIR_ID: different versions of the same pair in different languages have the same PAIR_ID), and a unique identifier for each pair in each language (ID), obtained by concatenating the PAIR_ID and LANG (e.g. "IT01").

[2] Note that the KN sentences are provided without distinguishing between those that are relevant or not to write the CS.

Target	N	%
Jews	400	17
LGBT+	408	17
Migrants	548	23
POC	352	15
Women	676	28
Total	2384	100

Table 2: The distribution of examples according to the target of hate.

3.1 Data collection

As it has been mentioned, ML-MTCONAN-KN contains triplets of HS, CS, and related KN. In the following, we describe how each of these elements was obtained.

HS We used the hate speech from the MT-CONAN dataset (Fanton et al., 2021), which comprises 5003 HS-CS pairs in English covering multiple targets of hate.

KN For each HS instance in the dataset, the knowledge retrieval and selection module from Chung et al. (2021a) was applied to retrieve relevant knowledge. More specifically, first a query for each HS is created, which is then used to search for relevant knowledge in an external repository (Newsroom from Grusky et al. (2018) and WikiText-103 from Merity et al. (2022)) via the Solr search engine[3]. The similarity between each article and the query is calculated with BM25 (Robertson et al., 1995), and the top 25 articles are retained. These documents are split into sentences, and the 5 most relevant according to ROUGE-L F1 (Lin, 2004) are kept as background knowledge for the dataset.

CS A graduate-level annotator with previous experience in CS writing is tasked with producing the CS starting from the provided KN. In particular, the annotation guidelines are the following: (i) if no relevant knowledge is available, discard the example, (ii) if relevant knowledge is available, use it to write a counterspeech message, adapting it if required and (iii), if several KN sentences are deemed relevant, the entry can be duplicated and two different CS for the same HS can be written, using different parts of the KN. On average, in one hour of annotation time, 17.5 examples can be obtained. At the end of this process, 596 CS examples in English were manually generated.

[3]https://lucene.apache.org/solr/

HS: Gli ebrei sono letteralmente dei pezzi di merda. Devono esserci delle leggi che proibiscano la loro religione nella nostra terra. **CS:** Il Primo Emendamento protegge la libertà di parola, ma anche la libertà di religione. Come per la libertà di parola e di stampa, la libertà di religione a volte implica la protezione di comportamenti che a qualcuno potrebbero non piacere. Tuttavia, negarla significherebbe negare un diritto umano fondamentale.
HS: Los judíos son literalmente pedazos de mierda. Debe haber leyes que prohíban su religión en nuestra tierra. **CS:** La Primera Enmienda protege la libertad de expresión, pero también la libertad religiosa. Al igual que ocurre con la libertad de expresión y la libertad de prensa, la libertad de religión a veces significa proteger conductas que algunas personas podrían no aprobar. Sin embargo, negarla significaría negar un derecho humano fundamental.
HS: Juduak kaka hutsak dira. Haien erlijioa gure lurraldean debekatzen duten legeak egon behar dira. **CS:** Lehen Zuzenketak adierazpen askatasuna babesten du, baina baita erlijio askatasuna ere. Adierazpen askatasunarekin eta prentsa askatasunarekin gertatzen den bezala, erlijio askatasunak, batzuetan, pertsona batzuek mesedegarri ez dituzten jokabideak babestea esan nahi du. Baina ukatzeak oinarrizko giza eskubide bat ukatzea esan nahiko luke.

Table 3: Translation of an HS-CS pair into IT, ES and EU.

3.2 Translation to other languages

Translating the English data into the other languages consisted of a two-step procedure. First, automatic translation was used: DeepL[4] for Spanish and Italian, and Itzuli[5] for Basque. Second, the automatic translations of the HS and CS were manually reviewed and post-edited by expert human annotators. Table 3 shows the HS and CS in Table 1 translated into Italian, Spanish, and Basque.

4 Evaluation

The evaluation of the shared task is based on two complementary approaches. First, on traditional overlap and similarity metrics commonly used in machine translation and text generation, including those specifically tailored for CS generation (Bengoetxea et al., 2024). Second, we use a recently proposed method based on JudgeLM which has a stronger correlation with human evaluations than traditionally used metrics (Zubiaga et al., 2024). The official ranking and task winner are determined by the pairwise ranking-based evaluation using JudgeLM.[6]

[4]https://www.deepl.com

[5]https://www.euskadi.eus/itzuli/

[6]The evaluation code is available at https://github.com/hitz-zentroa/eval-MCG-COLING-2025. It was also

4.1 Traditional Metrics

Reference-based metrics measure the overlap or embedding similarity between the generated and the reference CS. Furthermore, we also apply reference-free metrics to evaluate the generated CS without considering any ground-truth CS.

Reference-based metrics Building on prior work in CS generation (Tekiroglu et al., 2022; Bengoetxea et al., 2024), we chose to evaluate the submitted runs using BLEU (Papineni et al., 2002), ROUGE-L (Lin, 2004) and BERTScore (Zhang et al., 2020). BLEU (widely used in machine translation tasks) is a precision-focused metric that assesses the overlap between a candidate text and one or more reference texts. More specifically, it calculates the geometric mean of modified n-gram precision while applying a brevity penalty to discourage overly short outputs. In contrast, ROUGE-L emphasizes recall by identifying the longest common subsequence between the candidate and reference, normalized by the reference length. ROUGE-L is frequently applied in text summarization. Finally, BERTScore uses contextual embeddings from pretrained BERT models to measure the similarity between candidate and reference sentences.

Reference-Free Metrics We consider two different metrics: Novelty and Repetition Rate. Novelty (Wang and Wan, 2018) is calculated by identifying non-singleton n-grams in the generated text that also appear in the training data. Novelty aims to measure how distinct the generated content is from the training data. It should be noted that this metric is less informative when evaluating models in zero-shot settings, where no training data is involved. Regarding Repetition Rate (RR) (Bertoldi et al., 2013), the idea is to identify the non-singleton n-grams that are repeated within the generated text, providing a measure of self-similarity in the content. This metric focuses on capturing the diversity of the generated text.

4.2 JudgeLM Pairwise Rank Evaluation

The official scorer for the task is based on a new method to evaluate CS using JudgeLM which consists of a pairwise rank-based approach, originally proposed in Zubiaga et al. (2024). Given a pair of candidate CS, an LLM acts as a judge to determine the superior counterspeech. It has been shown that this method exhibits a high correlation with human judgments for this specific task. The model chosen for English, Spanish, and Italian is JudgeLM (Zhu et al., 2023), a scalable judge model built upon Vicuna. JudgeLM is trained using a large dataset of LLM-generated responses including various natural language generation (NLG) tasks, paired with detailed evaluations generated with GPT-4. Although JudgeLM supports various evaluation approaches, such as comparing single answers to a given reference or multiple answers simultaneously, we opted for a pairwise comparison of generated CS as proposed by Zubiaga et al. (2024). This approach eliminates the need for a ground-truth reference, focusing instead on selecting the best option among the available alternatives. By directly comparing two CS candidates, we also avoid the ambiguity inherent in evaluating them individually within an open-ended framework. Furthermore, and unlike traditional metrics, this method evaluates CS within the context of specific HS instances, rather than treating them as independent generations. Finally, in order to address the lack of Basque support of the original JudgeLM,we fine-tuned `Llama-eus-8B` (Corral et al., 2024) on the JudgeLM-100K dataset presented in Zhu et al. (2023), using the same settings outlined in the paper.

provided to the participants to assist them during system development.

Team	FT	Mul. FT	Kn. Fil.	Lan.
RSSN	✓	-	-	EN
Hyderabadi Pearls	✓	-	-	EN, EU
Counterspeech go	✓	✓	✓	All
Trenteam (run 1)	✓	✓	✓	All
Northeastern	✓	✓	-	All
NLP@IIMAS (run 1)	✓	✓	-	All
bhavanark	✓	✓	-	All
Trenteam (run 2-3)	-	-	✓	All
MilaNLP	-	-	✓	All
NLP@IIMAS (run 2-3)	-	-	-	All
CODEOFCONDUCT	-	-	-	All
HuaweiTSC	-	-	-	All

Table 4: Overview of the proposed systems, according to four distinguishing dimensions, namely, whether the model is fine-tuned (FT), fine-tuned over multilingual data (Mul. FT), whether the knowledge was filtered before being used (Kn. Fil.) and the language(s) of interest (Lan.).

5 Systems Overview

In Table 4 we report the participant teams and their approaches along four distinguishing dimensions, namely, whether (a) the system is fine-tuned, (b) fine-tuned over multilingual data, (c) background knowledge was filtered before being used and (d) the languages the system focuses on. Another issue worth mentioning is that every participant except the *bhavanark* team used the available knowledge. Moreover, only the *Counterspeech go* team employed additional data for training, while all the other teams only used the shared task dataset. Table 4 groups the systems according to common characteristics: from top to bottom, we can observe how the approaches focusing on a subset of the available languages all opted for fine-tuning, without filtering the knowledge. Furthermore, two groups of approaches performed multilingual fine-tuning, with or without knowledge filtering. Finally, those systems which did not perform any fine-tuning, with and without knowledge filtering, are listed. A summary of the submitted systems follows.

RSSN This team employs a language model fine-tuned to generate counterspeech in English, given as input a prompt including the hate target, the HS, and all the provided knowledge sentences. T5 (Raffel et al., 2020) is employed in the first run, while DistilBART (Lewis et al., 2020) in the second.

Hyderabadi Pearls They fine-tune Mistral 7B (Jiang et al., 2023a), Llama-base 3.1 8B (Dubey et al., 2024), and Llama-eus 8B (Corral et al., 2024) on the `ML-MTCONAN-KN` corpus to generate CS in English and Basque. Additionally, they experiment with GPT-4 to post-edit the generated CS for the aforementioned languages. The submitted systems are language-dependent. For Basque, run 1 and run 3 use LLaMa-base 3.1 models fine-tuned for 3,000 steps, while run 2 uses Llama-eus for 500 steps. For English, run 1 and run 2 are based on LLaMa-base 3.1 models, adjusted for 300 steps in the first run and 3,000 steps in the second one. Finally, run 3 uses the Mistral model with 300 steps.

Counterspeech go The same configuration was used for the three runs, i.e. a QWEN2.5-14B-Instruct model (Hui et al., 2024) fine-tuned on the provided dataset. Additionally, the knowledge sentences were filtered using GPT-4o (Hurst et al., 2024), Claude[7], and Gemini (Team et al., 2023). Moreover, the Alpaca dataset[8] was used as additional data for training to prevent overfitting. The runs focused on all four languages.

Trenteam The team proposes two main approaches: the Rerank-CS approach, where a multilingual reranker (bge-reranker-v2-m3[9] for run 1 and bge-reranker-v2-gemma[10] for run 2) is fine-tuned to identify the most relevant sentences in the KN, which are then passed to an LLM to guide the CS generation in a zero-shot-learning fashion. In the second approach (run 3) a multilingual LLM is fine-tuned over the entire set of KN sentences and prompted to identify the most relevant and use them to produce the CS in an end-to-end process (E2E Prompt-CS approach). For all three approaches, the employed LLM is Llama-eus-8B (Corral et al., 2024).

Northeastern Uni The Northeastern University team leverages Llama-3 in two main approaches for training: supervised fine-tuning (on the base model for run 1 and the instruct model for run 2) and the Direct Preference Optimization (DPO) strategy (run3). In all runs, they leverage the `ML-MTCONAN-KN` dataset in all four languages and use the provided background knowledge sentences. For the DPO strategy, they additionally incorporate negative examples of counterspeech generated with GPT-4o.

NLP@IIMAS Two systems are proposed to address the task depending on the language. The first system used for run 1 employs a graph-based generative model (Flan-T5, Chung et al., 2024) that encodes knowledge about HS to generate the CS. For Run 2, the system featured a LLM with personalized counterspeech prompts, applying Chain-of-Thought for Italian and zero-shot for rest of the languages. Finally, run 3 consists of using a LLM in zero-shot for English, while a graph-based approach was applied to the remaining languages. Both systems integrate background knowledge from the dataset: in the LLM-based system, relevant phrases are included in the prompt, while in the graph-based system, they are organized sequentially or interspersed with the offensive message.

Bhavanark The presented system consists of a GPT-2 model fine-tuned on the `ML-MTCONAN-KN` HS and CS only, in the English language.

[7]`https://claude.ai/`

[8]`https://huggingface.co/datasets/tatsu-lab/alpaca`

[9]`https://huggingface.co/BAAI/bge-reranker-v2-m3`

[10]`https://huggingface.co/BAAI/bge-reranker-v2-gemma`

English		Basque		Italian		Spanish	
MilaNLP	2523.0	CODEOFCONDUCT	2465.5	MilaNLP	1985.5	MilaNLP	2002.0
NLP@IIMAS	2498.5	MilaNLP	2242.5	CODEOFCONDUCT	1824.5	NLP@IIMAS	1919.0
CODEOFCONDUCT	2394.5	NLP@IIMAS	2086.0	HuaweiTSC	1792.0	CODEOFCONDUCT	1857.0
HuaweiTSC	2087.5	HuaweiTSC	1881.5	NLP@IIMAS	1630.5	HuaweiTSC	1728.0
Northeastern Uni	1191.0	ground truth	1534.5	SemanticCUETSync	1028.0	TrenTeam	987.5
ground truth	1175.5	TrenTeam	1394.5	Northeastern Uni	1004.0	SemanticCUETSync	974.5
TrenTeam	1145.5	Hyderabadi Pearls	1322.0	TrenTeam	965.5	ground truth	899.0
SemanticCUETSync	1079.0	SemanticCUETSync	1194.0	ground truth	929.5	Northeastern Uni	894.5
Hyderabadi Pearls	1058.5	Northeastern Uni	1158.0	Counterspeech go	685.0	Counterspeech go	652.5
Counterspeech go	924.5	Counterspeech go	904.0	Counterspeech go	667.5	bhavanark	54.0
RSSN	681.5	NLP@IIMAS	720.5	bhavanark	73.0		
bhavanark	301.5	bhavanark	74.0				

Table 5: Official results using Pairwise rank-based method with JudgeLM. The ranking is based on each team's best submission.

MilaNLP They adopt two distinct approaches to address the generation problem in English, Italian, Spanish, and Basque. For run 1, they use the Mistral-7B-Instruct-v0.3 model in a zero-shot approach to generate CS in English and then translate them into the target languages using the NLLB model (Costa-jussà et al., 2022). For runs 2 and 3, they directly generate the CS in the target languages. For all submitted runs, they implement a knowledge filtering step, either filtering the relevant sentences in a separate prompt before generation (runs 1-2) or asking the model to choose which sentences to use at inference time (run 3).

CODEOFCONDUCT First, a simulated annealing algorithm is used to generate the candidate CS, which is iteratively refined. k candidates are selected according to a Boltzmann-like distribution which accounts for the JudgeLM score of each candidate. Then, new candidates are generated starting from the selected ones and are evaluated with the same methodology. Finally, the best candidates are selected using a round-robin algorithm. Runs 1, 2 and 3 submitted by the team correspond to the candidates ranked first, second and fourth, respectively.

HuaweiTSC Three systems are proposed for the four languages: all employ few-shot learning with Chain-of-Thought to prompt GPT-4o-mini to generate CS candidates (run 1). Moreover, they also test two approaches to select the best CS candidate: a pair-wise comparison which selects the best candidate according to the highest Elo rating obtained using JudgeLM (run 2), and a point-wise scorer which integrates multiple metrics to evaluate each candidate individually, given a hate speech and its corresponding background knowledge (run 3).

SemanticCUETSync The developed system focuses on all languages and leverages the knowledge provided in the task dataset, as well as additional general information from external sources. However, details on how this external information was integrated or specifics of the system implementation were not provided. For this reason, the results of this team are not included in the following analyses.

6 Official Results

Table 5 reports the official ranking determined by the Pairwise rank-based JudgeLM method. Tables showcasing the rank per submitted run and all evaluation metrics considered for the task are provided in Appendix A.

The results across the four languages—English, Basque, Italian, and Spanish—reveal interesting trends and highlight the strong performances of certain teams. Thus, MilaNLP stands out as a consistent top performer, ranked first in English, Italian, and Spanish, and second in Basque, showcasing their adaptability across languages and thus representing the overall winner of the task. CODEOFCONDUCT also achieved impressive results, ranking first in Basque, second in Italian, third in English, and fourth in Spanish. NLP@IIMAS also obtained competitive results, ranked second in English, third in Basque, and fourth in both Italian and Spanish. Similarly, HuaweiTSC performed well, with strong rankings such as fourth in English and third in Italian. The ground truth scores, prominently included in each table, provide a benchmark for assessing the submissions, with several teams surpassing this baseline, reflecting the quality of their outputs. If we consider the systems proposed by these teams, we can observe some recurring patterns: in particular, they all use zero-shot learn-

English		Basque		Italian		Spanish	
TrenTeam	0.834	TrenTeam	0.776	TrenTeam	0.817	TrenTeam	0.828
Northeastern Uni	0.826	Counterspeech go	0.771	Northeastern Uni	0.813	Northeastern Uni	0.812
Hyderabadi Pearls	0.826	Northeastern Uni	0.762	Counterspeech go	0.811	Counterspeech go	0.811
SemanticCUETSync	0.824	Hyderabadi Pearls	0.755	SemanticCUETSync	0.81	SemanticCUETSync	0.808
Counterspeech go	0.819	SemanticCUETSync	0.751	HuaweiTSC	0.791	HuaweiTSC	0.794
NLP@IIMAS	0.808	NLP@IIMAS	0.749	NLP@IIMAS	0.772	NLP@IIMAS	0.782
HuaweiTSC	0.804	HuaweiTSC	0.742	MilaNLP	0.73	MilaNLP	0.735
RSSN	0.788	MilaNLP	0.707	CODEOFCONDUCT	0.686	CODEOFCONDUCT	0.698
MilaNLP	0.708	CODEOFCONDUCT	0.675	bhavanark	0.626	bhavanark	0.647
CODEOFCONDUCT	0.694	bhavanark	0.617				
bhavanark	0.671						

Table 6: Results with BERTscore. The ranking is based on each team's best submission.

ing, apart from HuaweiTSC which performs few-shot, and they all rely on the provided background knowledge, with MilaNLP's systems additionally filtering the knowledge sentences for generation.

By considering the results obtained using the traditional metrics (see the rankings for BERTscore in Table 6), it can be observed that Trenteam consistently obtains first place across all languages, followed by Counterspeech go, Northeastern University and Hyderabadi Pearls. When analyzing these systems, a common characteristic seems to be that the models were taught to select the relevant knowledge for generating counterspeech. This was done either explicitly via knowledge filtering (Trenteam run 2-3 and Counterspeech go run 1-2) or implicitly via fine-tuning (Northeastern run 3 and Hyderabadi Pearls run1). In fact, selecting specific knowledge sentences for generation allows to mimic the process in which the gold CS were created manually, thus reaching higher similarity with the references.

7 Discussion

In this section we discuss the results obtained by the proposed approaches from an aggregated point of view, first averaging across all languages, and then comparing their performance on English vs low-resourced languages. Results are reported in Table 7.

Overview of all languages Fine-tuned models achieve significantly higher scores on traditional metrics, and they also have shorter generations (in line with the length of the training data). Moreover, if we distinguish the non-fine-tuned systems between those using zero-shot and few-shot learning (only the HuaweiTSC team) it is possible to see how few-shot learning achieves an average generation length closer to that of fine-tuned models (41.1), in contrast to the average length from zero-shot generations (63.7). Fine-tuned models have lower Novelty, which is expected, as the generations are more similar to the training data. The best runs according to JudgeLM are those based on zero-shot, which turn out to be also the longest generations (Hu et al., 2024).

Moreover, fine-tuning over multilingual data benefits the performance on the overlap metrics, but it lowers the performance according to Novelty, RR and JudgeLM: the same trend can be observed for systems performing a knowledge filtering step before generation.

English vs low-resourced languages If we focus on the overlap metrics, the generation length and Novelty, similar trends can be seen across languages: fine-tuning is helpful in obtaining higher overlap scores, shorter generations (closer to those of the ground-truth references) and lower Novelty: all these trends are expected, as discussed previously.

Appendix B provides a preliminary manual qualitative analysis of the generated CS. The analysis indicates that the winning runs according to BERTScore focus on selecting knowledge from the provided options and tend to reproduce it more or less verbatim, achieving thus a high overlap with the reference. In contrast, the best runs according to JudgeLM, while also leveraging the provided knowledge, tend to rephrase it. This approach reduces the overlap with respect to the ground-truth CS but results in more natural generations.

The main differences across languages are registered for RR and JudgeLM. In particular, two different phenomena can be observed. First, fine-tuned models in English score worse according to RR and JudgeLM. However, when fine-tuned over multilingual data, repetitiveness is lower and JudgeLM assigns higher scores. Second, for low-

Lang	Approach		ROUGE-L	BLEU	BERTsc.	length	Novelty	RR	JudgeLM
All	Gold		1	1	1	32.835	0.790	3.773	1134.625
	FT	✓	**0.382**	**0.262**	**0.776**	31.720	0.798	3.992	785.3
		-	0.252	0.135	0.734	**58.151**	**0.819**	**3.882**	**1738.3**
	Mul. FT	✓	**0.393**	**0.270**	**0.780**	**31.269**	0.794	4.097	783.5
		-	0.374	0.263	0.770	30.466	**0.810**	**3.376**	**876.7**
	Kn. Fil.	✓	**0.362**	**0.234**	**0.775**	43.509	0.803	4.068	1207.4
		-	0.287	0.175	0.743	**46.232**	**0.813**	**3.857**	**1310.3**
EN	Gold		1	1	1	32.65	0.776	3.777	1175.5
	FT	✓	**0.447**	**0.337**	**0.793**	32.724	0.780	4.233	820.2
		-	0.277	0.151	0.737	**62.996**	**0.817**	**3.724**	**2066.3**
	Mul. FT	✓	**0.499**	**0.389**	**0.818**	30.070	0.773	**3.969**	**940.6**
		-	0.379	0.269	0.761	**36.262**	**0.788**	4.586	659.7
	Kn. Fil.	✓	**0.401**	**0.279**	**0.784**	43.793	0.793	**3.852**	**1447.4**
		-	0.348	0.233	0.757	**49.052**	**0.800**	4.056	1406.6
ES, EU, IT	Gold		1	1	1	32.897	0.794	3.771	1121.0
	FT	✓	**0.354**	**0.230**	**0.768**	31.294	0.806	**3.890**	770.5
		-	0.243	0.129	0.733	**56.401**	**0.820**	3.939	**1619.9**
	Mul. FT	✓	**0.371**	**0.245**	**0.773**	30.777	0.800	4.132	754.8
		-	0.245	0.131	0.734	**55.176**	**0.820**	**3.973**	**1538.6**
	Kn. Fil.	✓	**0.350**	**0.220**	**0.771**	43.414	0.807	4.140	1127.4
		-	0.261	0.150	0.736	**45.023**	**0.818**	**3.771**	**1269.1**

Table 7: From top to bottom: aggregated results for all languages, English and low-resourced languages respectively.

resourced languages, fine-tuned models are less repetitive, and fine-tuning over multilingual data actually worsens the RR scores and the performance according to JudgeLM.

Finally, filtering the background knowledge helps to improve RR and JudgeLM for English, but it degrades performance for the other languages. Therefore, we can conclude that overall, both fine-tuning over multilingual data and filtering the knowledge seem to benefit more in English than in the rest of the languages. Furthermore, for all languages, fine-tuning allows to obtain generations more similar to the gold references but with worse performance according to the pairwise ranking method used with JudgeLM.

8 Conclusion

The analysis of the results of the shared task highlights some patterns among the most successful approaches. In particular, zero-shot learning combined with the provided background knowledge allows to obtain better multilingual counterspeech generation in terms of overall quality, measured by JudgeLM. On the other hand, systems obtaining the best scores on the traditional overlap-based metrics demonstrate that teaching the systems to select relevant knowledge, either by explicitly filtering it or implicitly via fine-tuning, effectively replicates the manual creation process of counterspeech. Moreover, the differences between high-resource and low-resource languages suggest the need to apply different strategies across linguistic contexts.

In summary, the obtained results in the shared task not only advance the state of the art in automatic counterspeech generation but also highlight critical areas for future research, such as developing more robust methods for low-resource languages and the need for deeper exploration into the evaluation of these systems.

Limitations

This work provides an in-depth analysis of the systems developed to address the task but still has certain limitations. First, the dataset does not include information about which external knowledge sentences are relevant for developing the gold CS. This information could help future systems discriminate between what is relevant and what is not in CS generation.

Second, automatic evaluation remains a major challenge in language generation, especially in this task. As shown, traditional metrics based on n-gram or embedding similarity do not evaluate the quality of the counterspeech with respect to a given hate speech. Furthermore, previous work has shown a lower correlation of these metrics concerning human judgments. Therefore, we propose a new method based on JudgeLM as an alternative. However, despite its good correlation with human judgments, JudgeLM may introduce biases inherent in the models used as judges or it may show preferences for certain types of counter-narratives.

By highlighting these limitations we hope to encourage future research on multilingual counterspeech generation and evaluation.

Ethics Statement

Generating multilingual counterspeech to combat hate speech involves significant ethical and social considerations. Researchers and developers must take care to avoid reproducing harmful content, ensuring a responsible approach in creating automatic counterspeech systems.

First, the emotional well-being of researchers and annotators must be prioritized, as constant exposure to hateful content can harm mental health. Strategies like regular breaks and access to emotional support are essential when labeling datasets or evaluating systems that handle hate speech.

The dataset `ML-MTCONAN-KN` includes offensive messages, but it is designed to prevent models from generating abusive content. For this reason, our main focus in creating it was centered on achieving high-quality counterspeech replies, while the hateful messages are simple and stereotyped, to avoid possible misuses. Moreover, these messages were originally generated automatically, which allows us to preserve users' privacy.

Finally, automated systems may generate biased or harmful responses, especially when cultural and linguistic nuances are poorly addressed. For this reason, despite progress in automation, human involvement remains crucial: in this task, we always envision the deployment of counterspeech generation systems as assistant tools rather than to be deployed in the wild with no supervision.

Acknowledgements

This work has been partially supported by the European Union's CERV fund under grant agreement No. 101143249 (HATEDEMICS), and by the following MCIN/AEI/10.13039/501100011033 projects: CONSENSO (PID2021-122263OB-C21), MODERATES (TED2021-130145B-I00), SocialTox (PDC2022-133146-C21), DISARGUE (TED2021-130810B-C21), DEEPR3 (TED2021-130295B-C31) and European Union NextGenerationEU/PRTR, DeepMinor (CNS2023-144375) and European Union NextGenerationEU/PRTR, DeepKnowledge (PID2021-127777OB-C21) and by FEDER, EU.

References

Susan Benesch. 2014. Countering dangerous speech: New ideas for genocide prevention. *Available at SSRN 3686876*.

Jaione Bengoetxea, Yi-Ling Chung, Marco Guerini, and Rodrigo Agerri. 2024. Basque and Spanish counter narrative generation: Data creation and evaluation. In *Proceedings of the 2024 Joint International Conference on Computational Linguistics, Language Resources and Evaluation (LREC-COLING 2024)*, pages 2132–2141, Torino, Italia. ELRA and ICCL.

Nicola Bertoldi, Mauro Cettolo, and Marcello Federico. 2013. Cache-based online adaptation for machine translation enhanced computer assisted translation. In *Proceedings of Machine Translation Summit XIV: Papers*, Nice, France.

Helena Bonaldi, Greta Damo, Nicolás Ocampo, Elena Cabrio, Serena Villata, and Marco Guerini. 2024. Is safer better? the impact of guardrails on the argumentative strength of llms in hate speech countering. In *Proceedings of the 2024 Conference on Empirical Methods in Natural Language Processing*, pages 3446–3463.

Hyung Won Chung, Le Hou, Shayne Longpre, Barret Zoph, Yi Tay, William Fedus, Yunxuan Li, Xuezhi Wang, Mostafa Dehghani, Siddhartha Brahma, et al. 2024. Scaling instruction-finetuned language models. *Journal of Machine Learning Research*, 25(70):1–53.

Yi-Ling Chung, Elizaveta Kuzmenko, Serra Sinem Tekiroğlu, and Marco Guerini. 2019. CONAN - COunter NArratives through nichesourcing: a multilingual dataset of responses to fight online hate speech. In *Proceedings of the 57th Annual Meeting of the Association for Computational Linguistics*, pages 2819–2829, Florence, Italy. Association for Computational Linguistics.

Yi-Ling Chung, Serra Sinem Tekiroğlu, and Marco Guerini. 2020. Italian counter narrative generation to fight online hate speech. In *Proceedings of the Seventh Italian Conference on Computational Linguistics CLiC-it*.

Yi-Ling Chung, Serra Sinem Tekiroğlu, and Marco Guerini. 2021a. Towards knowledge-grounded counter narrative generation for hate speech. In *Findings of the Association for Computational Linguistics: ACL-IJCNLP 2021*, pages 899–914, Online. Association for Computational Linguistics.

Yi-Ling Chung, Serra Sinem Tekiroğlu, Sara Tonelli, and Marco Guerini. 2021b. Empowering NGOs in countering online hate messages. *Online Social Networks and Media*, 24:100150.

Ander Corral, Ixak Sarasua, and Xabier Saralegi. 2024. Llama-eus-8b, a foundational sub-10 billion parameter llm for basque.

Marta R Costa-jussà, James Cross, Onur Çelebi, Maha Elbayad, Kenneth Heafield, Kevin Heffernan, Elahe Kalbassi, Janice Lam, Daniel Licht, Jean Maillard, et al. 2022. No language left behind: Scaling human-centered machine translation. *arXiv preprint arXiv:2207.04672*.

Abhimanyu Dubey, Abhinav Jauhri, Abhinav Pandey, Abhishek Kadian, Ahmad Al-Dahle, Aiesha Letman, Akhil Mathur, Alan Schelten, Amy Yang, Angela Fan, et al. 2024. The llama 3 herd of models. *arXiv preprint arXiv:2407.21783*.

Margherita Fanton, Helena Bonaldi, Serra Sinem Tekiroğlu, and Marco Guerini. 2021. Human-in-the-loop for data collection: a multi-target counter narrative dataset to fight online hate speech. In *Proceedings of the 59th Annual Meeting of the Association for Computational Linguistics and the 11th International Joint Conference on Natural Language Processing (Volume 1: Long Papers)*, pages 3226–3240, Online. Association for Computational Linguistics.

Max Grusky, Mor Naaman, and Yoav Artzi. 2018. Newsroom: A dataset of 1.3 million summaries with diverse extractive strategies. In *Proceedings of the 2018 Conference of the North American Chapter of the Association for Computational Linguistics: Human Language Technologies, Volume 1 (Long Papers)*, pages 708–719, New Orleans, Louisiana. Association for Computational Linguistics.

Sadaf MD Halim, Saquib Irtiza, Yibo Hu, Latifur Khan, and Bhavani Thuraisingham. 2023. Wokegpt: Improving counterspeech generation against online hate speech by intelligently augmenting datasets using a novel metric. In *2023 International Joint Conference on Neural Networks (IJCNN)*, pages 1–10. IEEE.

Dominik Hangartner, Gloria Gennaro, Sary Alasiri, Nicholas Bahrich, Alexandra Bornhoft, Joseph Boucher, Buket Buse Demirci, Laurenz Derksen, Aldo Hall, Matthias Jochum, et al. 2021. Empathy-based counterspeech can reduce racist hate speech in a social media field experiment.

Zhengyu Hu, Linxin Song, Jieyu Zhang, Zheyuan Xiao, Jingang Wang, Zhenyu Chen, and Hui Xiong. 2024. Rethinking llm-based preference evaluation. *arXiv preprint arXiv:2407.01085*.

Binyuan Hui, Jian Yang, Zeyu Cui, Jiaxi Yang, Dayiheng Liu, Lei Zhang, Tianyu Liu, Jiajun Zhang, Bowen Yu, Keming Lu, et al. 2024. Qwen2. 5-coder technical report. *arXiv preprint arXiv:2409.12186*.

Aaron Hurst, Adam Lerer, Adam P Goucher, Adam Perelman, Aditya Ramesh, Aidan Clark, AJ Ostrow, Akila Welihinda, Alan Hayes, Alec Radford, et al. 2024. Gpt-4o system card. *arXiv preprint arXiv:2410.21276*.

AQ Jiang, A Sablayrolles, A Mensch, C Bamford, DS Chaplot, D de las Casas, F Bressand, G Lengyel, G Lample, L Saulnier, et al. 2023a. Mistral 7b (2023). *arXiv preprint arXiv:2310.06825*.

Shuyu Jiang, Wenyi Tang, Xingshu Chen, Rui Tanga, Haizhou Wang, and Wenxian Wang. 2023b. Raucg: Retrieval-augmented unsupervised counter narrative generation for hate speech. *arXiv preprint arXiv:2310.05650*.

Mike Lewis, Yinhan Liu, Naman Goyal, Marjan Ghazvininejad, Abdelrahman Mohamed, Omer Levy, Veselin Stoyanov, and Luke Zettlemoyer. 2020. BART: Denoising sequence-to-sequence pre-training for natural language generation, translation, and comprehension. In *Proceedings of the 58th Annual Meeting of the Association for Computational Linguistics*, pages 7871–7880, Online. Association for Computational Linguistics.

Chin-Yew Lin. 2004. ROUGE: A package for automatic evaluation of summaries. In *Text Summarization Branches Out*, pages 74–81, Barcelona, Spain. Association for Computational Linguistics.

Binny Mathew, Hardik Tharad, Subham Rajgaria, Prajwal Singhania, Suman Kalyan Maity, Pawan Goyal, and Animesh Mukherjee. 2018. Thou shalt not hate: Countering online hate speech. In *International Conference on Web and Social Media*.

Stephen Merity, Caiming Xiong, James Bradbury, and Richard Socher. 2022. Pointer sentinel mixture models. In *International Conference on Learning Representations*.

Kishore Papineni, Salim Roukos, Todd Ward, and Wei-Jing Zhu. 2002. Bleu: a method for automatic evaluation of machine translation. In *Proceedings of the 40th Annual Meeting of the Association for Computational Linguistics*, pages 311–318, Philadelphia, Pennsylvania, USA. Association for Computational Linguistics.

Jing Qian, Anna Bethke, Yinyin Liu, Elizabeth Belding, and William Yang Wang. 2019. A benchmark dataset for learning to intervene in online hate speech. In *Proceedings of the 2019 Conference on Empirical Methods in Natural Language Processing and the 9th International Joint Conference on Natural Language Processing (EMNLP-IJCNLP)*, pages 4755–4764, Hong Kong, China. Association for Computational Linguistics.

Colin Raffel, Noam Shazeer, Adam Roberts, Katherine Lee, Sharan Narang, Michael Matena, Yanqi Zhou, Wei Li, and Peter J. Liu. 2020. Exploring the limits of transfer learning with a unified text-to-text transformer. *Journal of Machine Learning Research*, 21(140):1–67.

Stephen E Robertson, Steve Walker, Susan Jones, Micheline M Hancock-Beaulieu, Mike Gatford, et al. 1995. Okapi at trec-3. *Nist Special Publication Sp*, 109:109.

Carla Schieb and Mike Preuss. 2016. Governing hate speech by means of counterspeech on facebook. In *66th ica annual conference, at fukuoka, japan*, pages 1–23.

Gemini Team, Rohan Anil, Sebastian Borgeaud, Jean-Baptiste Alayrac, Jiahui Yu, Radu Soricut, Johan Schalkwyk, Andrew M Dai, Anja Hauth, Katie Millican, et al. 2023. Gemini: a family of highly capable multimodal models. *arXiv preprint arXiv:2312.11805*.

Serra Tekiroglu, Helena Bonaldi, Margherita Fanton, and Marco Guerini. 2022. Using pre-trained language models for producing counter narratives against hate speech: a comparative study. In *Findings of the Association for Computational Linguistics: ACL 2022*, pages 3099–3114.

María-Estrella Vallecillo-Rodríguez, Maria-Victoria Cantero-Romero, Isabel Cabrera-De-Castro, Arturo Montejo-Ráez, and María-Teresa Martín-Valdivia. 2024. CONAN-MT-SP: A Spanish corpus for counternarrative using GPT models. In *Proceedings of the 2024 Joint International Conference on Computational Linguistics, Language Resources and Evaluation (LREC-COLING 2024)*, pages 3677–3688, Torino, Italy. ELRA and ICCL.

María Estrella Vallecillo-Rodríguez, María Victoria Cantero-Romero, Isabel Cabrera-de Castro, Luis Alfonso Ureña-López, Arturo Montejo-Ráez, and María Teresa Martín-Valdivia. 2024. Overview of refutes at iberlef 2024: Automatic generation of counter speech in spanish. *Procesamiento del Lenguaje Natural*, 73(0):449–459.

Ke Wang and Xiaojun Wan. 2018. Sentigan: Generating sentimental texts via mixture adversarial networks. In *Proceedings of the Twenty-Seventh International Joint Conference on Artificial Intelligence, IJCAI-18*, pages 4446–4452. International Joint Conferences on Artificial Intelligence Organization.

Tianyi Zhang, Varsha Kishore, Felix Wu, Kilian Q. Weinberger, and Yoav Artzi. 2020. Bertscore: Evaluating text generation with bert. *Preprint*, arXiv:1904.09675.

Lianghui Zhu, Xinggang Wang, and Xinlong Wang. 2023. Judgelm: Fine-tuned large language models are scalable judges.

Irune Zubiaga, Aitor Soroa, and Rodrigo Agerri. 2024. A LLM-based ranking method for the evaluation of automatic counter-narrative generation. In *Findings of the Association for Computational Linguistics: EMNLP 2024*, pages 9572–9585, Miami, Florida, USA. Association for Computational Linguistics.

A Official results

The official results of the shared task are presented. JudgeLM Score refers to the score obtained in the pairwise comparison setting described in Subsection 4.2. Generation Length corresponds to the average length of the generated outputs. Traditional metrics are those detailed in Subsection 4.1. The ranking was determined based on the JudgeLM Score for each of the languages.

Rank	Team Runs	JudgeLM Score	Traditional metrics(%)				generation length
			ROUGE-L	BLEU	BERTscore	Novelty	
1	MilaNLP run3	2523.0	19.0	4.9	70.8	83.0	84.7
2	NLP@IIMAS run2	2498.5	14.7	2.0	68.8	83.1	73.5
3	NLP@IIMAS run3	2494.5	14.7	2.0	68.8	83.1	73.5
4	CODEOFCONDUCT run3	2394.5	16.2	2.9	69.1	83.4	88.3
5	CODEOFCONDUCT run1	2374.5	16.2	2.8	69.4	83.4	84.8
6	MilaNLP run2	2357.5	18.5	3.8	70.8	82.5	66.7
7	CODEOFCONDUCT run2	2344.0	16.4	3.2	69.4	83.7	85.6
8	MilaNLP run1	2326.5	18.1	3.2	70.7	82.3	64.5
9	HuaweiTSC run2	2087.5	33.6	18.8	76.1	80.8	48.3
10	HuaweiTSC run3	1682.0	46.6	34.6	80.4	79.0	39.2
11	HuaweiTSC run1	1635.0	40.4	27.2	78.2	80.7	38.2
12	Northeastern Uni run3	1191.0	51.8	40.3	82.6	78.1	43.0
13	ground truth	1175.5	100.0	100.0	100.0	77.7	32.7
14	TrenTeam run2	1145.5	53.9	48.3	83.4	78.1	36.3
15	SemanticCUETSync run1	1079.0	51.8	44.4	82.4	77.5	33.4
16	Hyderabadi Pearls run2	1058.5	44.3	34.8	79.5	77.0	32.1
17	TrenTeam run1	1056.0	49.6	45.3	82.0	78.0	34.4
18	TrenTeam run3	999.5	52.5	43.3	82.2	79.0	35.4
19	Hyderabadi Pearls run3	996.5	45.2	35.2	79.5	77.0	30.9
20	Northeastern Uni run2	990.0	51.6	42.1	82.3	76.6	30.9
21	Northeastern Uni run1	965.5	48.3	40.1	81.0	76.8	30.4
22	Counterspeech go run1	924.5	49.6	34.0	81.9	76.5	24.4
23	Hyderabadi Pearls run1	861.0	53.1	40.9	82.6	78.2	28.7
24	Counterspeech go run2	854.0	49.7	34.0	81.8	77.2	24.0
25	Counterspeech go run3	840.0	49.8	33.9	81.9	77.4	23.6
26	NLP@IIMAS run1	704.0	48.8	41.2	80.8	78.2	29.8
27	RSSN run1	681.5	46.3	35.7	78.8	78.4	40.8
28	bhavanark run1	301.5	14.0	1.7	67.1	81.3	54.2
29	RSSN run2	59.0	24.5	13.2	69.2	80.8	31.0

Table 8: English Results.

Rank	Team Runs	JudgeLM Score	Traditional metrics(%)				generation length
			ROUGE-L	BLEU	BERTscore	Novelty	
1	CODEOFCONDUCT run1	2465.5	8.2	1.5	66.4	86.8	67.5
2	CODEOFCONDUCT run3	2382.5	10.4	2.2	67.5	87.5	69.1
3	CODEOFCONDUCT run2	2371.0	9.8	2.2	67.0	87.1	66.2
4	MilaNLP run1	2242.5	10.7	1.0	69.0	87.8	44.6
5	NLP@IIMAS run2	2086.0	8.9	0.6	67.7	87.5	34.6
6	HuaweiTSC run2	1881.5	17.7	5.6	72.4	86.8	34.5
7	HuaweiTSC run3	1722.0	23.3	10.5	74.2	86.5	32.1
8	ground truth	1534.5	100.0	100.0	100.0	85.3	26.5
9	HuaweiTSC run1	1484.5	18.3	6.3	72.1	87.2	30.2
10	TrenTeam run2	1394.5	32.8	20.9	77.1	85.7	27.5
11	TrenTeam run1	1364.5	33.8	22.4	77.6	85.2	28.2
12	Hyderabadi Pearls run2	1322.0	27.6	15.5	75.5	85.3	27.8
13	TrenTeam run3	1246.0	31.7	18.2	76.6	85.9	24.0
14	SemanticCUETSync run1	1194.0	26.5	15.4	75.1	85.4	26.0
15	Northeastern Uni run2	1158.0	27.6	13.5	75.7	83.4	24.5
16	Northeastern Uni run3	1145.0	30.9	17.6	76.2	85.2	29.6
17	Northeastern Uni run1	1107.5	25.6	13.3	74.6	84.3	24.8
18	Hyderabadi Pearls run3	1023.5	29.2	17.4	75.5	85.6	26.2
19	Hyderabadi Pearls run1	1011.5	29.2	17.4	75.5	85.6	26.2
20	Counterspeech go run1	904.0	31.8	15.6	76.7	84.9	18.0
21	Counterspeech go run3	855.5	31.6	15.3	76.5	85.1	17.7
22	Counterspeech go run2	837.0	32.4	15.8	77.1	85.1	18.0
23	NLP@IIMAS run1	720.5	29.2	17.6	74.9	86.0	24.9
24	NLP@IIMAS run3	720.0	29.2	17.6	74.9	86.0	24.9
25	MilaNLP run2	430.0	18.5	6.9	70.4	87.4	50.5
26	MilaNLP run3	422.5	17.9	6.8	70.7	88.3	72.8
27	bhavanark run1	74.0	5.5	0.5	61.7	88.7	32.4

Table 9: Basque Results.

Rank	Team Runs	JudgeLM Score	Traditional metrics(%)				generation length
			ROUGE-L	BLEU	BERTscore	Novelty	
1	MilaNLP run3	1985.5	21.1	8.9	72.6	82.1	101.4
2	MilaNLP run2	1912.0	22.7	9.1	73.0	81.1	73.4
3	CODEOFCONDUCT run1	1824.5	10.7	2.7	68.6	81.6	78.0
4	MilaNLP run1	1824.0	16.8	3.7	70.8	82.0	62.1
5	CODEOFCONDUCT run3	1803.5	10.1	2.4	68.3	81.6	75.2
6	HuaweiTSC run2	1792.0	30.8	16.6	75.9	80.3	49.5
7	CODEOFCONDUCT run2	1740.5	10.2	2.2	68.5	82.5	80.2
8	NLP@IIMAS run2	1630.5	13.6	1.9	68.4	81.9	50.1
9	HuaweiTSC run3	1372.5	41.1	26.6	79.1	79.1	41.9
10	HuaweiTSC run1	1260.5	36.1	21.7	77.2	80.9	40.8
11	SemanticCUETSync run1	1028.0	46.7	36.2	81.1	78.3	34.9
12	Northeastern Uni run3	1004.0	47.5	36.2	81.3	77.8	40.7
13	TrenTeam run2	965.5	48.6	41.2	81.7	77.8	37.0
14	ground truth	929.5	100.0	100.0	100.0	77.9	35.3
15	Northeastern Uni run2	905.5	45.4	33.7	80.8	76.9	33.5
16	TrenTeam run1	880.0	46.4	38.6	81.2	77.9	37.8
17	Northeastern Uni run1	830.0	42.6	30.8	79.7	77.8	32.0
18	TrenTeam run3	791.0	47.4	37.9	80.9	78.8	35.5
19	Counterspeech go run3	685.0	46.5	32.3	81.1	77.7	27.7
20	Counterspeech go run1	667.5	47.0	32.2	80.9	77.5	28.1
21	Counterspeech go run2	663.0	47.1	31.7	81.0	77.8	27.6
22	NLP@IIMAS run1	529.5	36.7	27.6	77.2	78.3	32.4
23	NLP@IIMAS run3	503.0	36.5	25.8	77.1	79.4	31.6
24	bhavanark run1	73.0	11.0	2.1	62.6	84.6	39.8

Table 10: Italian Results.

Rank	Team Runs	JudgeLM Score	Traditional metrics(%)				generation length
			ROUGE-L	BLEU	BERTscore	Novelty	
1	MilaNLP run3	2002.0	24.2	8.9	73.5	79.6	99.3
2	MilaNLP run2	1942.0	23.7	8.6	73.5	78.0	72.7
3	NLP@IIMAS run2	1919.0	16.7	3.3	69.6	79.6	64.9
4	CODEOFCONDUCT run1	1857.0	12.0	2.8	69.8	81.3	86.4
5	MilaNLP run1	1852.5	19.6	4.8	71.5	79.2	67.7
6	CODEOFCONDUCT run3	1839.0	11.5	3.0	69.5	81.8	87.8
7	CODEOFCONDUCT run2	1820.5	12.0	2.8	69.8	81.5	87.2
8	HuaweiTSC run2	1728.0	33.5	17.7	76.7	77.4	52.3
9	HuaweiTSC run3	1339.5	41.9	27.2	79.4	75.8	43.2
10	HuaweiTSC run1	1228.5	36.8	21.7	77.6	77.5	43.1
11	TrenTeam run2	987.5	51.6	42.9	82.8	75.6	40.9
12	SemanticCUETSync run1	974.5	46.5	35.6	80.8	75.3	36.5
13	ground truth	899.0	100.0	100.0	100.0	75.1	36.9
14	Northeastern Uni run1	894.5	45.6	34.5	80.6	74.0	35.1
15	TrenTeam run1	879.0	48.2	39.3	81.7	75.8	41.2
16	Northeastern Uni run3	873.0	45.3	33.4	80.5	76.6	43.8
17	Northeastern Uni run2	845.0	46.7	33.6	81.2	73.9	33.4
18	TrenTeam run3	769.0	50.2	40.3	82.0	75.4	37.9
19	Counterspeech go run3	652.5	47.4	29.7	80.9	75.7	26.5
20	Counterspeech go run2	646.5	46.7	29.8	80.9	75.6	27.1
21	Counterspeech go run1	639.0	47.6	29.9	81.1	75.3	27.1
22	NLP@IIMAS run1	492.5	39.7	30.7	78.2	77.3	36.3
23	NLP@IIMAS run3	466.0	38.5	27.6	78.1	76.1	33.6
24	bhavanark run1	54.0	14.7	2.5	64.7	81.0	42.7

Table 11: Spanish Results.

B Qualitative analysis of the results

We conducted a preliminary review of the winning runs by comparing the outputs from the winning systems according to the JudgeLM pairwise rank-based evaluation and BERTScore. Based on an initial assessment of a subset of 100 instances, we observed some trends in the characteristics of the outputs selected as winners by these two methods. Table 12 provides an illustrative example in each language where, according to the JudgeLM pairwise rank-based evaluation, the winner is Win_{PRB}, and according to BERTScore, the winner is Win_{BERT}.

When focusing on the English results, runs identified as winners by the JudgeLM pairwise rank-based evaluation tended to appear more natural overall while, those selected as winners based on BERTScore, often seemed less natural. Thus, the winner according to BERTScore closely mirrors the ground truth, using the same knowledge that informed the reference CN word for word, likely contributing to its high BERTScore. However, it also introduces an ungrammatical piece of knowledge (Knowledge 2), making the response seem incongruent. Throughout the submitted run, the CNs were combinations of pieces of knowledge without rephrasing, resulting in a high overlap with the reference but an unnatural, disjointed appearance. This made them perform poorly when evaluated by the JudgeLM pairwise rank-based evaluation method.

In contrast, the winner according to the JudgeLM rank-based evaluation also draws on the knowledge used in the reference CN, as well as Knowledge 3, but it combines it and rephrases it in a more natural manner. However, by rephrasing it, the overlap with the reference is reduced, which results in a lower BERTScore. This observation extends to other languages, where the winners according to BERTScore are those that select knowledge and reproduce it almost word by word, while the winners according to JudgeLM seem to be more focused on generation and adapting the knowledge to make it sound more natural.

English	
HS	Jews control Hollywood and the media.
Win$_{PRB}$	In Hollywood, many individuals of Jewish heritage have made significant contributions, yet it's inaccurate to suggest that they collectively "control" the industry. Historically, Hollywood Jews have been committed to assimilation and not religious celebration. They've been intermarried, secular, and ambivalent about their faith, often keeping Judaism a private matter. This misconception stems from a few prominent figures in the industry, rather than a coordinated effort or control.
Win$_{BERT}$	But almost from the inception of the American film industry, the Hollywood Jews were dedicated to assimilation, not religious celebration. Well, Jews last, which is why, in Hollywood, Judaism was always sotto voce.
ground truth	Almost from the inception of the American film industry, the Hollywood Jews were dedicated to assimilation, not religious celebration. Why should their religion be connected to an alleged "control of the media"?
KN	1. He began writing other Hollywood notables, asking them to sponsor endangered Jews. 2. well, Jews last, which is why, in Hollywood, Judaism was always sotto voce. 3. Secular, skeptical, intermarried, ambivalent, disenchanted, disengaged, sometimes Jews: on this day, Judaism and Jewish community briefly take center stage. **4. But almost from the inception of the American film industry, the Hollywood Jews were dedicated to assimilation, not religious celebration.** 5. And he urges that God himself would punish any king who tried to interfere with the Jews' practice of Judaism.

Spanish	
HS	Los judíos controlan el gobierno de EE.UU
Win$_{PRB}$	A pesar de que en el pasado hubo momentos de conflictos entre judíos y musulmanes, como en el caso de Israel, es importante recordar que hoy en día, la mayoría de los israelíes y musulmanes coexisten en paz. En cuanto al gobierno de los EE. UU., no hay evidencia de que los judíos lo controlen. En realidad, los judíos han sufrido persecuciones en países como China, Polonia y Turquía. Por lo tanto, es importante respetar a todos los ciudadanos y no asignar responsabilidades sin pruebas.
Win$_{BERT}$	El Gobierno debería perseguir activamente la liquidación de estos poderes antisemitas que trabajan dentro de las instituciones gubernamentales. En última instancia, el gobierno comunista patrocinó una campaña antisemita que resultó en que la mayoría de los judíos restantes se vieron obligados a abandonar Polonia.
ground truth	Esto no es cierto. Por el contrario, el Gobierno debería perseguir activamente la liquidación de los poderes antisemitas que actúan dentro de las instituciones gubernamentales.
KN	1. El Gobierno israelí apoyó a los musulmanes y envió policías para impedir el avance de los judíos. 2.Según el gobierno chino, no hay judíos de Kaifeng porque no hay judíos chinos. **3. El Gobierno debería perseguir activamente la liquidación de estos poderes antisemitas que trabajan dentro de las instituciones gubernamentales.** 4. En última instancia , el gobierno comunista patrocinó una campaña antisemita que resultó en la mayoría de los judíos restantes se vieron obligados a abandonar Polonia. 5. Resolvieron solicitar a los gobiernos britanico , austriaco y frances que intercedieran ante el gobierno otomano y detuvieran las persecuciones.

Basque	
HS	Juduek Hollywood eta komunikabideak kontrolatzen dituzte.
Win_{PRB}	Judu komunitateak ez du Hollywood eta komunikabideak kontrolatzen, baina beren jarduerei eta ekintzak moralitate eta arau berriak ezartzen dizkiete, eta eztabaidagarriak diren edukiak saihesten ditu. Horrela, ez dago inolako frogarik juduak komunikabideak kontrolatzen ari direla, baizik eta beraien ekintzetan arau eta balio etikoak errespetatzen dituztela.
Win_{BERT}	Baina ia AEBetako zinema industriaren hastapenetatik, Hollywoodeko juduak asimilazioan aritu ziren, ez ospakizun erlijiosoan. Gaur egun, judaismoa eta juduen komunitatea dira nagusi.
ground truth	Ia AEBetako zinema industriaren hastapenetatik, Hollywoodeko juduak asimilazioan zentratu ziren ziren, ez ospakizun erlijiosoan. Zergatik egon behar du lotuta haien erlijioa ustezko "komunikabideen kontrol" batekin?
KN	1. Hollywoodeko beste kontu batzuk idazten hasi zen, arriskuan zeuden juduak babesteko eskatuz. 2. Horregatik, Hollywooden, judaismoa sotto voce izan zen beti. 3. Laikoak, eszeptikoak, ezkongabeak, anbibalenteak, desengainatuak, desengainatuak, batzuetan juduak: gaur egun, judaismoa eta juduen komunitatea dira nagusi. **4. Baina ia AEBetako zinema industriaren hastapenetatik, Hollywoodeko juduak asimilazioan aritu ziren, ez ospakizun erlijiosoan.** 5. Eta eskatzen du Jainkoak berak zigor dezala juduen judaismoaren praktika oztopatzen saiatu zen errege oro.
Italian	
HS	Gli ebrei controllano Hollywood e i media.
Win_{PRB}	Gli ebrei non controllano Hollywood o i media: invece, molti ebrei laici, scettici, meticci e disincantati hanno contribuito all'industria cinematografica e alla produzione di media, come molti altri individui di diverse religioni e culture. La loro presenza è stata importante per la creazione di opere culturali diverse e significative.
Win_{BERT}	Ma quasi fin dall'inizio dell'industria cinematografica americana, gli ebrei di Hollywood si sono dedicati all'assimilazione, non alla celebrazione religiosa. Ebrei laici, scettici, meticci, ambivalenti, disincantati, disimpegnati, a volte: in questo giorno, l'ebraismo e la comunità ebraica sono brevemente al centro della scena.
ground truth	Quasi dalla nascita dell'industria cinematografica americana, gli ebrei di Hollywood si sono dedicati a integrarsi, non alla celebrazione religiosa. Perché la loro religione dovrebbe essere collegata a un presunto "controllo dei media"?
KN	1. Cominciò a scrivere ad altri notabili di Hollywood, chiedendo loro di sponsorizzare gli ebrei in pericolo. 2. Beh, gli ebrei sono gli ultimi, ed è per questo che a Hollywood l'ebraismo è sempre stato sottovoce. 3. Ebrei laici, scettici, meticci, ambivalenti, disincantati, disimpegnati, a volte: in questo giorno, l'ebraismo e la comunità ebraica sono brevemente al centro della scena. **4. Ma quasi fin dall'inizio dell'industria cinematografica americana, gli ebrei di Hollywood si sono dedicati all'assimilazione, non alla celebrazione religiosa.** 5. Ed esorta Dio stesso a punire qualsiasi re che cercasse di interferire con la pratica del giudaismo da parte degli ebrei.

Table 12: Example instances where according to pairwise rank-based evaluation the winner is Win_{PRB} and according to BERTScore Win_{BERT}. Here, HS refers to the instance of hate speech, Win_{PRB} denotes the counterspeech from the winning system according to the Pairwise Rank-Based Evaluation score, and Win_{BERT} refers to the counterspeech from the winning system according to BERTScore. Additionally, the ground truth represents the reference knowledge-based counterspeech, while KN indicates the provided knowledge. The knowledge shown in bold refers to the specific instance used to construct the gold standard.

Author Index